Still Alive

Still Alive

An Autobiographical Essay

Jan Kott

Translated by Jadwiga Kosicka

Yale University Press

New Haven and London

The publishers gratefully acknowledge the assistance of the
Alfred Jurzykowski Foundation, the Kosciusko Foundation, and
the Legion of Young Polish Women in the publication of this book.

This book is based on a work originally published in Polish
as *Przyczynek do biografii* (Footnote to the biography) by Aneks
Publishers, London. © Jan Kott, 1990.

Designed by Sonia L. Scanlon.
Printed in the United States of America.

Library of Congress Cataloging-in-Publication Data
Kott, Jan.
    [Przyczynek do biografii. English]
    Still alive : an autobiographical essay / Jan Kott ;
translated by Jadwiga Kosicka.
        p.   cm.
    ISBN 0-300-05276-6 (alk. paper)
    1. Kott, Jan.   2. Intellectuals—Poland—Biography.
3. Critics—Poland—Biography.   4. Poland—History—
1945–1980.   I. Title.
DK4435.K68A3   1994
943.805—dc20   93-29605
                    CIP

A catalogue record for this book is available from the British Library.

The paper in this book meets the guidelines for permanence and
durability of the Committee on Production Guidelines for Book
Longevity of the Council on Library Resources.

10 9 8 7 6 5 4 3 2 1

For Lidia

Contents

I don't write about myself, I write with myself

Preface

The first edition of this book was published in Polish by Aneks in London in 1990. The French and German translations contained new material. The present edition is based on an expanded text, which I hope will be the definitive one.

I wrote these biographical sketches at the dictation of my memory and its often intricate meanderings but also, unfortunately, of its alterations and lapses. Memory always has only one tense: the present. And in this present tense of mine, in this *praesens,* I have frequently recalled myself from half a century ago. Recalled myself and that world which I was discovering and experiencing. And which was experiencing me.

I have corrected some of the errors. But in this edition there are also new sections. Unexpectedly memory has brought back to me a store of reminiscences from childhood and, faithful to that memory, I have brought them back again in this edition. I have added a final essay, "The Fifth Heart Attack," in which characters from the earliest chapters return from among the dead. This final essay is a kind of ultimate reckoning.

As I read these texts in a language that is not alien to me but is nevertheless a second language, *Still Alive* suddenly seems to me the bringing back not of my life but of someone else's life, someone else who is not alien to me but is nevertheless a second self. As though these biographical essays were another's story, yet one occurring only in my tense. But whose story and what story?

The most discerning of my critics calls these essays "a philosophic tale." But if it is a philosophic tale, it takes place at a time when, as the master of my youth, Jerzy Stempowski, taught me, history has broken loose from its mooring. In this philosophic tale the role and fate of Candide have fallen to me.

Stony Brook
Autumn 1992

Chronology

Born in Warsaw	1914
Scholarship in Paris	1938–39
In Polish Army, defense of Warsaw	1939
In Lvov	1939–41
Resistance movement, Polish People's Army	1942–45.
Joins Polish Communist Party (PPR)	1943
Professor: Wroclaw, Warsaw	1949–69
Travel to China	1954
"Polish October," or October Thaw	1956
Resigns from Party	1957
Signs "Letter of the Thirty-Four," protesting government censorship	1964
Professor in the United States	after 1966
Request for political asylum in the United States	1969

Journey to the West

The last game of boccie I ever played was with Aleksander Wat, or at least it was in his presence: he was sitting on a bench under the plane trees in Messuguière sur Grasse, seeking shelter from the sharp rays of the afternoon sun. That was in 1962 or 1963, some thirty years ago. The last game of boccie I played before the war was with the future murderer of Trotsky either in May or June of 1939 in an exceptionally ugly Parisian suburb, or it might even have been an outlying district near one of the last metro stations.

In almost every village and every small town in the south of France and in all of Italy, men, especially older men who are still physically fit, play boccie from late afternoon until dusk. The French *boules* seem black and heavy, the Italian ones lighter and gilded as they gleam in the sun. Frenchmen play the game in collarless shirts fastened at the neck with a pin and cycling caps pushed far back on the head. Italians, particularly the younger men, play in brightly colored jerseys. On uneven ground, the players, knees slightly bent, throw the *boules* at a smaller ball, known as a *cochonnet,* or "little pig," which has been thrown several yards away. As in croquet, you can send the balls of your opponent flying when they get too close to the "little pig." A very exciting game passionately followed by groups of teenagers and older men. Frequently they bet on which side will win. The game requires a good eye and the ability to estimate the ball's weight and the distance it will carry. The future murderer of Trotsky was a much better player than I was. Less than a year after our last game of *boules* he smashed Trotsky's skull with an ice pick.

All four of us—Maria, Sylvia, Jacques, and I—usually went out together to that ugliest of Parisian suburbs. There was a run-down villa there that was either owned or rented by one of Maria's friends. Sylvia was a short, plump blond who had come to Paris from New York in the summer of 1938, a couple of months before me. Maria had waited for Sylvia at the Gare St.-Lazare. Now in September or November of 1938 Maria was again waiting—this time for me, at the Gare du Nord. Maria and Sylvia were Trotskyites.

I had met Maria two years before at my grandmother's on Senatorska Street in Warsaw. My grandfather, who was a gynecologist, always had the poorest patients, but under no circumstances would he perform abortions, even for those few who could afford to pay, so my grandmother regularly let out two rooms of the apartment to make ends meet. Maria had just arrived from Paris and was visiting a distant cousin of hers, who happened to be a tenant of my grandparents'. Maria had come from Paris, and her stay in Warsaw was very brief; she had no more than two days left after we met. I had just finished law school and was due to begin my military service. And for a couple of months yet I was only twenty years old. Maria must have been a year younger than I was, but she seemed to be much older, from another world and more mature than the girls I had been seeing so far. She was consumed by a fever that was unabating and tenacious, although it was a cold fever. That was the year of my fascination with Malraux, especially with *Days of Wrath* and, above all, with *The Conquerors*. Maria was straight out of a Malraux novel. But she came from a different Malraux, not the one I had learned about from my early mentor, Jerzy Stempowski. Maria and I hardly parted company for a moment during her two days in Warsaw. I wanted to show her the city, but she was interested only in the prisons where the Communists were held: the "Pawiak" for men and "Serbia" for women. I tried to kiss her at one of them, but she gave me such a powerful shove that I almost fell over backward. I took her to the prison on Daniłowiczowska Street where two years before I had spent a week or so in a cell for Communists after being picked up in the Jewish quarter during a demonstration commemorating the "three L's": Luxemburg, Liebknecht, and Lenin. I owed my release from prison to some older colleagues from the Association of Democratic Polish Youth (ZPMD: Związek Polskiej Młodzieży Demokratycznej), who were then working in the prosecutor's office. I was so proud of being imprisoned for those few days that immediately after my release I went to tell Zofia Nałkowska all about it, but I was actually more frightened than proud. That was the end of my prewar flirtation with Communism. Literature was almost all that was left. and if there was to be a revolution, it would have to be in my imagination.

I don't remember anything about what we said to each other in Warsaw. Maria did not speak Polish willingly or without coaxing. But somehow we must have been mutually intoxicated by those long conversations, since for the next two years we maintained an unceasing exchange of letters. Maria wrote in French, and I almost certainly did too. The following year I was in the army, doing my military service in Zambrów in a "disciplinary" unit, because my papers were marked "PS"—politically suspect. Day after day we had to crawl through the mud- and water-logged meadows. Every night we would gather in the latrine to drink vodka, wearing nothing but our "prison" long johns secured with tape at the ankles or our long white shirts. There were only three whores in Zambrów. But most of the time in the latrine we talked more about ways of committing suicide than about whores. In that late autumn, when even the squares in front of the barracks had sunk into the mud, suicide was on everybody's mind. It is not easy to kill oneself with a long rifle. The barrel of the rifle has to be placed against the chest and then the trigger must be pulled with the big toe of the right foot. And yet before winter came, three of my fellow soldiers from that disciplinary division in Zambrów had killed themselves that way. One of them was a fledgling poet just like me. That same autumn Maria became something of a legend in my eyes.

From the Gare du Nord she took me directly to her place. She lived almost at the very end of the rue de Vaugirard, one of the longest streets in Paris. She let me stay overnight on condition that I would leave at dawn with a map of Paris in hand and walk through half the city to the opposite end, where the Cité Universitaire is located. I was to live there at the Maison du Japon—Polish students on grants in Paris did not then have a residence of their own, nor do they now. I had to swear solemnly that I would not ask for directions on the way. But I was allowed to take a compass. Such was my first night in Paris.

During the weeks that followed I saw Maria almost daily. In the early morning we would go by bus or metro to forbidding suburbs and pay visits to suspicious-looking hotels or obscure bistros where Maria had meetings with strange bearded men. They were Greeks or Serbs for the most part. I was rarely permitted to join in the conversations unless I was needed to serve as a translator in that odd mixture of idioms. Often I would be abandoned in dark, stuffy corridors or left to sit for hours at a table all by myself. Whenever we went by Notre Dame, Maria would tell me to turn my head away. I was not allowed to go to the Louvre either. "You mustn't be a tourist," she would say. My fascination with Maria kept on growing.

That first night at her place Maria had told me that she was responsible for the world revolution. She was in the Youth Section of the Secretariat of the Fourth International. She had quit the French Communist party after the first Moscow trials. But she talked about herself only rarely and with obvious reluctance. Maria had left Poland when she was fourteen or barely fifteen years old. Her father was the director of some oil refineries in Drohobycz that were owned by a French joint company. The family lived outside the town in a villa with a garden the size of a park. Oil drillers wander throughout the entire world, from Java to Drohobycz. One of them, a young Frenchman or a Polish emigré who had returned home, got the director's daughter to help him set up a Communist hand printing press in the attic of her father's villa. Or it might have been a duplicating machine. In any case, the printing of Communist leaflets did not last long. The police made a raid, confiscating the duplicating machine and the leaflets. Maria was arrested, then suddenly released, and even more suddenly sent by her father to France.

She was enrolled in what I think was a convent school either in Nantes or in Strasbourg. The young girls wore uniforms and, always supervised by the sisters, they went on walks in columns of two, dressed in laced boots, small hats, and gloves. That is how I imagine Maria in Nantes. Or have I superimposed an image from a French movie? Two months later Maria ran away from the convent school. She joined the French Communist party immediately and didn't write her first letter to her parents until a year had passed. Threatened with deportation as an undesirable alien, she got married in less than a week's time. To a comrade in the party, of course. Their marriage was never consummated, but Maria's Communist husband followed her lead and went over to the Trotskyites. Even then Maria was known as *l'indomptable*—the invincible. She fought like a man against both the *flics* and the Communists during the Troskyite rallies that the police and the party storm troopers jointly tried to break up.

In Zambrów I mythologized the Maria whom I had met in Warsaw. Gifted with a perfidious memory given to fantasy, I mythologized the Maria from Drohobycz and the Maria from Paris for many years after that night on the rue de Vaugirard spent talking till dawn. In these phantasmagorias Bruno Schulz makes an unexpected appearance, diminutive and hunchbacked—as in the drawings in his *Book of Idolatry* —groveling at the all-powerful feet of the fourteen-year-old Maria. Schulz was in fact Maria's teacher at the gymnasium in Drohobycz, and as he bent over her, he would correct her drawings with thinly penciled lines. In my dreamlike memory, I am standing with the heavy-breasted Maria in a makeshift shower in her apartment on the rue de Vaugirard. Even after more than half a century the shock of that mutual nakedness still comes back to me. Not that I was a virgin by the time I came to Paris; I had served my time in the army, with all its brutalization of sex, but inhibitions and sexual taboos continued to be paralyzing. In those days young people of my age would make love with the lights turned off; they might switch them on for a moment, hurriedly and to the embarrassment of both. To tell the truth, the scene in the shower with Maria—

the water was actually ice-cold—never took place. Maria was very reserved. My imagination, not hers, was stimulated by *Les liaisons dangereuses*. In this phantasm of mine Maria had three passions: men, the Mediterranean Sea, and revolution. In reality "the Mediterranean Sea" was the run-down villa in the gloomy suburb where we used to go for the weekend and the small lake nearby in which we went swimming. I was no partner for Maria either in love or in revolution. She began to treat me worse and worse and made fun of me for turning everything into literature. Maria was probably right, because for me that "Trotskyite adventure" was certainly pure literature. The only lasting effect of my involvement with communism was obedience to the party. After the war it came back like an incurable disease.

I still remained under Maria's spell. But I had slowly started to explore Paris on my own. In that Trotskyite circle, besides Sylvia, there was also Ellen, a timid American girl, dark-haired and exceptionally tall, from a very rich old family of plantation owners. She was desperately trying to get rid of what she called "the family taint." But all in vain—she had it under her skin. Once she confided to me that if a Negro touched her she developed a rash. In Paris at the time, the Boule Blanche was a fashionable spot frequented by Negroes and the blondest Swedish girls in town. Ellen begged me to take her there late one night. There, for the first time in my life, I witnessed the mutual attraction of opposite skins. And for the first time in her life Ellen danced with Negroes. She did not develop a rash. From then on she went there all by herself. She claimed it had a healing effect on her.

After that, Ellen very rarely went with us to the run-down villa on the outskirts of Paris. But Sylvia and Jacques came every time. I couldn't understand what Sylvia saw in him. She never missed an opportunity to rub up against him. Jacques never took part in our conversations. He belonged to a different world. Maria told me that he had been thrown out of the Belgian army because of a duel or for cheating at cards. Jacques and Sylvia were together even before my arrival in Paris. They said he worked for some weekly as a reporter and photographer for sports events, mainly football, I think. For a long time I didn't even know his last name, but I remember he was always fooling around with his camera. His last name was Mornard. Jacques Mornard.

In actual fact, his name was Raṁon Mercader. His mother was a Stalinist secret agent of long standing who even during the Spanish civil war was still denouncing anarchists and Trotskyites to the GPU (later known as the NKVD). Ramón's mother must have signed him up while he was still a child. But it was only many years later that I learned about all that.

In 1960, twenty years after the murder of Trotsky, Mercader was released from a Mexican prison and immediately thereafter, with the help of Czech diplomats, he disappeared. I couldn't remember what he looked like until one day, skimming through old issues of *France Observateur*, I saw a photograph of Maria, Jacques, and Sylvia. Maria has her enormous chestnut eyes, Sylvia's hair is all in curls, and Jacques is wearing a dark suit, a tie, and a felt hat. He is smiling and looks like the leading man in an American movie. In the same issue there was another photo of Mercader, which must have been taken after his release from prison. His face is bloated and he is wearing dark glasses. He is hiding behind them. But I wouldn't have recognized him even in the first photograph. In that last game of boccie in that Parisian suburb I had an unexpected brush with History. But the one thing I really remember from that meeting with Trotsky's murderer is the view from Sylvia and Jacques's apartment. It must have been close to the Seine and on a high floor because from its windows the towers of Notre Dame could be seen. By then I was allowed to look at them.

2.

That same autumn I met Tristan Tzara. Some forty years later in London I was quite astonished to see Tristan Tzara on stage at the opening-night performance of Tom Stoppard's *Travesties*. Tzara was one of the play's three protagonists, along with Lenin and Joyce. I never would have suspected that everything turns into history and comes on stage so quickly. The action of *Travesties* takes place in Zurich in 1916. That year Tzara founded his Cabaret Voltaire, at which he himself appeared. The date marked the beginning of Dada. The cabaret was located in the old part of Zurich, in Spielgasse Strasse. According to what I read in Martin Esslin, Lenin lived right across the street at the same time. Something else I learned from Esslin is that eighty years earlier Georg Büchner lived on a neighboring street and it was there that he wrote his doctoral dissertation on the nervous system of the barbel, a small fish that is also found in Poland. Two years before that, Büchner wrote *Danton's Death*. The more my memory fails me, not only do different times— those belonging to me and to other people—seem to encroach on one another, as if everything that has happened happened *simultaneously,* but also the same places at different times, with different casts of characters, seem to be narrating the same stories. Thus for me many different Parises merge and blend: prewar Paris and postwar Paris, my own personal Paris and literary Paris, those I read about and those remembered as if in an evening fog and, even more distinctly, in the quivering light on the Seine during morning strolls through the Quartier Latin.

And there is a scene from my last short stay in Paris. It is of coming out of the Hôtel des Balcons (the window of my room looked out almost directly on the Odéon) early one morning and, after buying *Le monde,* going down to the corner of the boulevard St.-Germain, where, near the statue of Danton, there was a small bistro still bearing the name that I remembered from before the war. Through the window—which was as dirty as ever, wiped only perfunctorily for appearance's sake —I could see the same three female students I had seen some fifty, forty (or was it only ten?) years before, busily scribbling something in their notebooks, their hair hanging loose, one of them sitting on her leg with her skirt pulled up. When I ordered a croissant and café au lait at the counter, a sudden surge of happiness impossible to describe seized my entire being, as though once again in that diffused light and that air heavy with tobacco smoke in that Parisian bistro all different times merged and became one.

In that same late autumn of 1938 I saw a notice in *Le monde* that on the anniversary of Apollinaire's death there would be a gathering of friends and poets by his grave at Père Lachaise. I bought a bunch of flowers and went to the cemetery. That was when I met Mme Apollinaire, known as "the beautiful redhead," who was now white as snow, and Marie Laurencin, all wrapped in pink tulle and wearing a hat with an enormous feather. I remember Zofia Nałkowska wearing a similar hat in Moscow for the thirtieth anniversary of the Russian Revolution. I saw Marie Laurencin twice after that, when I was invited to have tea with her. It was chamomile or perhaps mint tea. I can still recall the sweetish taste. Marie Laurencin did two portraits of Apollinaire. And I can still see the double portrait of Marie Laurencin and Apollinaire that Rousseau Le Douanier did in 1908. Marie is in a full-length dress of an antique cut, Guillaume, in a dark suit, is holding a goose quill in his hand. At the foot of this "betrothal" portrait Rousseau painted nine large carnations since he believed that lovers dwell in paradise. I somehow connected one of them to that mint tea:

Colombe, l'amour de l'esprit
Qui engendrâtes Jésus-Christ,
Comme vous j'aime une Marie
Qu'avec elle je me marie.
("La colombe," *Le bestiaire ou Cortège d'Orphée*)

At that time my appetite for poets was insatiable. Tzara let me join him in his strolls through Paris. He liked to roam the streets in the evening and sometimes late into the night. Most often we would wander about Montparnasse. That was when he showed me the old women sitting on the glassed-in terraces of the Rotonde and Le Dôme—or perhaps it was during my second Paris, the year after the war—the old women with hooked noses like parrots, their faces plastered with white powder or thick layers of rouge. He showed me the model for Matisse's odalisques, and the two mulattos Hemingway had slept with, and the most terrifying of all the old crones, the "Russian Princess" from a brothel in Clichy so lovingly described by Henry Miller. Tzara called them by various nicknames: Poupette, Mini, Kiki, and Marysia. Who was the Marysia whom Tzara remembered? Coming back one evening past the Luxembourg Gardens along the tail end of the boulevard St.-Michel—I was living nearby, in the Hôtel des Mines, which had seen better times but was cheap—Tzara and I tried to get into the Clôserie des Lilas, deserted at that late hour. Outside the entrance an old woman who once sold flowers there recognized Tzara: "Monsieur used to come here with M. Apollinaire," she said.

My room at the Hôtel des Mines was huge but had a sloping floor. Friends jokingly suggested that it could be used for downhill skiing. Although there was no heat, the water was always hot. And there was a bidet almost in the middle of the room. In winter I used to sit on it and run the hot water to keep warm while I translated Apollinaire into Polish. It was Breton who told me that a bidet is the best place for translating poetry—and even better for writing it. "It frees one's imagination from all constraints," he said. "The bidet is a metonymy for woman." I failed to understand why sitting on a bidet would result in freeing my poetic imagination, but at least I wasn't as cold.

One day Breton invited me to his place. In the hall there was an enormous photograph, perhaps two meters long, of a naked woman. Cut off at the eyebrows. *"Je vous présente ma femme."* He wrote, *"Ma femme au sexe du miroir."* I considered myself quite conversant with surrealism, or at least well read in it; even before my trip to Paris, I had published in the *Contemporary Review* (*Przegląd Współczesny*), a highly respected monthly edited by Stanisław Wędkiewicz, one of my first "serious" essays, entitled "The Tragedy of Surrealism." I don't recall anymore what that tragedy was, but most likely I was trying to prove that the "subconscious" had eluded the surrealists even in their use of automatic writing. Jerzy Stempowski taught me that the avant-garde had much deeper sources. He got me to read Lautréamont. Breton's hatreds paled in comparison to the deadly venom of *Les chants de Maldoror*. But Breton told me to read de Sade.

At that time Breton was still, I think, publishing *Minotaure,* a continuation of *Le surréalisme au service de la révolution*. He had already become a Trotskyite. We can read the following about Trotsky: "An old comrade of Lenin's, a cosigner of the Brest-Litovsk peace treaty, an unforgettable emblem of revolutionary knowledge and intuition, the founder of the Red Army, which allowed the proletariat to hold on to power despite the capitalistic world, which closed ranks against it." This quotation is from *The Surrealist Revolution*. It gives the full flavor and frenzy of those years and of surrealism. But his brand of Trotskyism, mixed half and half with Freud like pure alcohol with absinthe, had nothing in common with the passions and hatreds of Maria and her bearded friends whom I used to meet in the northern part of Paris in dirty rooms on the top floors of cheap hotels, always, of course, without elevators. Despite that nude photograph of his "wife" in the hall and a display of African sculptures with protruding phalluses, Breton struck me as an affable old gentleman. Maria, too, had taught me to be mistrustful, although hers was a different kind of mistrust from that I learned from Jerzy Stempowski.

Undoubtedly it is to those lessons in surrealism that I owe my fascination with window displays, especially in the suburbs, where huge bras adorn flesh-colored mannequins, or jars of creams and hair pomades are carefully arranged amid of slips trimmed in lace. Many years have passed, but I still remember a hairdresser's window displaying a pink bust of a woman, her blond hair in curls; the bust was tiny—the smiling woman with blond curls was a midget. I also liked the stands with funeral wreaths of plaster flowers painted pink and blue in the midst of plaster statuettes of the Venus de Milo, newlyweds kissing, and Eiffel Towers of various sizes. Perhaps this predilection of mine for disorder, for sudden and unexpected affinities between objects, close as it was to the poetry of the dream as proposed by the surrealists, owed even more to Rimbaud's *Illuminations,* which I had just begun to translate, and of course to Apollinaire, whom I also translated, but only after the war.

Au-dessus de Paris un jour
    Combattaient deux grands avions
    L'un était rouge et l'autre noir
    Tandis qu'au zénith flamboyait
    L'éternel avion solaire
    ("Les Collines," *Calligrammes*)

I was fascinated with leaps of the imagination and I found them in the circus. I secretly shared these tastes with Adam Ważyk, even during the worst of the Stalinist years. But within ourselves we struggled against them resolutely and in others still more ruthlessly. During those Paris days I began to collect old postcards of Belle Epoque nudes.

Back then Zbyszek Bieńkowski (like me, a fledgling poet on scholarship in Paris) had similar inclinations, although he was more taken with Supervielle than with the surrealists. Once we stopped in front of a store selling sinks and toilets where, on display in the window, there was an ingenious mechanism for sucking water up and then releasing it. "It goes up the tube and it flows down the tube," Zbyszek commented. It became our favorite saying. We would repeat it on every occasion, almost obsessively. "It goes up the tube and it flows down the tube" was the principle of our existence, starting with our monthly stipends, which would melt away in no time at all, and including our erotic adventures, which ended quickly and without much success. Later we came up with another, equally obsessional saying. When we went on an excursion to Rouen and the white rosette of the cathedral emerged from the morning fog as in Monet's paintings, Zbyszek said, *"C'est pas mal comme cathédrale."* Only Julian Przyboś, immersed in his poetry and trying to keep pace with the rest of us with rapid little steps, his eyes cast upward, did not lose his habitual seriousness. Slowly and majestically he was borne off vertically into the sky until he stood suspended over the horizon along with the cathedral.

Of all my encounters and meetings during that first Parisian winter and spring, those with Paul Eluard have remained most deeply etched in my memory. Mutual tenderness developed between us despite the difference in our ages. I was attuned to all his poems, as though I had known them for a long time, even before I first read them. I had translated some of his poetry before my trip to Paris and I continued to translate it after the war. I remember his clear, bright eyes, which seemed translucent, seeing and yet unseeing. Those wide open eyes recur often in Eluard's poetry: *"Elle a toujours les yeux ouverts/Et ne me laisse pas dormir."* Eluard's fluttering fingers, which never stood still, not even for a moment, are something I shall never forget either. In his poetry, fluttering fingers turn into the fluttering wings of a bird. The fluttering of the pulsating wing is an aerial Eros, as utterly sensual as the touch of the tongue. It is intensely sharp.

Au-dessus des cheveux fous
    Le bruit de l'ecume entre les lèvres sans soleil
    Où l'aile battante de ton sang.

I was a frequent visitor at Eluard's. The walls and all the tables of his apartment were covered with nudes, always of the same woman, always luminous as though illuminated from within as when, in his poetry, the light penetrates the dark. Eluard's wife, Nush, was a great beauty. I never met her; in 1938 she was already dead. And I don't remember Nush's face from the many portraits of her that I saw in Eluard's apartment. It was only some fifty years later that I saw her face. On the first evening of my last visit to Paris, Michel took me to the place de la Contrescarpe, a favorite spot of mine from before the war. We stopped for a coffee; Michel disappeared for a moment and then presented me with a postcard of Eluard and Nush from a nearby kiosk. He found it among postcards showing generals from the First World War with pointed beards and curled mustaches, seminude women wearing ostrich feathers, and a whole series of scenes from an old movie about Archduke Rudolph and Maria von Vetsera. The postcard of Eluard and Nush must have been a reproduction of a photograph from the early thirties because Eluard looked younger than I remembered him from our first meeting and Nush's hair was all in curls like the hairdos of movie stars in those days. And once again various times have become entangled in my memory. *"Je suis debout sur tes paupières."* Fifty years ago that line from Eluard's poem was what I used to whisper to Lidia in bed just before falling asleep.

I don't remember exactly when I visited Eluard after the war or whether he still lived in the same place. I don't recall the name of the street, but I know that he lived in a working-class district, almost on the periphery, not far from the Stalingrad and Jaurès metro stations. In occupied France Eluard was one of the very few "clean" writers. He took part in the Resistance from the start and, if I'm not mistaken, joined the French Communist party at the same time. A year after the war ended, the names of those two metro stations near Eluard's apartment, on the red belt of Paris, seemed symbolic to me.

In the summer of 1947 Eluard came to Warsaw. Our daughter, Teresa, had just been born. Fingers trembling more than ever, Eluard put his hand on the baby's head. Like the good fairy in a fairy tale. And he gave me a large photograph of himself with the inscription "avec toutes nos raisons d'espérer." In 1947 my "hope" was a blind hope. But I still don't know what Eluard's "reasons for hope" might have been. Reasons for hope or reasons for despair? During the Occupation Eluard wrote: "L'Aube dissout les monstres." Did the Dawn continue dispersing monsters after the war? What kind of monsters were they and what sort of a Dawn was it in 1947?

3.

In the late winter or early spring of 1939 I became a frequent visitor at the home of Jacques and Raissa Maritain. In my memory Maritain has a long white beard and sometimes resembles the huge statues of the apostles on St. Peter's in Rome. But I really remember only his mouth, his drooping, inverted horseshoe mouth. Great sadness was written in that mouth. Raissa fares much better in my memory, although I can't recall her physical appearance. What I do remember is that, like Eluard, she was "illumined" by a light that seemed to emanate from within her. If ever in my lifetime I have met a saint, it was Raissa. Born into a Hasidic family in Lithuania, probably from Vilno or its environs, she had converted to Catholicism as a young girl, but she had retained the ardor of both faiths. Now, after many years, I think that in a profound sense she was like Simone Weil. The renewal of the covenant caused her anxiety, and she felt an all-consuming anguish as to whether she had received the gift of grace. Raissa was a poet. Fear and trembling are ever-present in her poetry, and although it uses a different poetics and different symbols, for Raissa as for Eluard, "Dawn disperses monsters."

I came to the Maritains with letters of recommendations from Father Władysław Korniłowicz and Sister Miriam of Laski. During that last year before I left for Paris, Father Korniłowicz was a frequent visitor to my grandmother Stefania's house on Senatorska Street. She was baptized either soon after I went to Paris or at the beginning of the war. In those years Father Korniłowicz baptized many of the Jews who were part of the long-assimilated Warsaw intelligentsia. I do not know how many of these conversions were truly religious and how many were prompted by the threat of a wave of anti-Semitism. Undoubtedly Father Korniłowicz's apostolic gift also played a major role.

I no longer remember whether I found my way to Laski through Father Korniłowicz or Sister Miriam. Sister Miriam belonged to the order of Franciscan nuns who ran the Institute for Blind Children in Laski. The fiancée of the talented poet Jerzy Liebert, she converted, I think, while he was still alive or perhaps she even joined the order during his terminal illness. She was not the only convert at Laski. Sister Teresa (Zofia Landy) coedited with Father Korniłowicz a religious and cultural quarterly, *Verbum,* to which, under the pseudonym Silvester, she contributed many articles on literature and philosophy, including one of the first and most enthusiastic reviews of Witold Gombrowicz's *Ferdydurke. Verbum* was a rather unusual journal for those times, like Laski and Father Korniłowicz's "Kółko" (the Circle, patterned after the French *cercles d'études*) an oasis within the parochial world of Polish Catholicism, which was openly, or at best secretly, anti-Semitic and shunned any sign of modernism like the plague. At a time when the word *ecumenism* was almost unknown, Laski was a meeting place for believers and agnostics, a dialogue of various creeds or, even more, a dialogue of anxieties.

In 1935 Wędkiewicz published my article "Catholicism in Liebert's Lyric Poetry." There was a cult for Liebert's poetry at Laski. Shortly before my departure for Paris, I published in *Verbum,* at Sister Teresa's invitation, what was probably the most theological of all my essays, "The Catholic Meaning of Rimbaud's Drama." At the same time I also wrote some articles on Mauriac. Ten years later—it may have been year two of the Stalinist asphyxiation in Poland—a friendly satirist characterized me in one of his poems with rare insight and perhaps excessive benevolence:

He steps to the right: a veritable Mauriac,
Plumbing the depths of Catholic creed;
He steps to the left: Marx, history,
And materialism, and Malraux.

Now I think that there was more to my oscillations than a protean skin. It was my status and my nature as a neophyte, which I had acquired along with my baptism, but I only began to realize it with the passage of many years. In one of my poems at that time I wrote:

To what Mary will you turn, where are your brothers and
    sisters?
The Star of David always runs after you.
In vain you wash with water, in vain you try to betray,
Your mirror shows a forehead furrowed with shades of
    ancestors.

I was baptized in 1919 in the Church of the Holy Cross in Warsaw. My mother's family had long been assimilated and had even become thoroughly Polonized. My great-great-grandfather Hilary Nusbaum published *A History of the Jews* and translated Moses's Pentateuch, the Torah, into Polish. He insisted that the sermons in the synagogue on Tłomackie Street be given in Polish and organized help for Polish exiles being sent to Siberia. I remember that one Saturday many years ago, after first going to confession, I was guided to visit that synagogue on Tłomackie Street by a puzzling mixture of emotions that were not entirely clear to me. My classmate Zdzisław Jeziorański—soon to be known as Jan Nowak, the "courier from Warsaw"—accompanied me on that pilgrimage. What was it that led us there?

There were converts in my mother's family going back three generations. Józef Nusbaum Hilarowicz, one of the first Polish Darwinists, was baptized as soon as he became a professor at the University of Lvov. Perhaps being baptized was a condition for getting the professorship. Christmas was solemnly celebrated with the traditional tree at the house of my grandparents, the Wertensteins. I was brought up by my aunt Maria Werten, a painter, who was like a mother to me when my parents moved to Bielsko; Aunt Marychna was in America when World War II broke out and died there. At my parents' house in Bielsko my sister always had a small Easter table complete with a traditional lamb holding a tiny red flag inscribed IHNS. My father was a nonbeliever and knew only a few words of Yiddish. I remember from my childhood that he would repeat, *"Meshuga i stumpf!"* Or perhaps I've got the expression mixed up in my faulty memory. At the house of my paternal grandparents, who came to Warsaw from Konin, Polish was the only language spoken and the kosher laws were not observed, although Passover and Purim were celebrated. I still remember the sweet cakes with almonds that my grandmother was famous for.

My father had me baptized when Poland regained its independence because he felt that otherwise there would be no future for me among Poles. He did not get baptized himself, but he insisted that my mother be baptized along with me. "The boy has to have at least one parent of the same faith as his," he said.

I remember when I was seven or eight or perhaps nine years old telling my father to kneel down and then waving a small crucifix at him. Or perhaps I was kneeling down and my father stood over me. I forgot all about that episode for years; it came back to me after my father's death. At no point did he have any doubt whatsoever that his decision to baptize me was the right one. Especially during the Nazi occupation.

I was searching for my proper place and the way to assert my identity. I was drawn to Laski because it was literally and figuratively a place of converts. Rafał Blüth introduced me to Laski, or perhaps I met him there. Or perhaps I met Blüth through Stempowski. In those final years before the outbreak of World War II, distinct and dissimilar waves of hope and despair alternated and intersected. Blüth wrote about the poet Adam Mickiewicz's final years in "The Constantinople Catastrophe"; Stempowski published his "Essay for Cassandra." Ludwik Fryde, my classmate from university, was also in some way connected to Laski and *Verbum*. Blüth, arrested by the Gestapo in October 1939, perished in one of the first mass executions. Ludwik Fryde was killed in the spring of 1942 in Byelorussia, where he had long been in hiding in a parish. He was baptized shortly before his death. It was Fryde who first got me to read Maritain.

During those months in Paris I was certainly one of the very few young people—if not the only person—who visited Breton, took part in the Thursday gatherings at Jacques and Raissa Maritain's, and almost simultaneously received surrealist and Thomist indoctrination from the very fountainhead. Only years later did I realize how similar those two milieus were—perhaps only in their tastes, but that is not without significance. In their discussions of poetry, both the Maritains and Breton would allude to Aloysius Bertrand, the *Romantische Schule,* and the dark Nerval, especially from his blackest period. Both admired Max Jacob, who was also a convert, and treated Lautréamont's youthful ravings reverentially and with deadly seriousness. I must admit I was well prepared. I had been introduced to Lautréamont by Stempowski, who was amazed that he included Adam Mickiewicz among the damned poets, and Stefan Napierski first gave me Max Jacob to read. Napierski was also a convert, but to a quite different faith. Whatever one's confiteor and ontology, one cannot escape the tastes of one's own period. Sister Teresa, a Thomist, was dazzled by Gombrowicz's *Ferdydurke*.

There were more similarities than differences between the "convulsive beauty" that Breton advocated and the "transcendental beauty" that is the *form* of being. There were differences in the language and in the metaphysics, but the saliva and earthly nourishment were the same. Neither the demonic Breton, who practiced training the imagination, nor the mystical Raissa, nor the last of the great scholastics, Maritain, had any confidence in nature. Neither art nor morality was supposed to serve nature or imitate it. Rather they were to conquer it, to subvert it, to irradiate it, or at least to shake loose everything that is simply natural. At about the same time Artaud called for the training of the body and invoked the plague as the double of the theater.

In those few years between the Spanish civil war and the outbreak of World War II the truly great philosophical debates took place between the disciples of the four sages—Augustine, Thomas Aquinas, Kant, and Hegel—between the phenomenologists and dialecticians of both faiths, between the once-again hungry devils of history and action and the elusive angels of pure knowledge. Husserl's angels were on the other side of the mirror. Try as one might, in the end one hit one's nose against a pane of glass. The angels were not even to be touched.

In the late spring of 1939, my friend Stefan Żółkiewski from Warsaw wrote to me in Paris:

I'm almost a Thomist by now. I'm up to my ears in the *Summa theologica* and I'm wild about it. What a splendid accomplishment! Not a single hole in it. Like the rounded sphere of Parmenides. But it lacks Marx's humor. My Persian cat gets fatter by the day. Remember, you called him Emil Meyersohn. In his philosophy (he certainly has one) my cat is anything but a relativist. And he certainly is not a Thomist. The cat bristles and raises his magnificent tail whenever I settle down to read Saint Thomas. Oh, if we could only dispense with metaphysics and stick to pure ontology. To remain intellectually honest and believe in God. Maybe that little old man with the beard is right after all—only by eating a pudding can one discover what it tastes like. But you cannot have your pudding and eat it at the same time. An eaten pudding is an intentional being, as Husserl might have said, the idea of an eaten pudding. Poor positivists: they will never understand that. Emil Meyersohn has bristled again and is spitting and hissing. He wants me to adopt his ontology first of all. To calm down, I read *The Pickwick Papers* in bed. Get thee to a brothel, Ophelia, go. Sam Weller sends his best regards.

4.

That spring I ended up in a monastery. I was fed up with Paris, with all the Parises. I had tried to grasp them all. I still continued my daily trips to the Bibliothèque Nationale on the rue Richelieu, passing by the now deserted Palais Royal, where the whores displayed their wares for the last time in Balzac's time. I did not go to the Bibliothèque's main reading room but instead went down to the basement, to what was called *l'enfer*, where I had special permission to read pornography from all over the world. My doctoral dissertation at the Sorbonne was to be on Apollinaire as editor of the Marquis de Sade. But I became sick of even that kind of literature. I was experiencing some sort of breakdown. I felt empty, as though I had suddenly vomited everything that I had eaten.

I went to see Maritain. He knew I was a nonbeliever. But I told him so again anyway. He smiled. And he rarely smiled. "Let your body and your soul rest for a while. Fresh air will do you a lot of good, my boy." And he wrote me a letter of recommendation to the rector of the Dominican order.

The monastery was located in the Massif Central. And there was in fact plenty of air there. The windows in the refectories were left open at all times, and through them came the strong scent of herbs from the garden. Birds would often stray in and flutter through the corridors. The whiteness of that monastery still dazzles my eyes. The walls were white, the corridors and the cells were white, the cassocks were white. Only the chapel was dark and empty except for the stained-glass window and the crucifix. And the hoods were dark-colored. We put them over our heads whenver the name of God was uttered in our prayers and in our hushed singing that was like humming. Starting at midnight, every three hours, eight times a day, the tinkling of tiny bells summoned us to the chapel for prayers and the singing of a Latin hymn. The seminarians were excused from two prayers: at midnight and at three o'clock in the morning. At six I would run to the chapel, still half-asleep and dreaming. Often what followed seemed a continuation of the dream. The dark hoods in that early-morning ballet of white cassocks flapped up and down with a life of their own; in the dark shadows, the beards, lighted by the swaying flames of candles, rose up in the air as in the paintings of Chagall.

I was one of the seminarians. But my stay wasn't a novitiate, not even the beginning of one. It was a *trial,* exactly as Raissa and Jacques had planned it. Immediately after my arrival I told my guide and mentor—who was in all likelihood the youngest of the brothers—that I was a nonbeliever. He was not surprised. "We don't believe that we believe," he said, "Go for long walks all by yourself. Preferably at dawn, before the first carillon has sounded. I give you dispensation from taking Communion, but you must go to confession regularly."

I went to confession, as was the practice, on the first Friday. "I don't believe," I said. "Don't you remember any other sins?" inquired a calm voice from behind the other side of the grill. And before the customary knock came dismissing me, the voice was heard again: "Take walks among the trees and read Pascal." I had already begun reading Pascal in Warsaw. "Man is neither an angel nor a beast." The legacy of the Jansenists had somehow survived in that cloister. These brothers didn't trust nature. But they didn't trust angels either. I had already come across that same kind of Christian pessimism in Laski. And on Maritain's lips, with their drooping corners.

There were over thirty seminarians there at the time, all either a few years older than I was or the same age; most were clerics or had various secular diplomas from different countries of Europe, Asia, and Africa. Usually there were two seminarians from a given country. It was only much later that I found out how carefully they were selected and how rigorous the requirements for selection were. The monastery was a Dominican university. After a long period of proving ourselves, we were destined for the order's highest distinctions, perhaps even in the entire Church. But that too I discovered much later, after I had left. Classes started at eight in the morning and lasted until the midday meal. Then, after an hour's walk, we would return to our "cells." They each had a window overlooking the garden, a large wooden table, two chairs, a washstand with a pitcher for hot or cold water, an iron bed with a crucifix over it—and a bookcase. We were allowed to take books out of the monastery library and bring them to our cells. There we did our "homework," which usually took the form of short essays or summaries of our readings. The courses consisted of philosophy, theology, Greek, and Hebrew—Latin was considered a "native" language, and from time to time we would be asked to write our *pensa* in it. There were also optional seminars like the history of art. It was my favorite seminar. A Spanish Dominican lectured on Goya and cruelty in art, and the reading list included Artaud. I first heard of Bataille at that point. But to my astonishment Sade, too, was on the reading list. For a moment I thought I was back in *l'enfer* in the basement of the Bibliothèque Nationale. The recommended reading by Sade was *The One Hundred and Twenty Days of Sodom*. But that was not the only unexpected thing in the Dominican monastery.

During the first month of my stay there was a mass and office of the dead for the Basques. The Basques were ardent Catholics, but in the Spanish civil war they sided with the Republicans and were fought against with special cruelty and then tortured in the camps both by Franco's Catholic regiments and by the Moslem units from Spanish Morocco. It was only then that I understood why the Spanish Dominican lecturer had chosen Goya's *Caprichos* and *Disasters of War* for his seminar on the history of painting. Briefly when I attended the obsequies for the Basques and the colloquium on the cruelty and bestiality of the Fascists, it seemed to me that I was back among Maria's circle of bearded Trotskyites on the top floors of cheap hotels or in the bistros thick with the smoke of Gauloises.

It was in that astonishing monastery in the early spring of 1939 that I felt for the first time something like the winds of approaching war. I certainly did not feel anything like that in Paris; during the day the air over the Seine was pearly, and at night, in Jan Brzękowski's words, it was like "a red sky of desire." The fathers in those long robes of white wool in that monastery in the midst of a vast garden may have had forebodings—that closed monastery was open to the world. The Dominicans were in Madrid and Berlin and, of course, Rome, although at the time relations between the curia and the order were far from reflecting the usual harmony and submissiveness to the hierarchy. The Dominicans' magazine, *Sept,* had been suspended on a sudden order from Rome. During my first weeks at the monastery, *Sept* was still to be found on the tables of the refectory; then it disappeared. The suspension of *Sept* was linked to the emergence of the "worker-priests," a movement that had originated in France. In the beginning six young priests abandoned their vicariates and left their parishes to go live like laborers and work as hired hands. Several of them were suspended. The Dominicans of *Sept* saw in this suppression a revival of the Church of the "powerful." Or perhaps they foresaw the movement toward a Church of the "poor," as happened half a century later in Latin America. I had met one of the new "apostles" at a get-together held by Maria and her bearded Trotskyites. Maria had been trained in party discipline as a young girl and had no confidence in dissidents. The Dominicans did.

I was happy in the monastery or at least I had what I would call, for lack of a better term, moments of lightness. From daybreak to the end of the evening meal, during which one of the brothers would read aloud, in Latin of course, either Thomas Aquinas's *Summa* or Augustine—the *Confessions,* not *De civitate Dei*—we were obliged to keep absolutely silent. We could only answer the questions posed by the fathers during the seminars and had to ask for permission to speak in the colloquia.

Friendships were formed during our evening walks in the garden. Never before had I encountered among my colleagues such a density of brilliant minds, such openness to everything, an almost perceptible vibration of thought. Nor would I later encounter anything comparable among my students. I too became more open and vibrating. The long hours of silence and concentration in the solitude of my bright cell, with the constant sharp scents of the garden, suited me well. I got used to the meatless diet, and the fish, both salt- and freshwater, was always excellent—even now my reminiscences about the monastery are linked to the crispness of the fried fish.

There were periods when I felt I could spend my whole life there in that fashion and, like Stendhal's Julian Sorel, dream of a bishop's miter or at least the purple belt of a prelate. But Julian Sorel sent secret letters to Madame de Renal from his monastery. When I left the monastery, I told my spiritual mentor that I was still a nonbeliever. He smiled just as he did that first day: "It only seems to us that we don't believe. Go for long morning walks and remember that this is your home forever and you can return any time."

Nearly forty years later, on the opposite side of the world, I heard almost the same words spoken again. It was in Thailand, near the border with Burma. I had spent all night getting there from Bangkok. During the day the heat was stifling; the nights were more bearable, although the air still felt like a wet rag stuck in one's mouth. I don't know why, but that night the bus was filled with vendors of straw hats and huge woven bags. At each stop—and there were many of them—half-naked boys sold bowls of rice and skewered chicken dripping with throat-burning red-pepper sauce. My destination was a small town in the mountains. It was famous for its young girls who, with their bare feet, ran back and forth along a man's spine in a highly refined yet risky massage, since one false step could result in permanent injury. But now, with summer drawing to a close in a relentless series of heat waves, the town seemed depopulated and its sanctuaries of pleasure tightly shut.

I had come to this town for a different purpose. In the surrounding mountains was one of the most famous Buddhist wooden temples. But in the town I was told that the monks were hostile toward visitors, that they sought to preserve their isolation, and that nobody was ever allowed to stay there overnight. None of this succeeded in frightening me away. I hired a guide with a donkey for what was a six-hour trip on the donkey or following it, and then another full hour of climbing the steep, stony path.

The temple was small, as though it had sunk into the ground. I knew the ritual. I struck the brass gong three times and lighted a resinous chip in front of the Buddha. He was different from the ones I knew. Like all other Buddhas, he had folds of fat hanging off his stomach, but his folds were cracked in places. And there were deep furrows on his cheeks resembling sword slashes. He was smiling, but the smile on his cracked face, eaten away by wood borers, was very sad. His eyelids drooped, as if he had lost all desire to see anything anymore. Several monks with clean-shaven heads were squatting by the walls as motionless as huge yellow beetles sound asleep. As I could not sit for long with my knees folded under me, I stretched my legs out, supporting myself on my elbows. In this position I contemplated the Buddha for a long time, until in that broiling heat my eyelids, too, closed tightly. The Buddha can be adored while one is asleep or awake. Perhaps asleep one is even closer to the Buddha, who watches and dozes beyond time. It was almost dark when I woke up. A very young monk, the youngest of them all, stood in front of me. Placing both his hands on his breast, fingers together as in prayer, he led me to a straw mat. Then he brought me a jug of green tea, cold and aromatic. The next morning when I awoke, he was already standing over me with a rice cake and herbal tea.

The following day, and the day after that, and the day after that did not in any way differ one from the other. The heat did not abate. After washing in the stream not far from our bedding, I would walk to the shrine of the Buddha with the scarred cheeks like those of Byzantine madonnas. I would strike the gong, light the little sticks of incense—from which there rose up unendingly a thin wisp of white smoke—fix my eyes on the drowsing Buddha, and fall asleep. I would wake up and fall asleep again. Gradually being asleep and waking up ceased to differ. Anymore than did all the days that followed.

It was a Zen Buddhist monastery devoted exclusively to meditation and contemplation. Zen tells you to be empty— like the limpid water from a mountain stream that you hold for a moment in the hollow of your bent hand. And free of any desires, for they only agitate, like the breeze that ripples the smooth surface of water. If you are hungry, appease your hunger; if you are thirsty, appease your thirst; if you are tormented by the stings of your body, lie with a woman, and when she leaves, your body will float away with her.

These Zen monks with shaven heads, who embraced total poverty, were not even allowed to beg. Every evening a few women from the neighboring villages would come to the shrine carrying baskets woven (as in Polish villages) out of wood bark and full of jugs of green tea, rice in small bags, and sometimes fruit, unfamiliar to me, that was sweetish in taste like the mango. Once or twice, as dusk fell, the women lay with the youngest monks in total silence and for a brief moment. In this union the man and woman seemed frozen like copulating insects. It was an offering, like the rice cakes and the slices of dried fish. These village women offered whatever they had.

The simplest gestures were my principal means of communicating with those monks in yellow cloaks. Only two of them knew a few words in English. I still do not understand how it actually happened that these monks with their clean-shaven heads and hostile attitude toward visitors kept me overnight, and I understand even less how it happened that they accepted me as though they hardly noticed my presence. As though my coming to that secluded spot in mountains was something perfectly natural. They did not ask me any questions, except in the evening of my second day there, when the eldest monk asked me what name he should use in addressing me and then repeated over and over again: Yon, Yon, Yan, until he had grasped the difference between "a" and "o." And on another occasion, on the third evening, I was asked what country I came from.

I have no idea whether "Poland" meant anything to them, but they did know that it was somewhere across the ocean.

They avoided looking me straight in the eye, which would have been a sign of arrogance according to accepted Eastern etiquette. Seemingly they were oblivious of my presence, yet they took care of me with touching delicateness. I was still smoking at the time and I soon ran out of cigarettes, but since my body was floating away, I did not experience any craving for nicotine. One morning I found four cigarettes on my bed. The monks must have asked the village women to bring some. Another time one of the women came over to me and gestured to me to take off my shirt. The next day she gave it back to me freshly laundered in the stream. I was losing my sense of time. The days and nights were all the same. In this half-sleeping, half-waking state, memories of my childhood kept returning to me more and more insistently: my father, my mother, my grandparents, Aunt Marychna, our apartment in Oboźna Street, and my grandparents' apartment in Senatorska Street; the dead returned, but there was nothing sad about it, as though they were still right next to me, only all the images I saw were dark, as on the negative of a strip of film, and they overlapped and had grown blurred.

It seemed to me that I spent weeks in that Buddhist monastery. In reality, I was there only seven or eight days, as I calculated with great difficulty, using my fingers and a pocket calendar I found when I returned to the small town where the naked girls ran barefoot over men's spines. On my last evening in the mountains, the sky was red in the west as though a storm was approaching. I said my farewells to the youngest and the eldest of the monks. The eldest said: "You are leaving for the West, but this is your home forever and you shall return."

5.

Barely two weeks after I left the Dominican monastery, I jumped off a moving bus pulling away from the place de la Concorde right at the corner of the rue de Rivoli. Standing there at the bus stop was a young girl of touching beauty, in a knee-length gray fur coat, her head uncovered. A few weeks before my departure for the monastery, I had met her at some Polish name-day party in Paris. We exchanged only a few words since she left early. But I found out that her name was Steinhaus. I thought about her often in the Dominican monastery. A couple of months before I left for Paris, Irena Krzemicka, who during the war married Tadeusz Kroński (nobody yet called him "Tiger," as he would later be known), had told me that I would marry Lidia, the daughter of a famous Polish mathematician, Hugo Steinhaus. Irena, who was a few years older than Lidia, had attended the same gymnasium in Lvov. Irena's brown eyes turned yellow when she was angry, which made her resemble an owl. She translated Plato and told fortunes. Since Lidia Steinhaus lived in Lvov at the time, we had never met and I took Irena's fortune-telling as a joke.

Three weeks after my jumping off the bus at the place de la Concorde, Lidia and I were living together in the small Hôtel Henri IV, in the triangular place Dauphine near the Pont Neuf. It was a beautiful spot, and it only became fashionable after the war. The hotel was very cheap but without modern conveniences; the bathroom was in the hallway. On the place Dauphine, at the rear of the Palais de Justice, there was only one restaurant, Chez Paul, famous for its *paupiettes de veau en papillottes*. We never ate there; it was far too expensive.

At the beginning of August 1939 we returned to Poland, leaving behind in the hotel my old suitcase with my diary and the notes for my dissertation on Apollinaire and the frightful Marquis de Sade. On our first trip to Paris a year after the war we went to the hotel to try to recover my papers. The suitcase and its contents had been lost. But we found our names in the guest book, which still had the same oilcloth cover, only now even more dog-eared than before.

During that first postwar trip to Paris, Lidia and I got to know Alexander Glasberg. Father Glasberg always wore the same greasy cassock. His eyesight was poor, so he also wore very thick, almost convex round glasses. I think he came from Vilno, where he had attended a cheder. I didn't ask him about his conversion. It must have occurred while he was still living in Poland. But he probably graduated from a French seminary well before the war. He was a good ten years older than I was. He must have suffered from a heart condition, too, since he was often short of breath.

The Polish ambassador to France at the time was Stanisław Skrzeszewski. We were invited to dinner at the Skrzeszewskis' along with Father Glasberg. "Your French, Father, is as good as your Polish," said the ambassador's wife while the cheeses were being served. "What language do you think in?"

"In what language?" Father Glasberg hesitated. I think that he must already have been a papal prelate then, as the red piping on his greasy cassock seemed to indicate. "In Yiddish, of course," he said.

Father Glasberg was awarded the highest French distinctions. He had taken part in the Resistance from the very beginning. His vocation was rescuing people. He saved Jews from both zones of France, the occupied and the unoccupied, and helped them get to Spain. Earlier, he had saved many Spaniards in the Republican army who had fled to France after the defeat and were threatened with deportation. I was told that after the war he saved Germans who were in hiding.

Father Glasberg took us to an orphanage just outside Paris. There were about thirty boys and girls ranging from five to twelve years old. All of them had been given the same last name, Korczak: Piotr Korczak, Izydor Korczak, Sally Korczak, Zuza Korczak. These Jewish orphans had been brought to France from Poland after the infamous pogrom in Kielce in 1946, when over a hundred thousand Jews left Poland for good. The great majority of these Jews had survived the war because they had been deported to various parts of the Soviet Union and had returned to Poland after 1945 only to confront vandalized cemeteries, burned-down synagogues, and homes to which they were refused entry. Whatever happened to those scores of French Korczaks? Nobody knows.

Here is yet another postscript or supplement to the theme of time recaptured. In 1959, or perhaps 1960, I attended a conference in Paris organized by UNESCO for the representatives of university radio. I had no connection with the university programs on Polish radio—if there ever were any—but I was sent to the conference anyway, following the Polish practice at the time, since I spoke French and was on hand. During the conference I noticed that someone at the opposite end of the table was studying me carefully. I could tell from his purple hat and his belt of the same color that he must be a bishop. It wasn't long before he threw his arms around me. He remembered me from our time together at the Dominican monastery. Now, as Monsignore Z., he was the director of radio programing for the Ecumenical University at the Città dei Vaticano.

The Occupations

For the first two or three weeks after my arrival in
Lvov, I hardly went out of the house. For a long time
I didn't even get out of bed. I was able to eat around
the clock. Lidia's mother or the maid, Pazia, used a
bowl—because even a deep dish wasn't enough—to
bring me dumplings, kasha, or noodles with milk.
In Lidia's room everything was white: the bed, the
walls, the furniture, even the bookshelves. But it
was precisely in this white room of hers, almost
unchanged since her childhood, that I realized that
everything that had existed before was over once
and for all. Not even four months had passed since
I said "See you" to Lidia. We spent the entire month
of August in Lvov with Lidia's parents. That was
probably the most idyllic month of all those we had
together. In the morning, we ate in our room off a
wooden tray—raspberries or wild strawberries, fruit
preserves in little saucers, freshly baked homemade
bread, often still warm, and coffee with cream. We
had time in the last days of August to make an excursion on foot to Worochta through pastures warmed
by the sun, where the freely grazing cows always
frightened Lidia. But the very first afternoon we
were sent back. The mobilization had been declared.

I had said farewell to Lidia—"See you" all too
often conveys a false promise of return—at the
railway station at Kamień Dobosza, not far from
the Romanian border, a day's trip by horse-drawn
wagon. The women on the platform, mothers and
wives, wept. But this scene has suddenly receded
into the distant past and I no longer remember it except as images from films of the First World War.
Our vacations at Kamień Dobosza and the Paris that

we had known belonged henceforth to a bygone era. I came back from the war to Lidia, but for us the war had just begun. And Paris came back to us again, but that was a year later, in the crackling and snapping of a muffled BBC newscast announcing the entry of the Germans into the French capital.

I still wasn't leaving the house much when Władysław Broniewski, Aleksander Wat, and several others were arrested after a contrived ruckus at a dinner party to which they and a Soviet visitor from Moscow had been invited. During those first weeks at Lvov, Gustaw Herling-Grudziński visited us with Krystyna Broniatowska. The road to Romania seemed to be blocked, but Lithuania was still free and the road to Grodno and Vilno apparently continued to be open. That was the direction that Gustaw and Krystyna took. Gustaw was seized a couple of months later a few miles from Grodno. Before my arrival, one of my cousins, Kazik Kott, visited Lidia and her parents. In Warsaw, almost immediately after the capitulation on 27 September, he joined the first military underground, perhaps even organized it. Picked up during a sweep and imprisoned in Aleja Szucha, where the Gestapo had its headquarters, he managed to jump from his cell onto the head of a guard and thus made his escape. Throughout Warsaw during the short time I was there, posters with his photograph were still posted everywhere, promising in Polish and in German a reward for his capture. He was supposed to drop by Lidia's again, but nothing more was seen of him. After my arrival in Lvov, various vague and never verified rumors circulated about attacks on military convoys headed for the General Government. Kazik must have been arrested, but whether he was killed on the spot or deported was never known.

Before I started to go out regularly, Mieczysław Jastrun often visited us. He spoke about the recently organized meetings of the *Profspiłka,* as the Writers' Union of the Western Ukraine was called. These meetings were held on Copernicus Street in Count Bielski's mansion. The union was immediately divided into three sections: Ukrainian, Polish, and Jewish. Each section held its meetings separately, but all three selected candidates according to the same procedure, which most resembled the interrogation of a suspect; Mieczysław Jastrun called it "mud baths." Being accepted in the *Profspiłka* gave one, or promised one, the right to food and, what was more important, fuel and, above all, housing authorization. But the price one had to pay was responding to the most insidious questions and engaging in "sincere self-criticism." In the Jewish section these interrogations were a dismal farce. When Z. finished telling about his life of constant misery, someone in the hall cried out: "But you didn't say that your father had a store!" The poor victim went pale, then turned red and replied triumphantly: "He had a store, but he went bankrupt."

Getting accepted in the Polish section was even more sinister. Sitting behind the table, with her teeth clenched, Elżbieta Szemplińska was the chief inquisitor of this commission; she seemed to hate absolutely everyone. The destinies of Poles are almost always complicated, but the knots that Szemplińska tied were as frightening as they were repulsive. I can still remember her one early morning when, after a night spent drinking, we suddenly decided to take a little trip to the country. "This is the first time," Elżbieta said, "that we've seen each other in the light of day." She had fuzzy light red hair and probably clenched teeth already. She had just published a collection of poems that were bitterly erotic but very daring for those times. On the eve of the Germans' entry into Lvov, she fled on a motorcycle with her frightful husband, Zygmunt Sobolewski, whom Jastrun nicknamed Pedro, and their several-month-old infant. In the depths of Russia their fate was, it appears, a terrible one, and the child died of hunger. They came back to Poland with the First Army in 1944, and not long afterward they were appointed to the Polish consulate in Luxembourg. A couple of months later they took documents and money out of the safe—at least that is what was said—and sought political asylum. For a number of years they remained exiles and led a difficult wandering life, finally ending up in Casablanca. Szemplińska's husband must have been involved in anti-Soviet activity; he was lured aboard a ship and thereafter lost sight of. Elżbieta next surfaced in Madrid. There she worked with Józef Łobodowski doing Polish-language broadcasts, which were probably terminated after Franco's death. Years passed. Szemplińska apparently grew depressed and wrote to Jerzy Putrament that she wanted to come back to Poland. Putrament finally arranged her return, but only in the 1960s. She had a small room on the top floor of the Writers' Union on Krakowskie Przedmieście. Once I saw her as she was coming down the stairs. I didn't actually recognize her; what I saw was a tiny, shriveled old lady who was, it seemed, already half-crazy. Hers is one of the most somber Polish stories, with a tragic dimension. And one of the many impressive stories in a Central European personal dossier, a disturbing *éducation européenne,* as yet unwritten.

At my admission interview for the *Profspiłka,* when I had finished the account of my wartime activities, Szemplińska, stony-faced, asked me why I didn't express joy at the fall of "manorial Poland" and the liberation of the Western Ukraine. In those days the phrase "manorial *Polsha*" was repeated endlessly like a password in every speech, and at least several times in the first few pages of every issue of the *Red Banner* (*Czerwony Sztandar*). I replied, to a murmur of approval from the auditorium, that I could not rejoice at the liberation of Lvov while Warsaw was occupied by the Germans. Szemplińska accorded my response a sour look, but I was accepted into the *Profspiłka* and I even took home some provisions.

A Ukrainian delegate from Kiev, Petro Panch, directed this new union and the mansion on Copernicus Street. He was very tall and had impeccable manners. Tea was served on the ground floor in the hall near the entrance, and sometimes there were even *chatka,* Siberian crabmeat. There were chess boards on the tables. Bruno Winawer, who was the best player, spent hours taking on all opponents. At least twice a day Panch would make a systematic tour of all the tables. "Winawer," he once said, "it's OK you play chess, but it's not OK you have so many different faces. I hear you write novels, comedies, and treatises on science. That's not OK: a writer ought to have only one face. Take me as an example. I only write fairy tales for children."

Registration was in progress in Lvov before my arrival.

There was registration of officers, of foresters, of those who wanted to cross to the other side of the Bug River. A number of Jews were even registering to return to German-occupied Poland. The future was uncertain, impossible to foresee both here and on the other side. But on the other side one's family and close relatives had often been left behind. In the General Government, Jews already had to wear the arm band with the Star of David, but the ghettos were not yet closed and no one then could have imagined the "final solution." But Lidia's father foresaw the worst. At the beginning of 1940, Maria Dąbrowska and Jerzy Stempowski's father, Stanisław, reached the General Government via Przemyśl. Lidia and I met them at Ineczek and Stasia Blumenfeld's before their departure. It was at this point that Winawer, crossed the border. (He died of tuberculosis in 1944.) Leon Grunwald, Lidia's mother's uncle, a former Piłsudski legionnaire who carried himself straight as a ramrod and wore a monocle, also decided to leave. He obviously ran the risk of deportation by the Soviets. My father-in-law hid him in our house in a small room in the attic and advised him not to leave. But Uncle Leon insisted, and he was shot by the Germans in Cracow, where everyone knew him.

Muta, Lidia's cousin, was taken from our house. She had decided to return but did not have time to get out and was sent to northern Siberia, close to the Arctic Circle. To the very end Lidia's mother sent her packages of kasha, flour, and sugar. My friend Roman Karst registered to stay but was also deported, sent to chop down trees in the land of the Arctic winter. Lidia's father told me not to register. As a member of the *Profspiłka* I was on the list of writers, and I thought that I wasn't threatened with deportation. But registration was required of all refugees (or *byezhentsy,* as they were known in Russian). Frightened, everyone went to the authorities to register. A kind of terror was in the air, slowly infecting everyone, and there was widespread belief in the omniscience and omnipresence of the NKVD. Besides, we were also being watched by the Ukrainians, who had gone overnight from nationalists to the most rabid of Communists.

They came to get me during the second or third wave of

mass deportations. At two in the morning, a corporal and a simple soldier. They asked to see me and told me to pack. They were, unlike the Germans in similar situations, silent and, in their own way, very human. Seeing Lidia's mother crying, they consoled her by saying that her son would come back, and if not, Mother Earth was vast, and humans lived everywhere. "You will find another husband," they told Lidia, "and your husband will find another wife." Deportation to the other end of the country, to the Arctic zones, or to the steppes of Kazakhstan, was, for those two Soviet soldiers, something quite ordinary and simple, devoid of cruelty. But those two, the corporal and the simple soldier—who it turned out had come here directly from the Urals—helped Lidia pack my things and made sure that I took with me soap and extra pairs of warm underwear. And that I didn't forget a blanket.

At the station at Zamarstynów the train waiting for us was still almost empty. It was a long train. As I went along the platform, I counted twenty wagons, and I hadn't reached the end. In an hour or two, before day broke, all the wagons were loaded with people, mostly young men but also women, even ones with small children.

By a strange coincidence, Boy-Żeleński was put in my wagon. I knew him only by sight, having seen him from afar at public readings in jammed lecture halls in Warsaw and then, more recently, at an official gathering in the Lvov theater, where he sat on the platform at a table draped in red, beneath immense portraits of Lenin, Stalin, and Mickiewicz. Now he was seated opposite me, hunched over, his square face wan, with huge circles under his eyes. He looked like an old man. He was then at least eight years younger than I am now as I write these lines.

As a schoolboy, I had devoured everything he wrote. I remember best his articles about voluntary maternity; I was completely flushed as I read them. After his "Betrothed" was published on the first page of the *Literary News* (*Wiadomości Literackie*) when I was in the eighth grade and getting ready to take my final gymnasium exams, I sent him a long letter—rewritten five times—in which I said that I was entirely in agreement with him and that the afianced should not have to wait for the Church's blessing but should immediately and without formalities enter into a marriage of equals. Boy answered me very quickly, on the back of one of his photos, thanking me for my letter and my support but saying that I should still wait a couple of years before entering into a marriage of equals. Boy was one of the emblems of that prewar rationalist tradition to which—despite its bourgeois baggage—we wished to be attached in our review the *Forge* (*Kuźnica*) in Łódź. I was labeled a follower of Boy when I began to publish my theatrical column, "As You Like It." At the beginning of the 1950s I edited Boy's *Little Words* (*Słówka*) and wrote an enthusiastic preface. I knew a good number of those "little words" by heart. And now we were sitting face to face in that train full of deportees being sent to the East.

Boy did not say a word. It must have been seven o'clock, because it was already bright, when, accompanied by two Soviets decorated with medals as if a Christmas tree, Wanda Wasilewska came running along the platform and rescued Boy, two painters whom I did not know, and me. When I got back to Kadecka Street, Lidia was standing on the balcony. From a distance I waved to her with my yellow blanket. The fate of objects is sometimes strange. They often have a surprising permanence, as though they had their own immortality. That yellow, warm, and eternally downy blanket went through the whole war and two occupations. Lidia's parents must have had it at Berdyczów, since it stayed to the very end in their house in Wrocław.

That winter and spring Wasilewska saved several dozen people from the mass deportations. Writers and actors. And once or twice entire families with young children. I had not known her before the war; I had only seen photos of her in the *Signals* (*Sygnały*) and read the pieces attacking against her as a "Communist ringleader" in the nationalist press, and even in *Flame* (*Płomyk*) or *Little Flame* (*Płomyczek*) (for kindergarteners). I had tried to read her novels, but they had seemed to me insipid and sentimental although decidedly red. From the beginning, she was the most important person in Lvov, at least among the Polish Communists. She hadn't yet become a delegate from Lvov to the Kiev Soviet—the "elections" hadn't yet taken place—but it was already said that Stalin himself had praised her novel *The Earth under the Yoke (Ziemia w jarzmie)*. She founded and edited *New Horizons (Nowe Widnokręgi)*, which was to become the principal literary and political monthly for Polish writers and scientists. Boy's long essay on Balzac appeared in the first or second issue.

One morning several months after our rescue from that train of deportees, Wasilewska's husband, Marian Bogatko, was shot dead in their apartment just before dawn. He also, it seems, occupied a very high position in the Communist hierarchy before the dissolution of the Polish Communist party. The perpetrators of the crime were never discovered. Many sorts of rumors circulated.

On the third day after Hitler attacked Russia, when the Germans were already approaching Lvov, Wasilewska burst into the hastily called general assembly at the mansion on Copernicus Street. She was in uniform and brandished a carbine. "We'll defend Lvov to the very end." This was a very Polish gesture on Wanda's part. And the next day at dawn she left Lvov for Kiev along with the entire *nachalstvo,* all the upper-echelon officials. It was that same day, I think, that a bomb fell very close to Copernicus Street and killed both Franek Parecki— who in the good old days frequented the Artistic Club "S" in the Baryczkas' townhouse in Warsaw's Old Town—and his very beautiful wife, who had incredibly limpid eyes in a cold face; they were thought to be extremely dangerous. The same bomb also killed Aleksander Havryluk, a former prisoner at Bereza Kartuska, where his fellow inmate was Leon Pasternak. Of the Ukrainian Communists, Havryluk was the most human, free of bitterness and hatred, and one of the few who not only understood but felt compassion for the refugees from "manorial *Polsha.*" He was certainly a good poet, in the tradition of Polish postromanticism. I have retained in my memory a few scraps of his poems evoking the smoke rising from the "famished flames" of the shepherds' stubble fires. I remembered those "famished flames."

In the procession of the dead that these pages inevitably call forth, different epochs merge and become superimposed because the dead live in multiple times. The first week after the Germans entered Lvov, Boy-Żeleński was shot, along with twenty-four other professors. Among them were Professor Stożek and his two sons and Professor Longchamp and his two sons, friends of Lidia's father. They were shot at dawn immediately after having been taken from their homes to Wólka Kadecka, a few hundred yards from our house. The same day, my father-in-law told us to leave the house immediately. We never went back again.

During that first winter of the war, I began to work, but I no longer remember if it was before Wasilewska saved me from deportation or after. I was in a group of refugees from Warsaw whose job it was to put back in order the totally disorganized and half-destroyed court archives housed in a building that had belonged to the Jesuits. Each morning we were assigned a specific number of documents, of which we burned a fair amount to keep warm in the freezing cold. I went to work in a heavy knee-length gray sweater and wide green trousers of thick flannel that my father-in-law wore to work in the garden. At home, that outfit—which made me look like an escapee from the circus—was called "stupid Bill."

Then, probably in late spring, I became *pombuch,* or assistant accountant, in the *Natsmenizdat,* that is, the publishing house, or *izdatelstvo,* for the Jewish and Polish national minorities. The head accountant, the *glavbuch,* was an important figure in the Soviet bureaucracy; in the big enterprises, the *glavbuch* belonged to the *nomenklatura.* He was the one who decided if the plan—and the premiums and medals that devolved from it—was judged as having been surpassed. Compared to the *glavbuch,* obviously, the *pombuch* was insignificant. When I came home, Lidia always greeted me with the following antic jingle: "The *glavbuch* and the *pombuch* together in one house, / The peaceful *glavbuch* wouldn't harm a mouse. / The *pombuch* did the mischief, the dirty louse." And what had to happen happened. On the day before a holiday, I had to pay all the employees a two-week advance and they all signed their names on a large sheet of paper indicating the amounts received. At the bottom of the sheet there was a large seal. I don't know how, but I immediately lost the paper with the signatures and the seal. Fortunately for me, after the holiday everyone acknowledged the amounts received. But I ceased to be the *pombuch* and was made a proofreader instead. The change was not a promotion, and I was less well paid, but the work seemed relaxing and not dangerous. The names of Lenin and Stalin, though, could never be separated and put on different lines. Once one of my unlucky coworkers did not catch a typo that rendered Stalin as Sralin, from the word *srać,* to shit, and she was accused of sabotage. She underwent hours of special interrogation and it was with the greatest difficulty that she was finally saved. But no one dared breathe when the following appeared in the *Red Banner,* to everyone's great amusement: "G. B. Shaw, the greatest joker of our time, has called Stalin the most eminent statesman of the twentieth century." Lidia's father invariably called the Soviets bandar-logs [the monkey people in Kipling's *Jungle Book*].

Adam Bromberg was in charge of the *Natsmenizdat*—the Polish section, in any case. I had known him in the 1930s when he was a salesman in a small bookstore on Senatorska Street, just behind Theater Square. I lived with my grandparents, also on Senatorska Street, but at the other end, at the corner of Miodowa Street. Bromberg was very thin and very tall and knew all the books in the bookstore by heart. He could locate them immediately and take them down, even from the highest shelves, just by standing on a low footstool. He seemed to know all books, even those that had never been in the bookstore. Steinsberg ran the bookstore and the publishing house, and perhaps he was the proprietor too. With the Mortkowiczes, he was the principal publisher of poets in Poland between the wars.

Of course, the authors got paid, but not very much. It was probably at the suggestion of Bromberg, with whom I often had long discussions at the bookstore on the avant-garde and revolution, that we published the first volumes of the Bibliothèque—as we gradiloquently called it—of the Artistic Club

"S." We began with a collective volume of poems entitled *S*. I had written some of my poems while still in school, but at the time the collection was published all three of us were in the second or third year of law school. Two years later, for an equally modest sum, which "subscribers" had helped to underwrite, my *The World in Double* was published by the same firm.

So this quite unusual salesman, full of astounding erudition and highly unusual thoughts, participated in the publication of my first book. I could not then foresee that he would once again have an influence on my literary career. And even on my personal destiny. Bromberg remembered me well and took me on at the *Natsmenvydav,* as the organization was officially called in Ukrainian. After the entry of Germans into Lvov, I learned that he had left town the day before on foot. For many years I did not hear anything about him. I didn't even known if he was still alive.

In July or August 1946—it was our first vacation after the war—I was sunning myself in the sand on the Baltic shore at Sopot. Suddenly, at high noon, a huge shadow fell across me. Bromberg was standing in front of me. He was thinner than ever, but he was wearing a splendid uniform. I thought I was dreaming. But sure enough, it was Bromberg in the dress uniform of a rear admiral. He had piping, insignia, and gold braid all over his chest and arms.

"I've been looking for you up and down the coast," he said. "I've come to ask you if you'd like to become a naval officer."

Again I had the impression I was dreaming. But dream or no dream, I asked, "Would I have to command a ship?"

Bromberg answered me in all seriousness. "No. You'd only get a motor launch with a boatswain and three sailors. You'd be my deputy officer. I'm responsible for the political indoctrination of the officers in the Gdynia admiralty. I'm opening a maritime publishing house."

I looked once again at Bromberg's insignia and braids.

"Listen," I said, regaining my presence of mind. "I'd have silver braid up to where?"

Rear Admiral Bromberg indicated the space between the cuffs and the elbow. And he added, "And on the collar, too."

I thought that it had taken a revolution, the Second World War, two occupations, and the destruction of half of Europe for someone to propose that I, Jan Kott, stretched out on the sand in a striped bathing suit, become a naval officer the next day. I might perhaps have accepted, knowing that I would never get such an offer twice in my life, but I didn't doubt for an instant that Lidia would never forgive me. All the same, later on I more than once regretted not having accepted it.

Bromberg soon stopped being a rear admiral. He was appointed editor in chief of the Scientific State Publishing House (Państwowe Wydawnictwo Naukowe). He turned out to be a superb editor. Under his leadership, PWN started the Library of the Classics of Philosophy and the *Encyclopedia*. The *Little Encyclopedia* came out during the October Thaw (1956), but with the *Great Encyclopedia* the censor became more and more ferocious as each of the thirteen volumes appeared. In the second edition of the *Little Encyclopedia,* which dated from the final Gomułka years (1969), not only were the great émigrés gone (Czesław Miłosz had been replaced by Miłosz Obrenowicz), but even Jerzy Andrzejewski, Paweł Jasienica, and Jerzy Turowicz had disappeared. My name is included in both the *Great Encyclopedia* (the volumes up to the letter *S* came out in the "good" period) and the first edition of the *Little Encyclopedia,* but I have evaporated in the second edition. In my place, undoubtedly for economy's sake so as not to throw the typesetting off, there are two new entries: "Cat, domestic" and "Cat, wild." In that mutilated edition of the *Little Encyclopedia,* as Lidia first noticed, the word *ham* disappeared as well, as bacon had disappeared from the shelves. The Marxist censors showed themselves to be quite unexpectedly nominalist.

After March 1968, in the purge of "Zionists," Bromberg and all the "encyclopedists" were thrown out of the PWN publishing house. Shortly thereafter, Bromberg, along with the other "Jews" forced to give up their Polish citizenship, took the train for Vienna from the Gdańsk station. He subsequently settled in Sweden, where, indomitable and tenacious as ever, he formed his own publishing house. He was the first to publish Miłosz in Swedish, long before the Nobel Prize. I am indebted to Bromberg for my own initial entry into the world. While still the director of PWN he suggested that I publish my *Shakespeare, Our Contemporary* in English. This was a year after the Polish edition came out. His idea seemed to me even more foolish than unexpected, but Bromberg commissioned the English translation by Bolesław Taborski and paid for it in hard currency. He had not only the imagination of a great editor but also the business sense. The English edition of my Shakespeare, published by Methuen, was printed in Poland. And paid for in hard currency.

During the second winter of the war or perhaps only in the spring of 1941, work began on a huge edition of Polish translations of Ukrainian poets, ancient and modern. The editors were Adam Ważyk and Mieczysław Jastrun. Mieczysław distributed the texts among his friends and I got my share. There were whole pages of poetry by Tychyna and Sosiora, Bazhan and Maksym Rylski to be translated. The pay was by the verse, that is to say, by the line, and it was very generous. Frozen sturgeon in supplies the size of an elephant (and with meat that tasted like turkey) was arriving in Lvov; for four lines of Sosiora or Rylski, a translator could buy two pounds of very good beluga sturgeon at the department store. The most profitable work, of course, was to translate poems written in "tiers," according to Mayakovsky's system. But most of the poems, unfortunately, were traditional, with rhymes, though so plentiful that Mieczysław distributed them by the yard. At the door he would cry: "Get to work! Poems! And more poems!" I got half a yard of Bazhan and a yard and a half of Sosiora. Lidia, too, began to translate for hire, and she did magnificently, handling versified poems better than I did and also much more quickly. She even translated a long epic by Taras Shevchenko. Mieczysław never tired of heaping praise on her.

In the second year of the war I began to think about my doctorate again. On French literature of course: at that point I didn't even dream about Shakespeare. My notes had been left behind in the Hôtel Henri IV on the place Dauphine in Paris, along with the books and Lidia's fur coat. My intended thesis, on Apollinaire as editor of the Marquis de Sade and the great pornographers of the Renaissance, seemed risky for the traditional prewar Sorbonne. In any case, it was out of the question to continue it in Soviet Lvov. But at the University of Lvov, hastily renamed Ivan Franko University, a competition for assistantships was announced. In this system the assistantships for doctoral students carried generous stipends, and there was an opening in Romance languages, the department in which Boy-Żeleński had begun his lectures. Apparently they were quite boring, but even so I dreamed of becoming his student and starting my new doctoral dissertation under his supervision. Zygmunt Czerny, the dean, was known for his strictness and his punctilious observance of all the rules, old and new, even at a university that had been brutally reorganized according to the Soviet model and with a Ukrainian rector, a certain Marchenko, who was appointed—as the *Red Banner* announced—"at his own request." I became friends with Czerny only many years later, after defending my doctoral thesis at Łódź, but even at the end of our first conversation he had already told me that climbers in the Dolomites wore soft shoes because the cliffs were extremely friable and that they used long, pointed hooks. Czerny was an amateur mountain climber. He must have felt very homesick for the mountains. I experienced such a longing many years later.

The examination for the competition consisted of questions on literature, grammar—both descriptive and historical—and Marxism-Leninism. The history of literature didn't frighten me, even though I knew Villon and Racine chiefly through Boy's translations, but I repeated whatever I could straight out of Lanson and Thibaudet. On the other hand, I had trouble, for the first time since graduating from the gymnasium, learning the grammar. It seemed to me that I would be impressive in "Marxism"; I had read *The Communist Manifesto* in the gymnasium, my cheeks afire, the year of my first Communist temptations; and then at the university, undoubtedly with Stefan Żółkiewski, I mastered the first chapter of *Capital* (I never got through the second); and finally I knew Lenin's *The State and Revolution*. But the examination in Marxism-Leninism was something quite different from what I had imagined. It was simply *A Short Course about the WKP(b)*. (The WKP(b) was the Bolshevik faction of the Communist party.) One had to learn it by heart, especially the fourth chapter, on dialectics, written by Stalin himself. It was impossible to learn it any other way. Lidia had me repeat it over and over again as if it were the multiplication tables. But it was precisely the test on Marxism that I failed. The literature and grammar examinations were of course in French, but the Marxism was in Ukrainian. I didn't understand the questions, I mixed up counterrevolutions and interventions, Denikin and Petlura, and I didn't get the assistantship.

That same spring, Helena Usijewicz came from Moscow, perhaps with Zofia Dzierżyńska, but I'm not sure about that. Usijewicz was the daughter of Feliks Kon, who was a legendary character, the last living member, if I am not mistaken, of the first Polish Socialist party, the Proletariat, founded in Warsaw in 1882. That, undoubtedly, is why his daughter escaped the purges and the liquidation of the Polish Communist party. Skinny, gray-haired, and at least twenty years older than I was, she spoke Polish correctly but with a distinct accent. She knew about the trials—if not everything, then a great deal. Almost all those in her father's circle and in her circle, Polish and Russian, had been executed or had disappeared, some forever, in the prisons and camps. But Helena Usijewicz never breathed a word. Besides, she had come to ask us what we thought would happen. She was apparently high up in the NKVD, and perhaps that was the reason she seemed so liberal. She questioned us about our hopes, and it is possible that in the deeply hidden recesses of her heart this daughter of Feliks Kon also hoped that things would be different. "If only Warsaw . . ." she once said, but she didn't finish the sentence. Clearly, it was already being said sotto voce in the Kremlin that there would be war with Germany.

A Professor Chernobayev, an eminent Slavicist from Leningrad, who it seems had never once left Russia, arrived in Lvov, probably for some Mickiewicz celebrations. To him Lvov, already badly destroyed, seemed a flourishing, wonderfully provisioned European city. Lidia went with him to buy warm socks and a watch. He was a very gentle man of great personal charm, and he talked with us openly. But when we remarked that after the war Poland would be reborn, he looked at us as though we were mad.

The house was full of visitors. In the afternoon or the evening, there was always someone who came to have tea with Lidia's parents or with us. People came not only from the other side of the border, as Chernobayev did, but also from closer by. During the first winter and spring of the war, Artur Rzeczyca came to see us; he was small, dark, and so slight that he hardly existed at all. I knew only the one or two of his poems that had been published in the Lublin review *Kamena*. His poems were intended to be like fairy tales, full of grasses and herbs. He was fascinated by Czechowicz and by Schulz, whom he had visited in the autumn of 1940 in Borysław or Truskawiec. Of this diminutive poet there remain by the unpredictable chance of fate nine words and a signature scribbled in pencil at the bottom of a letter from Schulz to Anna Płockier. A painter, Płockier was murdered with her fiancé in Borysław by the Ukrainian militia in November 1941. Schulz's letter, with a postscript by Rzeczyca, was found by friends on the floor of the couple's ransacked apartment. It was published only recently. But the postscript is not the only fragment of a text that remained behind after Rzeczyca's death. In her memoirs, *Faded Leaves and Flowers,* published in 1989, Alina Dawidowicz, Leon Chwistek's daughter, includes two lines of poetry that Rzeczyca wrote in her album shortly before his departure: "Who then drinks from the bottle full of the rooster's crowing / Optimistic as a mason or a postman bearing a money order? Artur Rzeczyca, Borysław, 28 November 1940." What is left behind after his death is this absurd question in two lines of verse, undoubtedly his last. He was shot in 1942, when he left Drohobycz and tried to cross the Hungarian border.

Of the visitors who came to see my father-in-law, Jakub Parnas made the greatest impression on me. He was an immense man, the size of an elephant; even his nose was like an elephant's trunk. An entry in the *Encyclopedia* credited him as one of the most eminent scholars in the field of biochemistry, and he had one of the most beautiful private libraries I have ever seen. When I went to visit him once with Lidia's father, he showed us the first printed editions of *The Aeneid, The Metamorphoses,* and Lucian to appear in the Renaissance. He also had ivory-colored Greek and Arabic papyrus scrolls that survived in only a few dozen copies. I shall never forget the feel of that paper when I touched it with my finger. It was like the softest flesh.

Parnas and his wife left Lvov the day before the Germans entered the city. With the rector of the medical school, they took the last train evacuating refugees. In Moscow he was given a magnificently equipped laboratory and he had an institute at his disposition. Almost immediately he became a member of the Academy of Sciences and soon received the Order of Lenin. When his son was wounded at Monte Cassino and evacuated to a field hospital with a perforated lung, he got Molotov himself to send a special plane to bring the young man to Moscow.

Parnas came to visit my father-in-law in Wrocław after the war. That must have been in 1946. Lidia's mother said that he was even fatter than before. Efforts were made to persuade him to stay and accept a chair in Wrocław. "I don't have many years ahead of me anymore," my father-in-law reported him as saying in their last conversation. "I don't have the equipment I need here and I still have some research to finish." At the beginning of the 1950s, I think, a letter came from Parnas's wife in Moscow telling their son, who lived in Wrocław, that his father was in the hospital. When, in subsequent letters, the same phrase was constantly repeated about Father's being in the hospital, it became clear that Parnas was dead. A year or two later, a biochemist came to Wrocław from Moscow. He, too, was an academician and a bearer of the Order of Lenin. Lidia's father asked him about Parnas. "Parnas?" this scientist asked in astonishment. "An academician? I never heard of him."

Not long after, Parnas's wife returned to Poland. She never spoke of the circumstances under which her husband died. It was only in the 1960s, a day or two before her death, that she

confided in a Mrs. Tuszkiewicz, the secretary of Rector Kul-
czyński, that Parnas was taken down the stairs early one morning and shot on the spot with a bullet through the back of his
neck. He had, it seems, criticized Lysenko. Jakub Parnas was
rehabilitated under Khrushchev.

Lidia and I often went to visit Leon Chwistek and his wife.
Chwistek, otherwise known as Uncle Leonek, had married the
beautiful Aunt Olga, the sister of Lidia's father. I had first met
him in Zakopane some years before the war, when he had invited Włodzimierz Pietrzak and me to a binge that turned out
to consist of downing water mixed with raspberry juice at the
Trzaska or Karpowicz restaurant. Chwistek's *Plurality of Reali-
ties* was one of the first "philosophical" books I read. At that
time I did not know all the doubles that Chwistek assumed
in the novels and plays of Witkiewicz. But Włodzimierz and
I knew that he had been in the circle of Karol Szymanowski and Bronisław Malinowski, and we were very impressed
with him. Włodzimierz called him Marchołt. For me there
was something Gargantuan about him—I was reading Rabe-
lais then. He was corpulent, an insatiable gourmand even in
the stories that reached us about his romances with ample-
bosomed nannies who came to the park with babies in car-
riages.

On the wall of Lidia's mother's bedroom on Kadecka Street,
Chwistek had painted a huge fresco depicting a beach. That
was his "spherical" period of painting. The fresco was in bright
colors, with green squares and orange cylinders. In the fore-
ground there was a big-bottomed spherical woman in a bathing suit. There were other paintings by Chwistek in the apartment on Kadecka Street, but by a strange turn of fortune, only
one was saved, a small abstract landscape in india ink. Lidia's
mother brought it to us in Warsaw and now it hangs on the
wall in our house in Stony Brook.

But in Lvov I was more interested in Chwistek's system of
logic than in his painting. He was an outstanding mathematical
logician, comparable to such giants as Russell and Whitehead.
In logic, as in painting, he was unbelievably inventive. He created his own system of binary notation for phrases and cardinal

numbers, which anticipated computer notation. It consisted of two signs: a dot and a dash. One was a dot, two a dot and a dash, three a dash and a dot, four two dots, and so on. This new system obsessed me. Once I was awakened in the middle of night by Lidia's laughing out loud when, in a dream, I repeated: "A dot, a dash, two dashes."

Chwistek, too, had to leave Lvov the day before the Germans arrived. He stayed a long time in Tiflis, then, toward the end of the war, in Moscow, where he lived in an apartment building for the privileged near the Kremlin. When the Russian armies reached the Vistula River, he was invited to a big reception attended by Stalin himself. On this occasion he apparently criticized socialist realist painting. Shortly thereafter he was hospitalized and died. There was talk of his having been poisoned. But these rumors have never been confirmed.

The whole period in Lvov, from December 1939 to June 1941, left me feeling suspended in time, frozen for a brief moment between prewar time and the three years spent in the Warsaw of the General Government. In Warsaw, night after night we lay squeezed close together, and whenever we heard the sound of steps on the staircase or the screeching tires of gendarmerie vans, Lidia and I would remember Lvov as a protected island, as a happy period in our life. We always slept in a very narrow bed, locked in each other's arms, and when we changed sides we had to make a simultaneous turn. We called one side "the silver," the other "the gold." We were very young, recently married, constantly hungry for each other, constantly curious about each other, and we separated only when I went to work. We had a real home. Lidia's parents treated me as their son, and her mother became reconciled to the idea that I was her daughter's husband.

There was much gentleness in that house. And much kindness for Lidia and me and for our friends, even if, after their departure, Lidia's mother would imitate them with real talent—which Lidia inherited—to the great joy of my father-in-law. He taught me the theory of numbers and the rudiments of the calculus of probabilities. For a while in my first year at the university, in addition to law, where I was officially registered, I attended classes in mathematics for students of natural sciences, thinking that they would be easier. But I soon had to give it up because without going to the seminars I began to get lost. I then took the courses in mathematical logic offered by Jan Łukasiewicz and the seminars given by Alfred Tarski, who must have been his assistant at that time. But I returned to pure mathematics only with Lidia's father, in Soviet Lvov. He thought that I could have been a good mathematician. But the mathematics that I discovered with him, without technical operations, was only thinking with numbers, relations, volumes, and spaces. It opened on a vertiginous world, which for Lidia's father was beauty and order. I spent numerous afternoons in his study as he prepared the second edition of *Kaleidoscope,* constructing—out of squares or rhomboids cut from colored paper and out of elastics—ingenious cubes that could be opened and folded flat. He was also working on an apparatus that would permit a localization in space on X rays. I remember a little glass pane, placed on a board, and a piece of wire between two balls. On the glass, the ball went into the interior of a potato as if it were transparent. This kind of an "X ray" had a new, "third" dimension.

Mathematics was not the only thing that Steinhaus taught me. He had two favorite authors: Joyce and Karl Kraus. He quoted Kraus's aphorisms in German and to the end of his days he refused to believe that I not only could not speak German but didn't even know two words of the language. Lidia's father also wrote aphorisms. After his death, they were published in a separate volume. I have always quoted one of them: "The earth: a ball at our feet." I think that only a "solar watchmaker" could conceive of such an aphorism.

Lidia's father and I also had heated discussions about the vicissitudes of language and about communism. He called the Soviets "the fathers of lies." It was only many years later, after his death, that I gradually concluded that he was absolutely right, both about language and about communism. And I recognized, although somewhat belatedly, that no one has had as much influence on my style of writing as Jerzy Stempowski and Hugo Steinhaus.

In occupied Warsaw, Lidia and I remembered Lvov as a lost haven. We knew that many people had been killed. But we were young and we could not imagine that a time would come when we would be the sole survivors of all the inhabitants and guests at the house on Kadecka Street.

2.

When the Germans shot the professors at the University of Lvov, Lidia's father told us to leave the house immediately. We moved in with the Ziemilskis, who lived in the center of town, on Czarnecki Street. Dr. Ziemilski was an excellent physician and not long before had cured Lidia of a bad case of hepatitis. He had been the family physician for many years.

We lived with the Ziemilskis for almost six months, from the end of June to mid-December 1941. I do not remember much from this period—nor does Lidia. It has become almost completely blacked out, as though it were merely a prolonged week, and only with the greatest difficulty can I order and date what little we have remembered.

I remember best the beginning and the end. On the last night before they left Lvov, the Soviets massacred the prisoners in Brygidki prison. It was said that the Ukrainians were responsible for the slaughter, but it took place before the Russians left. During that first week under the German Occupation the acts of terror seemed incomprehensible to us, as though they were only a nightmare. But very soon we came to understand that the nightmare was the rule.

Many Ukrainians, who while the Soviets were in Lvov served the Communists zealously, now put on the blue and yellow arm band. The streets were swarming with them. In the General Government, the Germans had closed the ghettos. In Lvov, they ordered the Jews to wear the arm bands with the blue star, beat them, forced them to perform hard labor, and often drove them out of their houses. Lidia's parents left their house soon after we did and moved in with Aunt Olga, Chwistek's wife, on Tarnowski Street. They never wore the arm band. Lidia's father knew that it meant a death sentence. We knew it too.

In those first weeks, I don't remember being afraid, only being hungry and, most of all, dying for a smoke. All the time. I walked the streets and gathered cigarette butts. I tore open the cigarette paper with my fingers, carefully took out the tobacco, which most often was very thick and didn't burn down to the end, and using the old soldiers' trick, rolled it in a scrap of newspaper and dragged on it like a madman, as if I wanted to swallow the whole thing at once.

Rubles lost all their value. One was forced to sell whatever one possessed. At the marketplace, food was available only in exchange for things. Or for new German *zlotys,* a currency in the General Government. One day Lidia went to the market to sell some dresses. She came back a few hours later. Her former gymnastics teacher at the Queen Jadwiga gymnasium had drawn her aside. "Everybody knows who you are. They'll kill you."

It was then, in Lvov, that I learned that, when death is cheap, food is expensive. And I found out that death and trade are war's closest neighbors. I began to engage in trade. The second week under the Germans, the former Soviet department stores were reopened to sell the remaining stock. At four in the morning, people started forming long lines. At eight o'clock the selling began. Two pairs of stockings were sold per person. These were long knit stockings. I resold them immediately at the local market, for three or four times the purchasing price. The market women bought eagerly. For those two pairs of stockings sold at a profit, I brought home potatoes, kasha, and sometimes even half a loaf of bread.

Then—I don't very well remember when or how it happened—I began to deal in sugar. And soon I had almost a wholesale trade. The Germans sold sugar illegally, in huge sacks. It wasn't a very secure business. I didn't say anything about it to Lidia. I got the key to the warehouses from a fat German corporal who was always drunk. Early in the morning I was to carry the sack full of sugar—actually to drag it, because it was too heavy for me to lift. Two soldiers waited behind the grating to carry it to our house. Lidia was terrified when they came into her bedroom and dumped the sugar on the bed. After having paid the German his share, I had enough left over to buy bread and meat for a week, but Lidia made me promise that I wouldn't become involved in that form of trade a second time.

At that point—or it must have been much later, because the trains for Warsaw and Cracow were no longer in service, but there was no control on the river San and even trucks could get through—I went into business with three specimens of a new subcategory: "merchants of war." They came to buy furs and rugs but most of all gold and diamonds. They knew that not only the Jews but also the Poles had to get rid of everything. Although honest in business in their own way, they were uninhibitedly voracious. Almost like Mother Courage, so unjustly called by Brecht "a hyena of war." Brecht wrote that theatrical masterpiece, which so blatantly contradicts his theories, in the same year as my Lvov trade activities. I lived off my "hyenas of war."

The circle of my activities expanded. Henceforth I traded mainly in dollars and gold. To say "traded in" is an exaggeration: I simply got from Mr. Lindenfeld, who was my "banker," dollars and sometimes rings and took them to my Warsaw speculators, who came once every two weeks to Lvov to trade, or rather to smuggle them back. Mr. Lindenfeld was a prewar merchant; he had had, as he told me one day, a magnificent jewelry shop on the main street of Stanisławów. Before the deportations, he had liquidated the whole business and taken refuge in Lvov. He called his store a counter and he did not cease to lament the loss of his precision scales of gilded copper. The last time I saw that kind of counter was in Athens, in the narrow streets that lead to the Acropolis. The merchants must have been Turks or Armenians, because they always wore a colored fabric cap. The shops were small as cellars, and the entrance was right on the street. On the counter, there was always a scale and small copper weights, like the ones I played with as a child. At Mr. Lindenfeld's, the transactions always took place in the bedroom, the back room of his apartment, with the curtains drawn. From his former counter, he had kept only his magnifying glass, always scrupulously clean.

One day I brought him several hundred German marks. These were profitable transactions: soldiers of the Third Reich brought that money with them and had to exchange it for *zlotys;* they couldn't buy anything with their marks. Mr. Lindenfeld threw up his arms and then held them up in front of him as if he wished to push me away. "I trade in money, not paper. Take that trash back." Mr. Lindenfeld had retained the principles of a jeweler from the main street in Stanisławów. My speculators from Warsaw had never read Marx, but for them everything was merchandise and nothing but merchandise: dollars and soap, candles and marks, false identity papers and birth certificates, and even two crates of Soviet brassieres that I brought them one day.

Even toward the end, my liquid capital never went above five dollars. The transactions were always conducted on one's word of honor, but usually a down payment was made to prevent backing out if the rate changed. I often gave Mr. Lindenfeld my five dollars. Once a customer backed out of a big transaction. I went to ask for the return of my down payment. "Mr. Kott," said Mr. Lindenfeld, "you aren't a man of letters anymore, you are a merchant. The word of a merchant is sacred." And in the end he didn't charge me more than a dollar for the lesson. That is how I learned to differentiate between wartime speculators and prewar merchants. But two weeks later, when I went to Mr. Lindenfeld, they warned me at the gate that the Germans had taken him and his wife off the day before.

I continued to trade with my "merchants," now mainly bartering things. One time I was given a raw-silk handbag to sell for acquaintances of acquaintances. Inside was a very beautiful Japanese kimono of the same material with painted flowers and birds in batik. As it wasn't very expensive, I decided not to sell it but to give it to Lidia. It had been a long time since I had bought her anything, except apples occasionally. My birthday was coming soon, and I wanted to buy her something as a present for me. Lidia's mother always bought herself a new hat for her husband's birthday. He was delighted with such a present. Lidia made some crepes and we invited the Ziemilskis to the birthday dinner. Lidia put on the kimono. I remember that evening because that kimono with the flowers and birds was a sudden and unexpected joy amidst the horror and misery of daily life.

We had visitors all the time. The well-known journalist Aleksander Bocheński found out that we had shoes for sale. He was very surprised to learn that Miss Steinhaus was selling them. Karol Kuryluk came to see us from time to time, as he had earlier at Kadecka Street. I knew him from before the war. In his *Signals,* which was pro-communist and common front, I had published in 1937 a long first-page essay, "Writers and Firemen," in which I advanced the idea that writers, like firemen, should put out blazes. The blaze, of course, was the conflagration of fascism. Karol was quite astonished to find Lidia sanding the floor of our apartment one day with a piece of glass from a broken bottle. Of course it wasn't possible to get steel pads. For Lidia, sanding the floor was an antidote to fear. But not only that; there was an inner need for order, which I did not experience but which never left Lidia. Perhaps it helped both of us survive the war.

By this time Lidia went out into the street only when she had to. Mieczysław Jastrun and his wife, too, came to see us very infrequently. Perhaps they had even left already. The final visit of Zuzanna Ginczanka was extremely dramatic. I had met her in Warsaw the year before I went to Paris, when she frequented Gombrowicz's table at the café Zodiak. She and Gizela Ważyk were the most beautiful women in that circle. And she was the youngest, I think. She looked like a Shulamite. One of her eyes was so black that the iris seemed to cover the pupil, while the other was brown with gold spots in the iris. Everyone was enthusiastic about her poetry, which, like her beauty, resembled a Persian miniature. Zuza came to see us one evening utterly terrified. The visa that one of her aunts was supposed to send her from a neutral country in South America hadn't come. An old woman who was the janitor in her apartment building had begun to blackmail her.

It was to this informer that Ginczanka wrote undoubtedly her last and one of her most moving poems. Somehow it got preserved and was published after the war. Ginczanka did not make it through the war. Janusz Woźniakowski, already an accomplished painter, got her safely from Lvov to Cracow. Whenever he went out, he shut her up in his room. One day the Gestapo picked him up on the street; he was deeply involved in the Communist Resistance. After several days he succeeded in sending a message to his friends so that they would tell Ginczanka, who was locked up in his room. But when they went to get her, the door was already open. When and by what means she left, and how she met her death, no one has ever learned.

Wikta Wittlin, Józef's sister, also came to visit us. She and her brother had been friends of Lidia's parents for many years. I had met Józef Wittlin before the war. Wikta was very tall, very blond—no one would have suspected that she was Jewish. By that time, in the second or third week of the German Occupation, there started to be talk in Lvov of "good" and "bad" looks. At that point they were a matter of life or death. Wikta told us that we should leave for Warsaw as soon as possible.

We had already thought about that earlier. I had heard from Ryszard Matuszewski that we could stay with them. But we kept putting off the decision because we were afraid of the trip. In the first half of December, though, the administrator of our building called me in. She was a Ukrainian. She asked me to sign a declaration saying that my wife was not Jewish. She had no suspicions about me; no one knew me in Lvov. I signed whatever she wanted—I would have signed a pact with the devil—but I knew that my signature wouldn't hold up for even twenty-four hours. Fortunately, my "merchants" from Warsaw were in town with their truck. They agreed to take us without asking why we had to leave so quickly. In time of war strange things come to the surface from the depths and recesses of the soul: courage and cowardice, greed and generosity, nobleness and the vilest baseness. But strangest of all, the most contradictory traits appear simultaneously more often than in times of peace and prosperity. My "hyenas of war" did not ask a single penny from us for the trip.

They covered us with a tarpaulin and some sacks. They must have had regular dealings with the Germans, because they talked with them for a long time, and quite boisterously, and always avoided a search. We arrived in Warsaw in the morning. One of them, the oldest, invited us to have breakfast with him and his wife. We were chilled to the bone. They gave us real hot tea and a large glass of vodka. Then he took us to Żoliborz, to the Matuszewskis' house, in his own car. And he carried our two heavy suitcases up to the second floor.

3.

We spent several weeks with the Matuszewskis before moving to Marysia Zarębińska's. I had met her before her marriage to Broniewski. One day she came to the café with Stempowski and Wichuna Rettinger. Zarębińska had just begun her career in the theater, and blond, tiny, rosy, she looked like a little girl. I asked Stempowski if she was Wichuna's daughter. I was not yet a frequent visitor to the apartment on Flora Street where Stempowski lived with the Rettingers. So my question was quite out of place and Stempowski explained to me at length and in a very complicated manner that slight differences of age did not necessarily signify any ties of kinship. After Broniewski's arrest, Marysia was not deported from Lvov, as was Ola Wat, but she rarely went out on the streets. She left for Warsaw shortly after the arrival of the Germans.

Zarębińska lived with her daughter, her father, and her brother in a little house on Dziennikarska Street, not far from the Matuszewskis. We stayed there briefly, barely two weeks. Marysia's brother, who was a very helpful and agreeable young man, belonged to the underground organization The Sword and the Plow. It was the most nationalistic of all the resistance groups. There were frequent meetings in Marysia's brother's room, and supposedly he had a cache of arms hidden somewhere. Marysia was very concerned about this, not so much for her own sake as for ours. We set about looking for another place, but we kept putting off moving until a neighbor came running up to Marysia to tell her that she had seen Lidia at the window, that she knew her from Lvov, and that she was well aware Lidia was Jewish. We left the next day. Beata Matuszewska acted as our new chaperone and rented a room for us nearby, at Mrs. Holnicka's, at the intersection of Zają-czek Street and Mickiewicz Street.

A few months later Marysia was arrested because of an informer or an indiscretion. Her brother was arrested also and tortured to death in the prison on Aleja Szucha. Marysia was imprisoned at Pawiak, then deported to Auschwitz. She returned after the war, full of energy; nothing indicated that she was terminally sick. Lidia talked with her for the last time by telephone when we went to Switzerland for a few days. Marysia was treated in a sanatorium in Zurich and died there in July 1947. Her ashes now rest in Warsaw. All the paths of fate cross for a moment in my narrative and then separate forever. In the autumn of 1939, Wichuna Rettinger was at Słoboda Rungurska, near Kołomyja, at the Vincenzes' house or somewhere nearby. She had been suffering for years from breast cancer. Jerzy Stempowski was taking care of her, treating her with herbal remedies known only to him. She died during that first winter of the war or the following spring. Lidia did not meet Stempowski until after the war, when we visited him in Bern. That was exactly when Lidia telephoned Marysia, who was already close to death.

Mrs. Holnicka's apartment was on the second floor of a big apartment building with six separate stairways, which one reached from the street by going through an open court with a trampled lawn where several rickety trees grew. The Zagórskis lived in the next-to-last hallway, but we didn't know them yet. One day Tadeusz Hollender pointed Maryna Zagórska out to me from the window as she walked across the courtyard. Her hair was a golden copper.

Lidia had been on a friendly footing with Tadeusz Hollender since the time in Lvov. Already a well-known poet, he associated with Stasia Blumenfeld, the Chwisteks, and Lidia's parents. When my sister came to Warsaw, he promised to get her an "authentic" birth certificate. Lidia was supposed to meet him, but he did not show up. He was shot in a mass execution with fifty other prisoners at Pawiak prison on the last day of May 1943. In November of that year, a small mimeographed volume of his *Satires and Fables* (*Satyry i fraszki*) was published under his Resistance pseudonym, Tomasz Wiatraczny.

Those three years in Warsaw under the German Occupation sometimes seem to me, more than Lvov under the Soviets, to be one long year or even an interminably long month; I mix up dates and even times of year. Perhaps it would be easier to arrange these months in my memory according to the apartments we occupied and abandoned, most often in haste. Lidia had acquired great skill in these unforeseen moves: she would wear two skirts and, if she had them handy, two coats; she would put what was most indispensable in a kerchief so as not to attract attention, and we would set off at a leisurely pace, almost always to find refuge at Ryszard and Beata's.

We stayed at Mrs. Holnicka's until the summer, most certainly in a state of relative calm, because I remember almost nothing of those months. Lidia already had new papers, brought by Irena Krzemicka's mother. The birth certificate was blank, but it had authentic seals. We wrote in: Lidia Janina Wójcicka. That became Lidia's maiden name to the end of the war. I found an old Polish identity card and, with the help of the technical service of the Home Delegation—or *Delegatura*, the central agency in Poland of the London-based government-in-exile—thanks again to Ryszard, changed my first name to Adam and dropped the second *t* of my last name. It turned out later that there was in fact another Kot with only one *t*.

In June or July of that year, Beata decided to make a two- or three-week trip to Kazimierz on the Vistula. As Ryszard was working at the town hall and had no vacation, Beata persuaded us to go with her. Neither Lidia nor I has retained any but the vaguest memory of that excursion. When we went back to Kazimierz after the war we tried to find the house where we had stayed with Beata. We knew that it was up from the town marketplace. Perhaps there exist profound reasons for such a case of amnesia.

Several days before our return to Warsaw, a German was killed near Puławy. Punitive roundups started, most of them at the Puławy train station. But we had no choice. An *Ausweis* from a German institution or from an enterprise working for the Germans was the best protection against the roundups. Beata had no fears for herself—she was then in a very advanced state of pregnancy. She gave Lidia her *Ausweis* with a Hitlerite "crow." And she also lent her signet ring with a Christian blazon for the trip. She had already given it to Lidia once before, when Lidia had had to go to the registration bureau. When the functionary had started to cross-examine her insistently, she had almost thrust Beata's ring under his nose.

At the Puławy train station, Lidia was the first to realize that the Germans were blocking all the exits. It was too late. Lidia, with her *Ausweis,* got through the cordon. But I was stopped. With the others, I was pushed onto a platform already jammed with people. The Germans had been emptying all the trains since morning. Wherever there were empty spaces we lay down to pass the night. Before dawn, when it was still dark, the Germans began to run along the platform with flashlights screaming, "*Arzt! Arzt!* [Doctor! Doctor!]" No one came forward. I had had some elementary training in first aid as a boy scout, so I followed the Germans to the end of the platform. I thought that someone had been beaten. But to my great horror, I saw lying on the platform a woman with a monstrously swollen stomach, who was moaning frightfully. Nearby some older women said that she was in labor. My knowledge of childbirth came exclusively—oh, time of profound ignorance!—from Żeromski's *Story of a Sin* (*Dzieje grzechu*). The poor heroine—I think her name was Ewa—had only a basin of hot water. And still drawing on that novel, which I had read with cheeks ablaze, I knew that she had cut the umbilical cord with a pair of scissors. But in what place? I stretched the woman out more comfortably, I slipped a blanket under her head so that she wouldn't hit it against the cement, and I asked for a bucket of hot water and scissors. I also gave her some drops that someone handed me. The woman stopped moaning and beating her feet. Her pain temporarily abated with the breaking of her water;

but I only learned that much later. The Germans, and even the older women, watched admiringly the attentions I proffered until the ambulance that had been sent for from the hospital arrived. The woman was put on a stretcher. Three people had been saved: the woman giving birth, the newborn, and me.

In the morning we were all loaded into cattle wagons. The trip wasn't very long. The women knew right away where they were being taken. Majdanek wasn't yet a name that inspired fear. It was a forced-labor transit camp on the way to the Reich, consisting of two or three scattered barracks in a wide field surrounded by ordinary barbed wire. It was perhaps no more than two kilometers from the station. I joined the column of men, but the Germans once again called out, *Arzt!* pulled me out, and put me with the women.

We were sent to the baths all together, men and women. There were stalls and primitive showers from which there streamed alternately boiling and ice-cold water. Years later that image of a steam room full of naked men and women, snorting, splashing, slapping one another on fat thighs, laughing and then crying, came back to me in one of Fellini's films. Or perhaps my memory is playing tricks on me. But I still remember distinctly that I was pulled out of the men's barracks that afternoon and that a member of the Gestapo in a black uniform led me into the women's block, into a room that must have been the infirmary: on the door there was an inscription in big letters, written in chalk, "*Kranken Stube* [Sick Room]," and four straw mattresses lay on the ground.

The German kept calling me "*Herr Doktor.*" He went on and on about something, of which I didn't understand a single word, and then he finally left me. After an extended interval I began to comprehend, as at the moment of awakening, when we are still wrestling with the remnants of a troubling dream, that I had become a doctor at Majdanek. And in the women's section. With their subalterns' logic, the Germans had instantly concluded, after my stepping forward with hot water and scissors on the platform at the Puławy train station, that I must be not only a doctor but an obstetrician. Now that time has passed, however, I think that my medical specialty wasn't of much concern to them.

There were mainly women in the transit camp at Majdanek. The railway line from Lublin was the chief route for smuggling contraband goods to Warsaw. Pigs were earmarked, and the gendarmes confiscated meat and bacon from the women at the station or even in the wagons. But the women's ingenuity was boundless, and the stocky ones especially put sides of bacon under their skirts to get past the guards.

These were my "patients." It was known that a medical commission was coming in a few days to conduct examinations before the trip to the Reich. The women asked what they could feign in order to be exempted. They came in twos and threes, taking off their skirts and blouses: "Look, doctor . . ." I was the only man in that barracks. Sometimes they really had something wrong with them, but I couldn't help them with my "medical knowledge." Nor, though, could I do them much harm; in the pharmacy of the infirmary, I found a laxative, something resembling cod-liver oil, iodine, several bandages, and cotton swabs. There was a bottle of what had probably been Lysol, because it smelled awful, but all that was left was the empty bottle. And an ointment for lice.

Lidia has no memory of ever suffering from hunger during the time we lived in Warsaw. Neither do I except for the first weeks after the Germans arrived in Lvov. That first year in Warsaw, however, I thought about food constantly. Mieczysław Jastrun was the person who came to see us the most, at Mrs. Holnicka's on Zajączek Street and then in other apartments. Many years later when he came to have tea with us, he used to say that during the Occupation I looked at him as if I wished to eat him alive. For my prescriptions and consultations, my women patients at Majdanek brought me white bread, meat, and fresh butter wrapped in cabbage leaves. Their brothers, their husbands, and their "fiancés" threw them baskets of food over the barbed wire. Then they shared them with me on an equal basis. During the entire war I never ate as well as at Majdanek.

That couldn't last longer than a couple of days. The medical commission arrived. In white uniforms and rubber gloves. But to be on the safe side they made the selection of the healthy and the sick at a respectable distance of several arm's lengths. They must have heard about me, because they only asked me my name. "Kot?" *"Jawohl!"* They took me to the office and gave me my things back. I was told to get dressed and given an official document saying that I could go home. One of the girls who had been to see me several times succeeded in handing me a sizable length of sausage with marjoram.

I was proud of my medical practice and of the sausage I brought home. But Lidia looked at me suspiciously and didn't have much faith in my story. Immediately after her return from Puławy to Warsaw, she hurried to the Matuszewskis'. Beata had also returned. They both were frightened. The following day, Tucha Dewitz, our mutual friend from prewar scouting days, had to go to Lublin. She had contacts in Lublin with the local commander of the Home Army (Armia Krajowa). Particularly during the early days, it was possible to get someone out of Majdanek for a small bribe, but we didn't have even that kind of money. Tucha promised to find out and do what she could. She came back a week after my return and told the whole story to Beata. In the roundup at Puławy, the personal chauffeur of a certain *Treuhänder,* an important German from Lublin, had been arrested. The *Treuhänder* had called the commander of the camp at Majdanek and had made a scene. The chauffeur was named Kot. He was sent to do forced labor in Germany. One Kot was freed instead of another. Lidia laughed at my performance as a new Schweik.

But I think that Lidia was wrong to ridicule me. My Majdanek story undoubtedly was something of a farce as absurd as it was vulgar. But if it had had a different ending, would it still have been a farce? In the everydayness of the deportations and forced labor, the endings are good or bad, but in those rare cases where one succeeds in escaping from the trap, there is something of an unforeseeable coincidence that can be considered as either miraculous or absurd depending on one's temperament or philosophy. In the transposition of these situations from life (perhaps it would be better to say "from death") into dramatic genres, one sees clearly the mixture of high and low, pure and impure, pathetic and vulgar. In *The Sorrow and the Pity,* Max Ophuls's disturbing film about the Occupation and Resistance in France, one often sees that mixture of courage and cowardice, humanity and bestiality in psychological or even moral categories. Happy endings, in this prevalence of misfortune, are somehow morally suspect.

On superficial reading, especially in times of prosperity and peace, the adventures of the good soldier Schweik in the Austrian army seem an anodyne and good-natured farce. During the First World War, occupations by the enemy were less deadly than they were a quarter of a century later, but behind these good-natured adventures of the Czech recruit there is often hidden terror. At least the terror of soullessness. It seems to me that Kundera has given the most penetrating analysis; in his interpretation laughter is somber, terror is ridiculous, and feelings of compassion and sensitivity are carefully concealed under the mask of vulgarity. Compassion and sensitivity are likewise present in Chaplin's irresistible farce, as is deeply hidden horror at the cruelty of the world.

A few months after my adventure at Majdanek—this must have been the beginning of our second winter in Warsaw—I came back from the university library early one afternoon. I had just begun the chapter on Tacitus that constituted the beginning of my *Mythology and Realism.* I was trying to show that classic texts contain contemporary horror. As I got off the streetcar on Mickiewicz Street, I noticed a German patrol. I escaped into the first doorway and then across a courtyard into a little garden where I couldn't get out. The fence was topped with barbed wire. I was wearing a heavy jacket of prewar British tweed that I had been given in Lvov. I was struggling with the barbed wire when the Germans surrounded me. They screamed, *"Hände hoch,"* and pointed their automatic rifles at me. But I couldn't raise my right hand, because my sleeve was caught in the barbed wire. Fascists salute with the arm outstretched, Communists with the fist clenched. In the situation I was in, I could only freely move my open hands at the height of my thighs. In the system of signs, it was the salute of a helpless intellectual. The Germans took my notebook away from me; it contained my notes on Tacitus's *De moribus et populis Germaniae*. "Germania, Tacitus, Deutsche, Deutsche," I kept saying. The Germans helped me out of that cul-de-sac.

At that point we were staying in our third place on Mickiewicz Street but this time behind Wilson Square, at Kamilla Olsienkiewicz's apartment in a building belonging to an insurance company. Her real first name was Irena, but I had called her Kamilla ever since our student days and she had continued to be Kamilla not only to her friends but also to herself. We had taken Tatarkiewicz's course in aesthetics together. It had really been a seminar, but the next year it had become a private course given in his house. Rumor had it that Tatarkiewicz had asked twelve tall blond women with blue eyes and twelve of the most brilliant male students to take part in this *privatissimum*. That wasn't quite true. Kamilla was tall, she had a beautiful neck, black eyebrows, and blue eyes, but she had brown hair, which she sometimes dyed red. She could be very attractive, but she would suddenly become dreamy, somnolent, and insipid, like Goplana in Słowacki's *Balladyna,* for a Grabiec of flesh and blood.

Along with Włodzimierz Pietrzak and Alfred Łaszowski—who soon stopped coming—I was one of the youngest to attend Tatarkiewicz's seminars in aesthetics. The oldest of us was Władysław Sobociński, tall, thin, and already stooped, always dressed in a black suit with a starched collar. He gave promise of being an excellent logician, but I didn't know at that point that he was a rabid anti-Semite. The seminar had as its topic the concept of the beautiful. The year preceding the Warsaw uprising, Hanna Krahelska and Professor Marceli Handelsman were kidnapped and shot. They had been picked up for "interrogation" by one of the nationalist underground groups because they had had contacts with the Communists. After the war, Sobociński was accused of having been responsible for the outcome. But the affair was never completely elucidated. Sobociński emigrated to the United States, where he was a professor of philosophy at Notre Dame University, and he died there in the 1960s, I think.

The "stars" of the seminar were Stępniewski, nicknamed the "Devil," Bolesław Miciński, and Tadeusz Kroński. Stępniewski, thickset, with feverish eyes and streaming hair, could really have passed for the evil one when, following the lead of Trentowski and Hoene-Wroński, he spoke of the omnipresence of the devil in history. Like Jerzy Braun, the leading neo-Hegelian, whom he once brought to the seminar, he used the strangest terminology, and it was in vain that Tatarkiewicz asked him to explain the meaning of the "duality" and "biality" of Being. Bolek Miciński, always pale—he was already suffering from a lung ailment—himself a symbolist poet, wrote reviews of poetry for a nationalist weekly but he was even more fascinated by Stempowski than I was and devoid of all nationalism. He was preparing a book on a French philosopher who, like Kant, had never left the confines of his hometown. The war led the Micińskis, with their little daughter, through long and difficult wanderings. He died in May 1943 of tuberculosis that could not be arrested. Tadeusz Kroński was the most devious of polemicists; he led each argument to utterly unexpected conclusions. He had a round face, a neck that grew red, and eyes that caught fire. Miłosz in his *Native Realm* calls Kroński "Tiger," but that was the name Irena Krzemicka gave him at the very start. Kroński, who had an astonishing ability to mimic people and give them nicknames, must have been the first one to call Tatarkiewicz "Apcio," the diminutive of "Apollon." Tatarkiewicz was always very elegant, in a stylishly cut sea-blue suit and every day a different matching tie. As a rule the female students were in love with him.

Kamilla paid no attention to me in the seminars until the day she had to give a report. I no longer remember the subject, probably Plato's concept of the beautiful. What she said was clever and even rather erudite, but I attacked her as violently as I could, and the professor himself had to interrupt to remind me, with his habitual courtesy, that a philosopher must maintain a certain gentility of tone. After the seminar, I walked Kamilla home for the first time and we spent a long evening together. I lost sight of her when, after earning my degree, I had to do a year of military service. I met her again in Żoliborz during the third year of the war, when Lidia and I were living at Mrs. Holnicka's. Kamilla suggested that we stay with her. Her husband was a prisoner of war in a German camp. She had two rooms; she kept the bigger one—with a portrait by Tymon Niesiołowski of her in a summer dress of white tulle—and let us have the smaller.

At this point I got my new *Kennkarte,* an identity card valid in the General Government. One had to carry it with one at all times. I got it, I don't know how, through Rysiek Matuszewski's intermediary at the Home Delegation. It was "authentic," that is to say, it bore the authentic seals, while the different rubrics were left blank. Now, to be legally registered in new lodgings, I had to produce a certificate showing that I had legally moved out of the previous one—always with the same first and last names: Adam Kot. That was not very difficult. The "technical service" had different authentic seals for the different districts and suburbs of Warsaw. I could choose freely. I chose Świdry Dolne.

It was the beginning of August, a few days after I received my new *Kennkarte.* I remember that day well because to mark the temporary end of our troubles Lidia made pierogi with blackberries, and somewhere she even bought a half-pint of sour cream. That was a great treat. We were no longer suffering from hunger, but our daily fare was gluey rationed bread, sometimes chicory coffee or ersatz tea bought from an old crone at the market, marmalade made of beets—also rationed—and most often potato pancakes fried in rancid black oil that smelled so bad it was necessary to air the kitchen afterward. Lidia made half a bowlful of the blackberry pierogis. They were wonderful; I decided to leave half of them for supper. Suddenly, toward the end of the afternoon, while it was still light, two policemen came to get me—they were Polish, but from the German criminal department.

They took me to the prison on Daniłowiczowska Street, which I knew from before the war, when I had been picked up at a "demo," to use party jargon. We had set out in a procession through the Jewish streets—Twarda, Nowolipki, and Złota—waving red banners. Our "technicians" threw them over the streetcar wires. We can't have been more than two hundred, mainly adolescents but also a few older comrades. The police dispersed us with their nightsticks. We scattered, only to regroup at a previously agreed-on corner. I ran off through a doorway but was caught by a plainclothes officer at the landing of the stairway.

At the Daniłowiczowska prison I was photographed and had my fingerprints taken. That was in 1934, when I was in my second year of law school. But now, when I was arrested for the second time, they only took my belt and tie, which I still wore at the time, and I was immediately taken to be interrogated. There were three officers in the room, one fat and two thin, wearing uniforms without insignia. "All right, you better confess right away. How did you cut their throats? With a butcher knife? Where did you throw it?" And one of the thin ones punched me in the face. I didn't respond, and I got punched in the face again. For a long time I didn't understand what it was all about. "Kot? Adam? From Świdry Dolne? Butcher's apprentice? . . ." It all added up. Kot, Adam, had killed three people at Świdry Dolne a week before. "Confess!" And I was punched in the face for a third time. This time it was the fat one, who was the oldest of the three. "It wasn't me," I said. "Have him show us his hands," the fat one said to the thin one. I showed them. The fat one came up to me, looked me in the face, and then examined my *Kennkarte* again. "Those aren't the hands of a butcher." And then he turned to me: "Just who are you, prick?" I had no choice. My fingerprints, taken ten years earlier, were right there in the prison. "Who I am is none of your fucking business. And I advise you shitheads not to concern yourselves with it," I shot back. They were dumbstruck. The fat one glanced again at my *Kennkarte*. "Take him away!"

I spent the night in a common cell on the ground floor. We were piled up one on top of the other, forbidden to go out during the night. Streams of urine flowed from all sides. Some, badly beaten, moaned. I thought only of the blackberry-filled pierogi that I had left for supper. That I would never eat. In the morning we were given coffee without sugar, and they start taking prisoners up to the next floor for interrogation. I was left behind. It was only after several hours that I was called. This time they took me to the fourth floor. In an office with a wide-open window the three guys were sitting in chairs: the fat one and the two thin ones. But they were all in plain clothes. They immediately had me sit down. "Excuse us, colonel, for the misunderstanding. You'll have some coffee, won't you? . . ." I drank it. "And now," they said, "let's have a bite to eat." I wasn't at all sure where they were taking me. I breathed more easily only when I saw that they had taken me to a bar in Wilanów that survived the war and the Occupation, Stalinism and Gierek, and blossomed again in the Warsaw of Glemp and Jaruzelski. On the second glass of vodka, the fat one said, "Remember us after the war, colonel, sir." Only then did I begin to understand. My *Kennkarte* came from a stock the Home Delegation got by means known only to them. These policemen from the criminal division must have known the erased numbers. My *Kennkarte* had one of them, and the Home Army was already executing informers.

They took me back home only after curfew and deposited me directly on the bed. Lidia thought they were bringing a corpse. As a matter of fact, I was dead drunk. But in the morning I ate the blackberry pierogi; Lidia had saved them. A few weeks later we read in the *Information Bulletin* (*Biuletyn Informacyjny*) that the fat one had been executed by the underground for having blackmailed Jews and handed them over to the Gestapo. I had once again succeeded in getting out of a trap.

The year we spent with Kamilla on Mickiewicz Street was a peaceful one. But only for us. All around us the horrors mounted day by day. Slowly the ghettos were starting to be liquidated throughout Poland. Sealed trains were leaving for Bełżec, Treblinka, and Auschwitz. We already knew about the gas chambers. More and more alarming reports came from the Grünhuts, who lived in Truskawiec. We had visited them in Cracow in 1939 on our way back from Paris. Grünhut, the patron of many painters, had one of the best collections of Moise Kisling's paintings. He was a well-known doctor; his wife was Lidia's grandmother's sister. After September 1939, they ended up in Lvov, but as refugees they couldn't register, and therefore they went to Truskawiec. They were living there when the Germans occupied the city.

Before we left Lvov for Warsaw, Lidia's father had told me where in the garden I should dig to find a small bag with gold coins and jewelry. The Grünhuts had entrusted Lidia's parents with it. I sold the gold coins over the course of the Occupation. Lidia was in charge of the bag I dug up, which sustained a number of families. Rysiek's mother, when she was being evacuated after the Warsaw uprising, took the few remaining coins tucked in a ball of yarn. A teacher of geography for many years and a woman of great kindness and presence of mind, she thought, in that moment of panic, of saving the "treasure" confided to Jewish friends of her son. Lidia succeeded in getting papers for the Grünhuts and finding an apartment for them in Warsaw. One of our close friends was to go get them and bring them from Truskawiec. When everything was ready, word came from the Grünhuts on a scrap of paper torn out of a notebook: "We are going out into the unknown." At almost the same time, in Drohobycz, Bruno Schulz was caught in a roundup and shot on the street. People from the underground had prepared "Aryan" papers for Schulz and secured a hideaway for him in Warsaw, but the arrangements were too late. At almost the same time, my father disappeared and was killed when he was supposed to be released from prison in Cracow. In the summer of that year, my mother came wearing a black veil and stayed with us at Kamilla's before going briefly to Józefów, a suburb near Warsaw.

For a long time Kamilla's apartment seemed safe to us. The large building had many different entrances, no one paid any attention to us, and there was no caretaker. Among the first people who came to visit us there were the young Aleksander Węgierko and his very pretty wife, a young actress who had barely had time to make her debut before the war. Węgierko— who had the same first name as his uncle, a famous and distinguished director—had finished, along with Erwin Axer, the program in directing at the PIST (State Institute of Theater Arts). Naturally, he was fascinated by Leon Schiller and, in a different way but no less markedly, by Stempowski. The Węgierkos came to say good-bye to us; they were about to leave for Switzerland via the Reich, in a special convoy of Jews organized by the Germans in exchange for a huge bribe in dollars. (It was to be known as the Hotel Polski affair.) The preceding convoy got through safely. But the second one, which Aleksander took with his young Aryan wife, never reached Switzerland. That trip to the gas chambers paid for in dollars was one of the most diabolical hoaxes invented by the Gestapo.

Kamilla often went away for weeks at a time to stay with her mother in Starachowice. On those occasions we had two rooms to ourselves. We took advantage of Kamilla's absence and put up many people. For one night, for two nights, sometimes for a whole week—but often the very night when they had no other place to go. It was just such a night, perhaps one of the last, that Antoni Rosental's father spent with us. Antoni had been my scout leader (and Rysiek's) when I was in the third grade at the Mickiewicz gymnasium in Warsaw. He looked very Jewish, a fact that was becoming more and more important. Every one of us made a thorough self-examination in the mirror before going out; Lidia debated whether she should dye her hair blond. I put Antoni's father in the basement because that night we already had other "guests." Soon after, I learned that he had committed suicide; he no longer had anywhere to go. Antoni's mother, too, stayed with us for several days, then she went to the Matuszewskis. She survived the war. Antoni survived as well, became a doctor after the war, but never used his real name again.

My uncle Ludwik Wertenstein, my mother's brother, spent one night with us, sleeping in an armchair because there was no spare bed. That was the last time I ever saw him. After the Germans occupied Turczynek, he spent a few weeks in Komorów with his family. In December 1942, he went to Cracow. In 1943, he remained hidden for a while in the estate at Rzędowice, but in February 1944, friends of his, physicists from Cracow, succeeded in smuggling him to Hungary. He lived in Budapest and was killed just before the end of the war, when the Germans blew up the Elizabeth Bridge.

A former assistant to Marie Curie-Skłodowska in Paris, Ludwik was an outstanding experimental physicist, reputed to have hands that accomplished miracles. Along with Bruno Winawer, he was the best popularizer of physics. In my mother's family, almost everyone for four generations had been writers. Uncle Ludwik came to our family dinners on Senatorska Street on Fridays, if I'm not mistaken. But I don't remember much of those conversations. I remember him much better from the three war weeks in Turczynek. He was tall and slightly stooped, with a closely trimmed black moustache and crewcut hair that was still black. It was in Turczynek that he talked with me about Marie Curie, saying that she was quarrelsome and very ambitious. I had heard of her affair with Langevin, but I was astonished to learn that she slept with her assistants—not with Ludwik but with another young Polish assistant. I imagined Marie Curie—I don't know why—in black lace, like my great-grandmother Bronisława in an old family photo. And it seemed to me for a long time that she was of the same generation. It wasn't ignorance but, back then, youthful contempt for everything that was even just a little antiquated. Now that I am a quarter of a century older than Ludwik was when we talked about Marie Curie in Turczynek in 1939, time has caught up with me.

From those days in Turczynek I still remember a young girl with hair combed straight, in a dark gown buttoned to the collar, like Marie Curie in the photograph in the encyclopedia. Zosia M. was a domestic who ran the household. Uncle Ludwik confided in me one night that he was in love with her and was very unhappy. The girl was barely a few years older than I was and it seemed to me ridiculous that my old uncle could say such things. I still remember my embarrassment. Torn shreds of remembrance, or rather of shaky memory, return sometimes like the ripples when a stone is thrown into the middle of a lake. Many years later Jadwiga M. wrote to me from Kansas that when she crossed the Hungarian border not long before the end of war, the guide told her that a few weeks before he had helped a middle-aged Polish professor and his young daughter make the same journey. Was the "young daughter" Zosia from Turczynek?

It must have been at Kamilla's, too, that we were visited by Tomek Koral, the son of my Aunt Luta, my father's sister. I doubt he was even eighteen at the time. He was very tall, wore knee-high boots, and belonged to an underground unit of the Home Army. He was killed in the Warsaw uprising. We also had staying with us—for a week, I think—the mother of Leon Kasman, who after the war was for many years the editor in chief of the party daily, *Tribune of the People* (*Trybuna Ludu*), and the most inflexible one it ever had. She survived the war. In 1961, when I had the upper lobe of my right lung removed in an operation for tuberculosis and we had difficulty getting permission to go to France for a rest cure—I had quit the party four years earlier—Lidia went to see Kasman. A week later we got our passports.

We lived almost a year at Kamilla's without any troubles. But one morning in June or July 1943—we were then staying in Józefów, only Lidia had gone to Warsaw for the day—an officer with black trim on his cap came to the house accompanied by a soldier and without much ado asked for me. Then he went right into Kamilla's room. She was in her enormous bed, her dressing gown unbuttoned as usual, surrounded by a huge pile of newspapers. Clandestine, obviously—all Home Army publications. She blushed to the very roots of her hair. We had laughed at her in Tatarkiewicz's seminars for constantly blushing. The Gestapo officer thought that it was because of him, so he bowed and discreetly retired. For a long time that visit had no repercussions, but the apartment was no longer safe and Lidia decided never to go back there again.

Answering an advertisement, Lidia then rented a room with a Mrs. Majewska, once again in Żoliborz. It was in that district that the war had started for me; on the first day, the company I was serving in had been transfered from the Citadel to the apartment buildings behind Wilson Square. That was where we endured the first bombardment, and from there we reached the "front" at Bielany and Młociny. During the Occupation, all our Warsaw apartments except for the last one were in Żoliborz. At the other end of Warsaw, far from German Mokotów, it was a relatively safe district; it had its old and its new inhabitants but kept its own intellectual character. Of course, there were instances of Jews being denounced, but these were infrequent, and more often, in this district in particular, Jews found at least a temporary refuge with the tacit approval of the neighbors. And there weren't any police informers in the streets.

Even after we had moved to Mrs. Majewska's, I kept the key to Kamilla's apartment and went there, when she was away, to see if there were any messages for us. That was when Fryda Kalinowska found us again. She had already changed her name to Michalinka. In Lvov, we had worked together at Bromberg's; she knew several foreign languages and was an editor at the *Natsmenvydav*. With her distinctively Jewish looks, she had undergone horrible things in Warsaw. She had been blackmailed repeatedly, her coat had been taken and a chain she wore around her neck ripped off; she was even raped and had spent several nights in garden plots on the outskirts of town. She didn't have anywhere to go. I locked her in Kamilla's apartment and brought her something to eat once a day.

After the visit by the Germans, though, the apartment was no longer safe. But for a tracked animal there are no good choices. Not many months later I became convinced of that when our apartment, too, became suspect. For more than a week I didn't know where I was going to sleep the following night. In those last years of the war all the places where I could go were already endangered: there were either Jews in them or weapons or caches of underground publications. And I was not willingly received. A principle of clandestine activity has always been not to multiply the risks. But I often had no choice, and neither did Michalinka. During the week she stayed at Kamilla's, she knitted a sweater for Lidia with some remnants of yarn left by my mother. Michalinka survived the war; later she worked at the Ministry of Foreign Affairs and served in various positions overseas. She sent us presents from abroad: a gold pen for me, dresses for Teresa, stockings for

Lidia. Being a Jew, she lost her job after March 1968 and so emigrated to Sweden.

Although we didn't stay at Mrs. Majewska's very long, those months were our most difficult in Warsaw. The ghetto uprising began then, and Adolf Rudnicki, who had started to come see us back in Lvov and later often dropped in on us at Kamilla's, came every day, often early in the morning. We went out without saying a word, trying not to look each other in the eye. Even before we reached the viaduct, we could hear the sounds of gunfire. And after the viaduct we could see the flames. The carousel was set up in Krasiński Square, facing the wall. It was going full steam, the little cars bobbing up and down amidst squeals of laughter. The smell of burning came from the other side. The wind blew scraps of burning rags. Someone near us said, "The kikes are burning." But almost a half-century later, Czesław Miłosz's poem is the most enduring testimony of that carousel in Krasiński Square:

I thought of the Campo dei Fiori
in Warsaw by the carousel
one clear spring evening
to the strains of a carnival tune.
The bright melody drowned
the salvos from the ghetto wall,
and couples were flying
high in the cloudless sky.
("Campo dei Fiori," trans. David Brooks and Louis Iribarne,
from *The Separate Notebooks,* trans. Robert Hass and Robert
Pinsky, with the author and Renata Gorczyński)

Sometimes Mieczysław Jastrun joined us. But most often, we were alone, just Adolf and I. We could walk along the wall for a long time. On this side. Without those hours spent walking the length of the wall, Adolf would never have written so many phrases heavy as tears of stone. And all that I could write about our silence would ring hollow. At that point, or perhaps when the uprising had died out and all that remained were the ashes and the smell of burning, which lasted almost until the end of summer, I wrote the poem "To the Defenders of the Ghetto." After years of my not writing any poetry, this was my last poem. Adolf took it. He assumed the job of collecting poems on the ghetto. I think it was that same summer or in early autumn that a little book the size of half a notebook page appeared, printed on thin newspaper stock and covered in brown wrapping paper. The title was *From the Abyss* (*Z otchłani*). It included Czesław's poem on the carousel, three striking poems by Mieczysław, and I think two poems by Boruchowicz. I had known Borwicz-Boruchowicz at the university, and he had come to see us several times in Lvov. He spent the entire war in the armed Resistance. We met again only years later, in Paris, at one of my readings at the Bibliothèque Polonaise. It was a few months before his death. There are only a few copies left of that little collection *From the Abyss*. I have one of them. Of all the books that I have published or have contributed to, this tiny book on newspaper stock of almost as bad as the paper used for the underground edition of my *Stony Brook* (*Kamienny Potok*)—which appeared in the 1980s in Poland under martial law—is for me the most precious. As is the memory of Adolf, who remained silent throughout that week while the ghetto was dying. He, too, one of my last friends from occupied Warsaw, is dead now.

Lidia found Warsaw more and more difficult. She scarcely went out of the house anymore. She wanted to leave the city at all costs if she could find work as a private tutor—that was the only possibility of getting away. Kamilla was going to visit her mother, and it seemed the family of a forester not far from Starachowice was looking for a governess for their ten-year-old daughter in exchange for food and lodging. Perhaps there would even be some extra pin money. Kamilla and Lidia went by train; then at Starachowice a carriage came to get them at the station.

I remained alone. And I tolerated solitude very poorly. I wrote to Lidia every other day, but it was not enough. The house of the forester did not have a telephone, so I telegraphed time and again: "Come back quickly" or "I love you very much" or "It's sad without you." And yet again: "Come back no matter what." The forester, as I found out later, flew into a rage. There were partisans in the forest. After two telegrams, he began to suspect that they were coded messages from Warsaw. He could not imagine that one could telegraph the same thing all over again. After the seven or eighth telegram, he put Lidia in a harnessed carriage and sent her to the station.

Lidia would not admit defeat. She made me promise to send no more telegrams and set out in quest of a new job, this time by advertisement. She found a position with two children in the Sandomierz district, in a village called Kotkowo, which because of its inclusion of the word *kot* amused her. She thought that it was a good omen.

Mr. Wizbek, the father of the children whom Lidia was to care for, came to get her in a hired automobile that had three other passengers. At the outskirts of Warsaw, the car was stopped by gendarmes, who ordered everyone to get out and checked their papers. They looked Lidia over carefully, called her *"Jude,"* and took her off to the nearest station of the criminal police. She was not interrogated there but rather put in a carriage and, accompanied by two Polish policemen in navy-blue uniforms, taken to the Gestapo. There one of the policemen delivered Lidia in return for a written receipt, and as he was leaving, he said, "She's a dirty Jew. She screamed, 'Ay vay! Where's my umbrella?' "

Lidia was interrogated by two officers, tall blonds beautiful as archangels in their black uniforms. They told her to say her prayers, asked her to tell them the shape of the host, and tried to get her to say that it was square. Next they sent her to the "anthropologist," whom they addressed as *Herr Doktor.* He had the rank of major. He examined her from all angles and came to the conclusion that the build of her body was Nordic and her type Euro-Asiatic. The investigations began all over again, now with the assistance of three experts: a Jew, a Ukrainian, and a Pole. When they expressed their astonishment that Lidia was so dark, she said that she was a Tartar and that Kotkowo was her native village. Mr. Wizbek, as she subsequently learned, was a Tartar. Lidia was taken out into the corridor and told to wait. Police informers were running around the corridors constantly, several times bringing in Jews. They had all been beaten. It was after the liquidation of the ghetto, and Jews were shot on the spot. Lidia was calm; she didn't have the slightest hope. After an hour or two, she was ordered to go home and send her husband.

Lidia went first to a close friend of hers, but only the woman's mother was there. There were weapons in the house, and to shelter Lidia, who came directly from the Gestapo, was too risky. Grażyna's mother telephoned Ryszard and Beata Matuszewski. They already knew that Lidia had been taken to Aleja Szucha. Although it seemed to Lidia and me that no one knew us except those closest to us, Warsaw during the Occupation was a strange and unusual city, where parallel, but sometimes intersecting, lines of resistance and commerce ran, comparable only to the system of communications in a stirred-up anthill. W.—we didn't even imagine that she could know us by sight—saw Lidia accompanied by the two policemen in an open carriage going in the direction of the Gestapo, and she immediately telephoned Beata: "Tell Jan that his wife won't be coming back for the night."

Not much time had elapsed since Lidia had left that morning for her new job. I arrived at the Matuszewskis' a good two hours before the second call came announcing that Lidia had come back. Ryszard brought her over immediately. Lidia was pale but composed. She told us that they had let her go on the condition that her husband appear. I decided to go to the Gestapo immediately. Lidia, Ryszard, and Beata thought I was crazy. But I insisted and tore myself away from them almost by force. I am now of the opinion that a lack of imagination was always stronger in me than courage. That and a reluctance to face any kind of change. Not to go meant to "evacuate," to change the *Kennkarte* and all the documents, to adopt new first and last names, to invent a new biography. And to move from Mrs. Majewska's involved not only looking for a new place of refuge but also stopping writing for weeks. And precisely at that moment my writing was going well. I had just begun an essay on Voltaire's *Candide*.

To go to the Gestapo meant to have peace for many months —of course, provided that . . . I wasn't afraid. All my papers with the name Adam Kot were "authentic." And, most important of all, I wasn't circumcised. Several times already, informers or the Polish police had taken me into doorways and ordered me to open my fly. If there was no special informer's report and only one's face was suspect, that proof of identity sufficed. At the Gestapo, they gave me a pass and I was taken to an upper-story room used by the black archangels.

They weren't there. They told me to come back in the evening or the next day. When they had let Lidia go, she had said to the Jewish informer, with her usual sangfroid, *"Au revoir."* "Don't say *'Au revoir'* and never come back here. It's a horrible place." I hadn't seen anything horrible when they took me up and down the stairs and through the corridor that led to the room where interrogations could prove fatal. There were only corridors, doors that opened with a twist of the knob only from the outside, black uniforms, the sound of boots, and dead silence. But I knew that it was a horrible place. And I knew that I would never return there of my own free will. Lidia, who always knew that I would return to her from the ends of the earth, burst into tears when she saw me.

The next day I wrote a long letter to Lidia's parents in Stróże telling all that had happened. In great detail. How she went to her job, how they came for her in an automobile, how she was arrested at the tollgate, how the Matuszewskis were informed, how she went to the Gestapo—everything up to the happy ending. But this ending, following the rules of suspense, came at the conclusion of the letter. Lidia's father almost had a heart attack reading that letter. Lidia could never forgive me for writing it.

That day when Lidia went off to her first job was endless. And then there were the endless weeks before we were together again. The evening of my return Maryna Zagórska came to the Matuszewskis'. "You'll come with me," she said to Lidia. The Zagórskis' son, little Włodzimierz, was four years old; Lidia was to be his nanny. The Zagórskis took Lidia in at the most difficult period of our lives—without a word.

I went back to our apartment at Mrs. Majewska's. Ryszard, Beata, and Lidia considered that a new manifestation of my folly. I could find other places to sleep at night even if they weren't the safest, and I could always go to Ryszard and Beata's, but I wanted to continue writing my chapter on the philosophic tale. I could write only in my own house, or rather where I at least had a table and a roof over my head. I decided to trust fate and to give it an equal chance. I went to Mrs. Majewska's every other day. The Germans did not come, but after about two weeks Mr. Wizbek let us know by indirect means that the Gestapo was looking for me. By then I had moved out of Mrs. Majewska's. I only dropped in occasionally, to see if there was a letter for me. The last time I found Mrs. Majewska very agitated. She was a rabid anti-Semite; even the destruction of the ghetto had not affected her. But the previous day the police had come for her second lodger, who lived in the little room next to ours. He was a pharmacist from a small town in the south of Poland, a very quiet elderly gentleman. He rarely went out. Lidia and I were almost certain he was Jewish. And he must have thought the same thing about us. But neither he nor Lidia and I gave any sign of knowing what we all knew. That was the fundamental rule. Mrs. Majewska told me that the police had dragged him down the stairs and beaten him.

Maryna Zagórska found us an apartment on Szreger Street, in a house next to theirs and the Andrzejewskis'. It was in Bielany, far from the center of town, on a little street lost among other, similar little streets where two- and three-story houses stood in the midst of pitiful little gardens surrounded by broken fences. This was our last dwelling place in Warsaw before the uprising, and it was the happiest for us. We felt almost safe from the very start. We had our *Kennkarte* with authentic seals, and I even had two, with different first and last names, one for the house and one for venturing out into the town. For greater security, Ryszard's contacts had arranged to have our names taken off the central registry of the Bureau of Population. The presence of the Zagórskis and the Andrzejewskis nearby was also reassuring.

I had started to become good friends with Jerzy and Maryna the year before. Black-market dealings had brought us together. Jerzy was my broker and banker and, above all, my expert when, after Lvov, I once again began to trade in money and gold. We met regularly at noon on the other side of Marszałkowska Street, in a little restaurant on Złota Street a few steps from the main brothel for the *Wehrmacht*. In that restaurant, At the Golden Orange, unless it was the one right next to it, the waitress was Natalia Gałczyńska, who was then very beautiful in the Gypsy or Caucasian style. She, too, helped us in our business deals and found us clients. Jerzy almost always came with Maryna.

Of all the married couples I knew they were the most inseparable. Not in a figurative sense but physically, on a daily basis, night and day, and then, after the war, at theatrical premieres in Warsaw and all the provincial towns and at author's evenings organized by the Writers' Union throughout Poland and abroad—in London, the Crimea, and Rome, where I saw them for the last time before Jerzy's death. Maryna would come to that miserable joint on Złota Street wearing strange hats and shawls; with her copper hair she succeeded in looking like Botticelli's Primavera one day and a witch the next. Even back then, when Jerzy got angry his lower denture would fall out, and he got angry often. He was capable of the looniest ravings, but in the midst of his apocalyptic visions there would suddenly and unexpectedly arise intuitions, or rather predictions, that were astonishingly accurate and realistic.

In his *Coming of the Enemy* (*Przyjście wroga*), which dates from the Vilno years, Zagórski was the first and no doubt the most authentic catastrophic surrealist, but his visionary gift helped him in surprising ways when it came to gambling on the underground market. Stempowski in his remarkable essay "The Chimera as a Beast of Burden," had observed many years before the war, that the new art characterized as insane was the best school for training the imaginations of the big gamblers on the world markets. Jerzy infallibly foresaw the daily rises of "hard," or czarist, "piglets," the Russian five-ruble gold pieces that in the Congress Kingdom of Poland were the surest investment through two world wars and a revolution. Hoarders are the last traditionalists in a world that is crumbling.

Jerzy played the Warsaw black market with assurance and

no hesitation. Even if he lost, he always succeeded in recouping. But unfortunately not only my working capital but his as well was limited. Nonetheless, thanks to the expeditions to Złota Street that Jerzy and Maryna undertook each morning like two birds of prey, they succeeded in sustaining the entire household: in addition to little Włodzimierz, there were two daughters, Bożena and Elżbieta, and the maid, Rózia. After Lidia, Maryna took on Danuta, who was also Jewish. Maryna had absolutely no sense of danger, at least not for herself. To save people was for her as natural as to serve hot soup at dinner. "You'll come with me," Maryna said to Lidia when, after that adventure at the Gestapo headquarters, Lidia could not, and did not want to, go back to our room at Mrs. Majewska's and had no other place to stay. Folly and practical sense, love and hatred were so entangled in Maryna's nature that it was impossible to separate them. Like Jerzy's surrealist visions and his market evaluations. Jerzy and Maryna were very different but in a profound sense very similar.

Warsaw had an underground literary life as well as a political and commercial one. I didn't take part in it. We didn't go eat at the Literary Kitchen on Pieracki Street, even go for the traditional Christmas Eve. The reason was obvious: we were simply afraid of human imprudence and gossip. Jastrun told us that one day, as he stood on a streetcar step, hanging on, he heard Allan Kosko, on another step at the other end of the car, ask him in a booming whisper, "Mieczysław, are you in hiding?"

The two Jerzys, Andrzejewski and Zagórski, were very careful in these matters. One evening, we went through the hedges to pay Jerzy Andrzejewski a visit after the curfew. We found him cutting out sheets of colored cardboard. They were for the cover of an underground edition of poetry, he told us. But he didn't tell us whose. It was Czesław Miłosz's. I had met Miłosz at that tumultuous literary morning or evening called "The Avant-Garde Attack on Warsaw." That must have been in 1937. I knew that he was in Warsaw, but after that forgotten episode from before the war, I saw him again only at someone's birthday or something of the sort, at the actress Kropka's, an event that, after the curfew, turned into an interminable night of drinking. When I woke up at dawn and went to the kitchen to get a glass of water, I saw Miłosz and Andrzejewski kneeling opposite each other. They were making horrible faces like Siphon and Miętus in Gombrowicz's *Ferdydurke*. They beat their heads on the floor, then—one, two, three!—they got up and made faces. They made private faces and public faces, innocent faces and obscene faces, faces of generals and of statesmen, of virgins and of homosexuals, and of historical figures—of Beck, Hitler, and Stalin. And of the Father and of the King. And Czesław's last face was of the Good Lord, at the sight of which Jerzy fell flat on his stomach. For whom were they making those faces? For the years before the war or those that were to come?

4.

In the spring of 1978 I had to appear for a final interview at the Immigration and Naturalization Service. I finally had a green card, which had been refused me repeatedly. Lidia and the children were already American citizens, but my efforts had always ended in a denial. The reason, of course, was my having been a party member. "Our regulations take into account a variety of circumstances;" explained the middle-aged gentleman (crew cut, navy-blue suit, tie of the same color, with the stripes of one of Yale's colleges) conducting the interview. "If someone joined the Communist party to save his life, that is a circumstance that justifies itself and there is no obstacle to granting him citizenship. If someone joined an organization of that sort to save his family, that, too, is an extenuating circumstance. If," and he looked at me briefly and put his hand on his clean-shaven cheek—he wore the ring of all Yale graduates—"If someone has joined a subversive party to obtain obvious material advantages, then"—he again rubbed his cheek with the hand bearing the ring—"that is perhaps not in moral terms an act worthy of praise, but we are all only human . . . But you," he looked at me without smiling, "joined the illegal Communist party"—he glanced at a thick notebook full of documents—"in Warsaw during the war, when the death penalty was the punishment for that. That cannot be justified in any way. You are hard-core."

When, in December 1941, we came from Lvov to Warsaw, Stefan Żółkiewski was already deeply involved in the Communist underground. Władysław Bieńkowski was perhaps even more deeply involved than Stefan, and so was Dawid Hopensztand, as I found out after his death a few days before the unsuccessful attempt to get him out of the ghetto. Franciszek Siedlecki was also in the intellectual Communist movement. They were all from the prewar Circle of Polonists at the Warsaw University. But both then, in the circle, and after my return to Warsaw, Żółkiewski exerted the greatest influence on me. He was one of the three people who most fascinated me during my university years and the two years before my trip to Paris.

Julian Przyboś was the first of these three sources of fascination, going back to my days at the gymnasium. I was writing poetry then, but I chose him not only as a model and a basis of a poetics. I think that I was fascinated above all by his determination and by his relentless pursuit of innovation rather than by his artistic manifestos, his ardent profession of faith in poetic creation, a faith that never abandoned him, even during his strolls in the quiet streets of the provincial town of Cieszyn, where he lived. For many years I remained fascinated by the avant-garde—incarnated at that time by that thirty-year-old angel traversing with shuffling steps the hills above Olza, an inquisitor with clenched teeth, tiny hands, and beautiful, sometimes astonishingly gentle eyes—even when Przyboś's poetry seemed to me dry and his poetics a straitjacket.

When I consider them from the perspective of my later years, my fascinations with Stempowski and Żółkiewski have been more enduring. They have come back and still come back alternately, at different times and with different intensities. But in the thirties they intersected and sometimes were not so deeply alien, despite the disparities of age, experience, and intellectual filiations. Jerzy Stempowski's favorite book was Gide's *Lafcadio's Adventures,* of which he cited whole pages in a hushed whisper; Stefan Żółkiewski could not be separated from *The Pickwick Papers,* and at social gatherings he mouthed the sayings of Sam Weller in a deep bass. He had not only the agile and abundant body of Mr. Pickwick but also the deeply concealed goodness of soul.

Stefan taught me to read and forced me to undertake theoretical studies. Jerzy Stempowski taught me to write. He proved a better teacher than Stefan, who often repeated, always as surprised as ever, "How is it that you are able to write better than you can think? In my case, it's quite the opposite!" But my dual fascination with Stempowski and Żółkiewski extended likewise to their personalities. Everyone called Stefan "Hetman" [the name for a Cossack chief]. He was never apart from Wanda, one of the most beautiful young women studying Polish literature, tall and handsome, with a beauty that was very Polish and perhaps even peasantlike. They married only a year or two after completing their studies, but they hugged and embraced in all the corridors of the university and even in the great reading room of the library. In those years of puritanical taboos, couples did not kiss in public and only Stefan and Wanda had that privilege.

To tell the truth, among my university professors I did not have any masters. With few exceptions, the university authorities and the subjects of study met with Jerzy's and Stefan's sarcastic scorn. In the very first semester of law I realized that going to class was a pure waste of time. So I would give the factotum my student book to sign, and for the annual examinations I needed only a few weeks of morning-to-evening, or rather evening-to-daybreak, immersion in the previous year's textbooks, bought at half price.

In the Romance language department, I went to Stanisław Wędkiewicz's seminar. Wędkiewicz was a stocky, slightly stooped gentleman with a large, almost square face who seemed to me very old. His memory and his erudition were prodigious, as if he had a whole library, particularly French and Swedish, in his head. The seminars began with a reading of work in progress by one of the doctoral students. But after a few sentences Wędkiewicz interrupted the reading to conduct an unending lecture, full of citations in the most varied languages. By the end of the year the unfortunate candidate for the diploma would not yet have succeeded in reading more than three pages of his work. Wędkiewicz was one of the few professors to whose home I was invited. He lived at the professors' residence on Skarpa Street, not far from the Vistula. In his study, on the work table, on the floor, on the sofa, and on all the chairs there were books and magazines piled in heaps. I once asked him timidly how he succeeded in finding, in those mountains of papers, the particular book that he was looking for. "What do you mean?" Wędkiewicz seemed surprised. "The books that I need are on top and when I stop using them they slide in a natural fashion to the bottom." I am grateful to Wędkiewicz for three things: the choice of Romance languages for my doctorate and a year spent at the Sorbonne, the publication of the first of my literary essays in the *Contemporary Review,* which he edited, and finally, valid still, his natural method for arranging and locating books in the reference section of my library at home.

At the end of my studies I also took the seminars and courses of Stefan Czarnowski. He had a chair in sociology, but cultural anthropology was the discipline that he taught and that his own writings belonged to. In the 1930s that field's type of research and reflection was practiced by few in the West, except in France; and it was completely unknown in Poland. Czarnowski was certainly influenced by George Dumézil (a precursor of structuralist anthropology before Claude Lévi-Strauss). Czarnowski's seminar, which was more like a lecture course, except that it took place around a table for a small group, was about the ancient civilization of the Celts. But as it unfolded— thanks to a pattern of interrelations and interpretations—the myths, the economy, the manufactured products, the tribal emblems of otherness and kinship, the rites of birth, marriage, and burial, the bracelets, the vases, and the tombs took their place in a homogeneous and perfectly lucid system. Czarnowski must have been the only professor to wear an open collar à la Słowacki; I never saw him with a tie. He was sympathetic to the Polish Communist party and perhaps even had closer ties to it. His courses had the reputation of being "Marxist," but the Marxism was of a very different kind from that of Kautsky and Plekhanov—what was called Marxist sociology. Czarnowski's lectures were still too difficult for me; I came out of them with my head spinning. Later they came to me in dreams.

But that wasn't the only reason I was attracted to Czarnowski. The Circle of Positivist Sociology in his department was the only scholarly group in the whole university except the Circle of Polonists to which Jews could belong. That was where I met Rafał Gerber, who with his egg-shaped face and fleshy lips seemed to have just escaped from Pudovkin's film *Storm over Asia*. He was already working on his history of the assimilation of Polish Jews. I lent him the diaries of my great-grandmother, Grandmother Bronia, as my mother called her, Bronisława Lande, whose maiden name was Nusbaum. The diaries were in three volumes bound between thick covers of gray cloth. I remember the covers but have no recollection of the diaries themselves. Grandmother Bronia corresponded with Eliza Orzeszkowa, and in her diaries she had copied the letters she sent and received. She wrote in Polish, but the letters to her fiancé were in French and, after her marriage, in German when they concerned family and financial problems. Rafał copied portions of these diaries and at the first convention of historians after the war, in 1948, he gave a speech on the assimilation of Jews in the Congress Kingdom of Poland in the second half of the nineteenth century. The speech was based entirely on the notes that he made before the war from the diaries of my great-grandmother. Unfortunately, I didn't ask him for a copy of his lecture; at that point I was not interested in my family traditions, close or distant. Subsequently it was too late. Great-grandmother's diaries were burned in Warsaw in my grandparents' apartment on Senatorska Street. Rafał died in 1970. There is not a trace of his speech at the convention of historians.

The Circle of Positivist Sociology was small, invisible, almost lost within the university. The Circle of Polonists, on the other hand, was one of the largest and most influential groups. The student organizations at all the universities, except in Vilno—where for a short time a common front of

Catholics and leftists headed by Stefan Jędrychowski and Henryk Dembiński was victorious—were in the hands of partisans of the National Radical Camp (ONR, Obóz Narodowo-Radykalny) and the old rightist party. For a long time there had been *numerus nullus* for Jews. In the Circle of Polonists, the governing board had for years been chosen by the Popular Front, which grouped together many different democratic and leftist organizations. But the real organizer and driving force of the entire electoral campaign and negotiations was the small Communist cell called Life (Życie), which, though illegal, acted almost openly in the circle and included the discreet, pale, and timid Wanda Markowska and Władysław Bieńkowski, who thundered from behind his desk as from a revolutionary tribunal. During my last year at the university, I became the head of one of its sections. The National Democrats' newspaper, the *Warsaw Gazette* (*Gazeta Warszawska*), published on its first page a small notice, no doubt at the instigation of Alfred Łaszowski, who—after a brief period of friendship—spewed his bloodthirsty anti-Semitism at me: "Chaya Skwara and Yonah Kott at the head of the Circle of Polonists." Kind-hearted Irena Skwara came from a pious middle-class Catholic family. But she wasn't alarmed at being called Chaya.

The Circle of Polonists was my university. In the most literal sense. Its members began to conduct their own courses twice a week, in the afternoon and evening. The initiative came from Franciszek Siedlecki; he was the oldest of all of us and also the most mature. Stooped, narrow-chested (he already had an advanced case of tuberculosis), gentle, seemingly lost behind his glasses, Franciszek had not only written original works but also developed his own theory of Polish versification. He was a pupil and follower of Kazimierz Wójcicki, but above all of the Russian formalists and the Prague School of linguistics headed by Mukařovský and Jakobson. At this "university," Siedlecki taught Polish versification, and it was from him that I heard for the first time about Saussure's linguistics and the phoneme. Siedlecki said that as Einstein had split the atom the Prague Circle had split the word. Einstein did not split the atom: Siedlecki was more of an expert in phonetics than in physics. But words suddenly acquired a certain transparency. They no longer consisted of letters, prefixes, suffixes, and roots; phonemes existed because of mutual oppositions and formed morphemes that differentiated meanings.

The driving force behind these independent studies was of course the "Hetman," Stefan Żółkiewski. He directed the evening seminar on the theory of the humanities, and from him I learned about structuralism. Dawid Hopensztand spoke in his group about the sociology of literature. His was the most Marxist of all the seminars, but the Marxism was heavily tinged with a new formalism. Ludwik Fryde led the fourth seminar, which dealt with literary criticism. Tall, extremely thin, with ears that stood out, very Jewish, and quite preoccupied with the social mission and didactic function of literature, he had the largest number of students and I, too, went to hear him as often as I could. He accused Zofia Nałkowska of being mannered, shallow, and gossipy; for him the model of what a novel should be was Maria Dąbrowska's *Days and Nights* (*Noce i dnie*), in which human destinies attain the truth and moral objectivity of the epic. Ludwik was then under the influence of Maritain and Thomism. His last essay on the transcendence of poetry appeared in the final issue of the *Pen* (*Pióro*), which came out the first week of the war. One yellowed copy is left. Napierski, who financed the *Pen,* was executed by the Germans in 1940. His apartment, including his library and files, was burned. Fryde succeeded in getting to Lithuania. After the Germans attacked the Soviet Union, he hid in the little Byelorussian town of Dzięcioł, in a presbytery, I think. Arrested in the winter of 1942, he was baptized in prison. He had already been a believer for a long time. He was shot in February 1942. Another chapter in the fate of Polish Jews.

Not only the university law school but also Tatarkiewicz's philosophical salon and even Wędkiewicz's geysers of erudition seemed tepid and insipid compared to the passionate discussions that we had in the evenings and often late into the night on long walks from the Copernicus statue to the Zygmunt Column and back again. In the mid-1930s, the Circle of Polonists brought together a group of quite exceptional people. Almost all of them were a few years older than I was, and even if, like Ludwik and Franciszek, they did not survive the war or they died prematurely, they left behind them enduring achievements. Those of us who have survived will forever remain entangled in the bitter and confused history of the four postwar decades.

In those night seminars in the second half of the 1930s I experienced for the first time the temptation of a universal system and a universal method, of a different Marxism and a new Thomism. I was always very attracted to grandiose systems; facts interested me far less. At that time—it must have been after my graduation—we got together every Sunday at noon for group readings in an old building that had belonged to the Jesuits, next to the Church of the Sisters of Visitation. Stefan directed these Sunday "gospels." We read in French, page by page, Husserl's *Cartesian Meditations* and Carnap's *The Logical Structure of the World*. For young men in their early twenties in the second half of the 1930s such reading was quite advanced.

Today, when I consider it from the perspective of half a century, I can see how out of the group of young people in the prewar Circle of Polonists and out of the traditions of its "university" there subsequently grew the Institute of Literary Research, which took what was most valuable from it. And the Łódź Communist weekly, the *Forge,* at its inception and during its first years also extracted what was best of the circle.

After returning to Warsaw from Lvov with Lidia, I once again found myself in Bieńkowski and Żółkiewski's circle. Of course, Stefan was now far removed from those group readings of Carnap and Husserl. But when, in Kamilla's kitchen, I took the oath of a soldier in the People's Army (Armia Ludowa), reading the words off cigarette paper, it was not only because of Żółkiewski's influence. Certainly I did not realize that those few sentences on cigarette paper, burned immediately thereafter in the gas flame of the stove, would weigh so heavily on my life, but I knew that I was making a choice. Many causes contributed to that choice. Some of these did not go far back—although they soon seemed to belong to the distant past—some were quite complex, others were clear-cut, and still others even appeared to be in contradiction with one another.

I had been attracted to communism at the university; I belonged to the Polish Democratic Youth, which was in some way a bridge between the Communists and the orthodox Piłsudski Legion of Youth. I installed a mail drop in my grandparents' apartment on Senatorska Street, I got clubbed on the head at illegal demonstrations almost always held in the Jewish district, I spent nearly a week in a separate cell for Communists in the prison on Daniłowiczowska Street, then for a long time afterward I was afraid. Soon thereafter the Polish Communist party was dissolved by the Comintern on Stalin's orders. Polish Communists were summoned to Moscow from Poland, France, and Germany; they ended up with a bullet through the back of the neck in the basement of Lubyanka prison, having never had a trial or even heard their sentence. The most fortunate were sent to the gulags. In Paris, during the last year before the war, I had associated with an international group of Trotskyites. All of them had previously been in the party, and some in the Comintern; a number of them, having served long prison sentences in their own countries, quit the party after the great purge trials and the "betrayal of the revolution" by Stalin. I could scarcely claim ignorance.

And then, during the first two years of the war, there was Lvov and the vast deportations ordered by "the fathers of lies," as Lidia's father called the Soviets. Seen, however, from the perspective of Warsaw—with its mass public executions of hostages, their mouths stuffed with plaster so they could not cry out; the enslavement of the Polish population; and the final extermination of the Jews—the experiences in Lvov took on a different meaning. My friends from Żoliborz and from Szreger Street, with their ties to the Home Delegation, to socialist groups, or to the Home Army, believed firmly that liberation would come at the hands of the Allies. That was the belief of the great majority of Poles. It seems to me that it was a delusion willingly embraced. The experience of Lvov was bitter, but in the second year of the war between the Germans and the

Russians, especially after Stalingrad, it did not exclude hope. The liberation could only come from the *other* side.

Mieczysław Jastrun made fun of the meetings and the new forms of devotion at the *Profspiłka* in Lvov. Adolf Rudnicki, like me, tried to remain silent and be as invisible as possible. None of us wrote for the *Red Banner* or for the *New Horizons* or took part in the public ceremonies or sat at the red table beneath the portraits. But now not only I but also Mieczysław and Adolf had more or less close ties to the party. Mieczysław published only poems, I think, in the *Turning Point* (*Przełom*), edited by Żółkiewski and Bieńkowski. After the war, Adolf and Mieczysław were part of the first *Forge* in Łódź. So were Paweł Hertz, who was one of the earliest to be sent from Lvov to the camps, and Adam Ważyk, who left Lvov on the eve of the arrival of Germans—he came back to Poland with the First Army and paraded about in Łódź for a long time in a captain's uniform with a huge Mauser hanging from the long straps of a holster.

Shortly after getting settled in Warsaw, we went to visit the Krońskis. Tadeusz had not set foot in Soviet Lvov, but he took pleasure in evoking the interminable May Day procession of starving hordes carrying immense icons—three stories high and identically multiplied thousands of times—of a smiling Stalin and a Lenin forever with the same pointed beard. And yet scarcely a few weeks later this guffawing "Tiger" became an apostle of Marxism. Tadeusz was always the most perverse Hegelian, and I suspect that Miłosz came up with the concept of the "Hegelian sting" with Kroński's metamorphoses in mind. But for me in Warsaw at that time, and still more for Mieczysław and Adolf, it was a question not of the final sense of history illuminated by reason but of a last attempt to find some hope in the future.

Man's Hope was the title of Malraux's novel about the Spanish civil war. Once again, different threads crossed strangely. Jerzy Stempowski was the first to speak to me about Malraux. He considered *The Royal Way* an important book. Stempowski was fascinated by the new rules of action revealed by Malraux, which were different both from those of the artistic bohemia

and from those of the well-to-do and well-situated. They were
the rules of the game for adventurers. At times Stempowski
called Malraux a new brand of conquistador. The new attitude
was full of contempt for bourgeois morality. In Malraux's subsequent novels, which took place in China, Stempowski discovered the same rules of the game (the word *game* has replaced
the word *morality,* and that was not only a semantic difference)
in the principles and behavior of terrorists. But at that period
I read those novels differently: each generation has its "heretical" books; for me and for many others, Malraux's novels were
the heretical books. They not only inflamed the imagination,
they also showed that one could experience life on a grand
scale only through action. Revolution was immersion in the
"destructive element," destructive and intoxicating, as Conrad
once called it.

Man's Hope was the book that affected me the most deeply.
For a number of intellectuals of my generation or a few years
older in France, England, and even America who had gone
through communism, the Spanish civil war represented the
beginning of political consciousness and the first choice in
their lives. *No pasaran!* They shall not pass. They passed. But
from then on the world was divided into reds and blacks. And
that was the sole choice. And the sole hope. Bitter but hope
nonetheless.

There were other motivations that led me to make the choice
I did during the Occupation. Fear is degrading, especially fear
thrust on one, from which there is no escape. Only the fear that
is a deliberate act of freedom, a choice, is not degrading. One
can measure oneself against it. It acts as therapy against the degrading fear. I started to go mountain climbing in the Tatras
many years after the war. My hands were too weak and I was
very afraid. But I myself had chosen that fear. Of my own free
will I could measure myself against it. The fear I experienced
during the Occupation was paralyzing. Adhering to the party
was the choice of one's own fear. I was afraid when I went
to meet with our group. But that was another fear. Malraux's
revolutionaries also knew that fear. In *The Conquerors* and in
Man's Fate, they grow drunk on it. It is a measure of the human.

But to tell the truth, in my cell in the People's Army I didn't have many reasons to be afraid. My tasks consisted almost exclusively of writing articles for *Young Democracy* (*Młoda Demokracja*), which I then brought to my meeting with Hedda Bartoszek, always held at the same hour on the same day of the week at our "spot," a vulcanizer's workshop on Żurawia Street. Hedda was our liaison. In addition, our whole group met once or twice a week. Most often we met separately, so as not to attract attention, at the suburban railway station on Nowogrodzka Street. It was the favorite meeting place for almost all the factions of the Warsaw underground. After a couple of weeks, we all knew one another by sight, we had sniffed one another, and we had sometimes even exchanged information and tips about the roundups that had taken place here and there.

That last winter before the uprising, Władek, Stefan, and Hedda were coming back from a meeting in the "district" shortly after the curfew. I think Stefan described that episode in one of the first issues of the *Forge*. At the next corner they noticed a patrol with automatic rifles. It must have been Hoża Street, not far from the vulcanizer's workshop where we usually met Hedda. The patrol was heading straight for them. They turned, but it was too late. The gendarmes took them into the entryway of an apartment building, then into the janitor's. It was hot in the room: a fire roared in the little cast-iron stove fed with coal dust. The German officer threw the janitor and his kids out and ordered the three to strip. Hedda was "clean" and Stefan was "clean" too. But Władek had in the side pocket of his thick winter coat a package of Communist bulletins and fliers. Stefan undressed first and stood in his shirt. When Hedda began to unbutton her blouse, the German was struck with a sudden and unexpected feeling of decency, because he went out the door and turned away. *"Schnell!"* he said. Through the door Hedda passed him, item by item, her skirt, her blouse, her brassiere, and even, one after the other, her thick wool stockings. At the same time, with her left hand she threw, piece by piece, in the open flue of the cast-iron stove the fliers handed her by Władek. In Brechtian terminology, this double movement of Hedda's hands—simultaneously feeding the stove with fliers and passing her clothing and underwear to be searched by a German soldier—would certainly be called *gestus*. For Brecht, *gestus* is at one and the same time a gesture and a situation that reveal the dramatic contradictions that are suspended for an instant and, as it were, become frozen in his epic theater. In this gesture of Hedda's, as she stood in her panties in front of the smoking flue of the little stove, one can discern both the pathos and the vulgarity. They were often linked. In those days pathos without vulgarity meant death.

I went more and more frequently to Wanda and Stefan's place on Tarczyńska Street. Even today, at the sound of the word *Tarczyńska,* the smell of fresh planks comes back to me and I have a taste in my mouth of sawdust floating through the air. But perhaps it is only an illusion and there never was a sawmill on Tarczyńska Street. The staircase leading to Stefan and Wanda's apartment was dark and the corridor was even darker. The dining room was dark too, the balcony window covered with a blanket; a lightbulb hung above a table covered with papers and with several glasses of partially drunk tea.

At Stefan's I met Comrade Tomasz. During the Occupation, Tomasz was the pseudonym of Bolesław Bierut, which of course I learned only after the war. But I knew that he was a member of the National Council (Rada Krajowa) and that he was "important." The National Council had been created the previous New Year's Eve on Twarda Street. I knew that Stefan, as well as another member of our group, Szczęsny ("Lucky") Dobrowolski, had taken part in that meeting; as usual, Hedda was the liaison. Tomasz seemed to me much older than I was; he kept his coat on, although it was not at all cold in the room. He was clean-shaven. The impression he made on me was that of a municipal functionary. I had imagined a top party comrade quite differently. Tomasz was nondescript. He spoke in a very low monotone. I had a strange feeling that although he was talking to me he wasn't actually talking to me at all but rather repeating to himself phrases that he had learned by heart.

At that point, I think, Comrade Tomasz was editing, in collaboration with Stefan, the "theoretical" monthly the *National*

Council, which back then was reproduced on a duplicator. He wanted me to write an article on the cooperative system. I told him I didn't have the slightest idea about the cooperative system. Tomasz looked at me sternly and said very gently, "That doesn't matter, comrade. You'll learn. It will be useful for you later on." It was only many years later that I realized that reality for Bierut was similar to those wooden blocks children use to construct houses, bridges, and towers, always according to the same pattern. Finally I wrote a long article for the *National Council* on the future organization of the universities in liberated Poland.

There were always "guests" at Stefan and Wanda's. Jews who had no place to go came for a night or two. So did liaison officers and delegates. Stefan rarely introduced me to them. Sometimes the bedclothes were still lying on the floor. I think that the apartment also served as a warehouse for all sorts of clandestine "literature." It struck me as a powderkeg that would blow up at the strike of a match. And then there was the problem of "stupid Zośka." That's what Wanda called her subtenant, who occupied the little room at the entryway to the left of the dark corridor. She was a young girl, not very pretty, with a turned-up nose and an ample bosom. She worked in a factory. She must have been popular with men, because Wanda complained that she was always bringing them home with her. One of them gave her a camera, and she played with her gift at the window one day. The window opened on a courtyard and, beyond it, a low wall and another courtyard, which faced an SS barracks where the soldiers were training. A few minutes later the clatter of boots could be heard in the hall and the Germans burst in, grabbed the camera from the girl, knocked her about, and screamed that she was a spy. Zośka started to weep and said that she hadn't taken any pictures. A few days later the officer in charge, a tall blond Austrian from the Tyrol, very handsome, as Wanda later told me, came back and gave Zośka her camera. But the trouble was that he had fallen for her. And what was worse, she took a fancy to him too. He started to come regularly. The risk became greater and greater. But for Wanda, the issue was not only safety. Even the self-respecting whores of Warsaw wouldn't sleep with the Germans. Wanda was very emphatic on this point. "If you sleep with him," she told her, "I'll teach you such a lesson that your own mother won't recognize you. I'll throw you down the stairs and toss your junk out into the street." The Austrian stopped coming. He had been sent somewhere, fortunately.

When, after several weeks, I went back to Stefan and Wanda's, the dining room was black with cigarette smoke and on the table there were even more glasses of partially drunk tea than usual. The guests were already gone. Wanda put her finger to my lips. "They just left," she said. "Tomasz and three others." They had had a war council; there was still a map lying on the table. "The Austrian had to come at just that moment. In the doorway he explained that he had come to say good-bye, because he was being sent to the front. I pushed Zośka into her room and told her to go to bed with him immediately and not let him out for three hours." She glanced at the clock on the wall. "They are still . . ." Wanda never used vulgar expressions. And she laughed a laugh that I had never heard from her before.

Zośka was happy—with Wanda's permission she had her German lover, and he, too, was lucky that afternoon. But "stupid Zośka" never found out that by wiggling her ass she had saved the entire upper echelon of the People's Army from being caught. She didn't survive the war. She died in the rubble of Tarczyńska Street during the uprising.

In that last year before the uprising, my life in Warsaw—my political as well as my interior life, if I can put it that way—was divided between Tarczyńska Street and Bielany. The ideological differences were not yet very marked, and our various commitments did not shatter friendships or mutual trust, particularly in this partially literary milieu. And then, Ryszard did not take my Communist activity seriously, and Maryna openly ridiculed it. Besides, the different milieus frequently intersected and merged, and not only on social occasions and at name-day parties. There were also joint gatherings, half-literary, half-political.

At the Matuszewskis' apartment Andrzejewski read his

story "At the Court" ("Przed sądem"). Miłosz, Żółkiewski, and Bieńkowski came. So did Mieczysław Jastrun and his wife, Krystyna. In the story, one of the last written by Andrzejewski during the war, the hero betrays his friend to the Germans because he does not want to die alone.

That gloomy tale was undoubtedly haunted by the ghosts of Bernanos. When Jerzy finished reading, a heated discussion ensued. More heated than was usual at such gatherings. Bieńkowski was the first to attack Andrzejewski, accusing him of justifying betrayal in a covert fashion. The group split into two distinct camps. Miłosz defended Andrzejewski. Stefan, Jastrun, and I attacked the story. We talked of the judgment of history that would decide . . . The light went out: the electricity was often cut off in those days. In the flickering gleam of an acetylene lamp it was hard to distinguish the voices because everyone shouted at the same time.

In that passionate discussion which divided us so sharply, not once was the term *Home Army* used. And only later that night, when I could not sleep, did I realize that the discussion was all about the Home Army, about the defense or condemnation of loyalty in defeat. A few weeks later the uprising began. I succeeded in finishing my chapter on Conrad and the morality of the captains of ships that go down, which even many years after the war my enemies could not pardon me. Nor could my friends.

For my generation, choices and destinies are intertwined. In those strange destinies that separate and reunite people, almost all the participants in that discussion at the Matuszewskis' apartment during the Occupation met for the last time at a triumphal evening at the PEN Club in Warsaw after Miłosz had been awarded the Nobel Prize.

The Overcoat

Three or four weeks before the uprising I left our apartment on Szreger Street in the distant district of Bielany, where for almost two years we had been living next to the Zagórskis and the Andrzejewskis. After our precipitous departure from Lvov, this was our last apartment in Warsaw (the sixth or seventh), a room with a kitchen where we lived happily. I moved to Słupecka Street, near Filtrowa Street. By myself this time. I wanted to divide the chances and the risks. The circle around me was drawing tighter and tighter. Arrests were taking place closer and closer to home. At that point I had my two *Kennkarten* and two work certificates, both of course almost authentic, because they came from friends. Two pairs, one for day and one for night. When I returned to the house, I hid the *Kennkarten* for going out in a little wooden stool that had a hiding place for documents under a sliding piece of plywood. Friends had given it to me as a present; it had been made by their "technical" service, which was better than ours. In case I was arrested in town or at one of my meeting places, the *Kennkarte* for going out would prevent the Gestapo from coming to our apartment. I constantly made mistakes. Once I even went out with the two documents, each in a different pocket. Every morning before I went to town Lidia made me repeat my second biography: names of mother and father, date and place of birth. And most important of all, what my name was. For my part, every evening I taught Lidia the Our Father, Hail Mary, and the Credo. Lidia was a good pupil.

I moved to Słupecka Street two or three weeks after our meeting place on Żurawia Street was discovered following the arrest of the vulcanizer. And that was not the only arrest in my group; people who "looked Jewish" whom I knew more or less well, sometimes only by their prewar names, were picked up on the street or at home because someone had informed on them. I had still other reasons for moving to the opposite end of town. The Soviet offensive was close, and drawing closer almost every day. There was no doubt that the liberation would come in only a few weeks or perhaps even a few days. And with it the final showdown and seizing of power. Friends on the "other side" warned me that the Information Bureau at the Home Delegation or one of its special sections was drawing up a list of Communists with addresses and often pseudonyms. And that I was on that list. The bulletin was supposed to be strictly confidential and to exist in only five copies. But there was always the risk that one of the copies would fall into the wrong hands. I never had the opportunity to verify this information.

Behind Narutowicz Square, Słupecka was a quiet, peaceful little street. It was almost like the country. There were small gardens all around and, just a little farther out, plots of land with vegetables. I rented a room from an elderly lady who lived alone. I was her only tenant in an apartment consisting of three rooms. It was on the fourth floor facing the courtyard and very quiet. There was no telephone; we didn't have one on Szreger Street either—there was one at the Zagórskis'—but I often returned to Bielany for the night.

On Monday, the thirty-first of July (I spent all of Sunday with Lidia), Bieńkowski and Żółkiewski came to see me at Słupecka Street early in the morning. That night we had heard a bombardment in the direction of Grójec, and the sky was lighted red from the glare. Bieńkowski said that the uprising could break out at any moment. But he didn't believe it himself. It seemed to us pure folly, especially now. The Soviet troops were on the other side of the Vistula; they might enter the city that very night.

We were seized with frenzy. We began to write proclamations on the entry of the Polish First Army and the Fraternal Army of Liberation (the Red Army). "Citizens . . ." Żółkiewski and I took turns dictating as Bieńkowski took it down on narrow strips of paper. "Democratic teachers . . ." Then an appeal from the scouts, in the name of liberty and the fulfillment of Mickiewicz's prophecy, to all the patriotic youth of the liberated capital. And then a proclamation for the Independent Socialist Youth about the shared traditions and brotherhood. And a declaration from the Circle of Catholic Intellectuals saying that believers and nonbelievers should work hand in hand. . . .

The word *fałszywka*—a deliberate manipulation of the truth, from *false*—did not yet exist. My specialty, and the assignment given to me a year earlier, was to publish brochures and compose tracts in the name of progressive Catholics. To conclude our work, Bieńkowski wrote a fiery proclamation for writers and scholars. He wanted to sign it "The Forge Group." If I remember rightly, he had been writing or planning to write about Hugo Kołłątaj. We finished toward noon, and Bieńkowski took the pages that we had written and left for Praga. No doubt he was going to the printer's. Żółkiewski stayed behind. I made tea. We began to talk about Voltaire's *Candide*. I was still writing about it for what was to be the last chapter of my book. "Only in a philosophical tale can the insanity of the world be shown without any illusions."

"But where is this garden that we are supposed to cultivate?" asked Żółkiewski. "Perhaps we should plant potatoes in a garden plot." And then, as he was going out the door, "But those madmen are capable of starting an uprising."

I did not believe in the uprising even when, the next day around three o'clock in the afternoon, people started running through the gate, saying that white and red flags were flying in Narutowicz Square and that a tank was burning in Grójecka Street. Then in the early evening shooting could be heard quite nearby. A glare rose above Śródmieście, the center of the town, in the direction of Czerniaków. At night the sky was red everywhere and the smell of burning was overpowering. That smell would hang in the air night and day until the very end.

At dawn the building began to shake. Heavy shells started to fly overhead with a whistling sound. During that first night, the landlady had gone down into the cellar. She appeared again briefly at noon, took her bed linen, and bundled up her belongings. She shared with me the provisions on the shelves and in the pantry: bacon, lard, marmalade, and a sack of potatoes. She made the sign of the cross over me and the apartment. I helped her take her things down into the cellar, from which she appeared only once or twice until the end of the uprising.

I remained by myself in the empty apartment. A growing number of people were camping out by the gate of the building, in the courtyard, in the stairways. The uprising had broken out at noon, and these were people who could not reach their homes or who were looking desperately for their families and dear ones. They had nothing to eat, nowhere to sleep, not even a place to rest their heads. The second evening I picked a man and a woman out of this nomadic band. They were not much older than I was; he was huge, she was small and thin. I no longer remember if they were husband and wife or brother and sister. Or what significance that could have. I put them in the landlady's bedroom. Three days later, three couples were occupying the three rooms. I had taken my mattress and sheets into the kitchen. That was where the pantry was. But I shared the provisions equitably. We took turns making potato pancakes.

News was hard to come by. There were only rumors, which grew stranger and stranger and became increasingly improbable. No one in the building had a radio. The Home Army news sheets reached us three or four times. Their reports did not correspond with the fiery glare that could be seen over Śródmieście at night. In the middle of the second week, three young women appeared at the gate to the building—which had become, when the firing of shells quieted down, a meeting place, a spot for exchanging news and predictions about the future, and above all a small market for foodstuffs. The oldest of the women could not have been more than twenty; the youngest did not even look sixteen. They were exhausted and out of breath, as though they had been running for a long time. They were different from all of those who had so far become stranded on our doorsteps.

I took them upstairs and made them tea, sharing the remaining sugar. Soon I knew all the news. They had come from the Home Army outpost in Ochota to take a report to the command headquarters in the center of town. Słupecka Street was still quiet, but we were cut off from the city. Grójecka Street was under fire from machine gunners and illuminated by searchlights all night. From the very start the Germans held the main artery, Aleje Niepodległości. It was impossible to get across. The girls did not want to hear this. They had been told: they must get through at all costs.

That evening at dusk—the days were still long—when the cannonade stopped for two or three hours, I took them through the underground passageways and cellars with holes knocked through the walls that led out to Grójecka Street. The houses were still standing on both sides of the street, but here and there the upper stories were burned out. The street was totally deserted and it seemed that no one had been living in the houses for a long, long time. Only at the next corner, when we leaned around the side of the building, could we see two burned-out trucks.

The oldest of the girls ran out first and was cut down by bullets on the sidewalk. I managed to pull her back by the leg. But she was dead. A few moments later the second one ran out. She was hit in the middle of the street. She tried to pull herself to the other sidewalk, but that's as far as she got. Now the third one wanted to dash out. I grabbed her around the waist and we started to wrestle. I hit her repeatedly in the face until she fell. Then we sat huddled against each other on the steps of the nearest cellar until late at night. Without moving, without saying a word. I only learned that her name was Anna.

Of the days that followed I do not remember much. There weren't many of them in any case before the liquidation of Ochota and our being driven out of Słupecka Street. Three weeks or, at most, four weeks. I remember that we buried the first girl in the garden, right behind the house; we had managed to drag her up to the gate of our building. I remember, too, that several days later a "cupboard"—the slang term for a shell—hit the house next to ours. I happened to be in the toilet, and when I pulled the chain everything shook and I found myself half a flight lower, covered with plaster but without a scratch. I started to laugh like a madman; that movement of my arm, so ordinary, so innocent, repeated thousands of times since childhood—and because of it a five-story apartment building began to shake and then collapsed.

From then until the end, the days begin to blur in my memory, as if they all were only one long day and one long night. Each morning, just before dawn, in the gray light, we all went together or one after the other to dig for potatoes or beets in the garden plots. Once we found onions. I remember that expedition because afterward I wrote a whole page of my chapter on *Candide* that I had begun but never finished. Precisely on the utility of cultivating one's garden when faced with the end of the world. For a long time there hadn't been any bacon or lard. Anna prepared kasha in the mornings and evenings and made some kind of pancakes or pasta. For several evenings in a row, they were made with onions.

I don't remember much more. "Cupboards" and "cows" (bombs) that produced a terrible howling sound flew over us lower and lower and landed closer and closer. The fires also were drawing nearer. The glare lit up the whole sky. But from the direction of Czerniaków the dull cannonade had stopped. We had no need of news sheets: it was clear that the Russian offensive had pulled back. The end was approaching with alarming rapidity—the end of the city and, even before that, the end of people like us. At the gate to the building the talk more and more often was of people driven out of buildings and shot in mass executions on the spot.

I don't know about what I talked with Anna about during those two or three weeks. But we talked endlessly night and day. When everyone else went down into the cellars, we stayed alone in the kitchen. I read her poems. I had brought a few books and my translations of Rimbaud with me to Słupecka Street. I knew "Le Départ" by heart:

Assez vu. La vision s'est recontrée à tous les airs.
Assez eu. Rumeurs des villes, le soir, et au soleil, et toujours.

Assez connu. Les arrêts de la vie.—O Rumeurs et Visions!
Départ dans l'affection et le bruit neufs!

It seems to me now that we lived through that last week
in full awareness of death and quite intoxicated. We were
together, but we saw our own nakedness for the first time in
the red glow of a rocket that for an instant seemed to hang immobile outside the kitchen window. Then I waited a long time
for a new rocket. We both were embarrassed.

The end came sooner than we expected. The Germans appeared at high noon and made everyone go out in the street.
"Schnell! Schnell!" I managed to run down to the cellar and hide
the manuscript of my book in the farthest corner, under a pile
of rubble. I had worked on it over the past two years, very
often at the university library, which for a long time was a
quiet spot. A friend got me in with a false *Ausweis.* I would sit
there for hours in the reading room, hidden up to my eyes behind a mound of German encyclopedias. On Słupecka Street
I had one of the three copies of my manuscript, the only one
that survived. When I returned to Warsaw for the first time
in February 1945, I immediately went to Słupecka Street. The
building had been burned to the ground. But I was still able
to get to the cellar. In a corner under the rubble lay my manuscript. All the edges were singed, and they crumbled at the
slightest touch. But the interior of the pages, in the shape of
a large egg, remained intact. Like an archaeologist, I recon-
structed my book from these eggs. *Mythology and Reality (Mito-
logia i Realizm)* was published in 1946, one of the first Polish
books to appear after the war.

When I ran back up again from the cellar, the selection was
already taking place in front of the building. Through the window I saw men and women standing with their faces toward
the wall and their hands on their heads. My landlady was one
of them.

I had with me at Słupecka Street a very fine green prewar
jacket of excellent English tweed whose pockets, lapels, and
collar were trimmed in leather. Lidia and I called it the count's
jacket because at what was called the time of "the first Soviets"

I got it in Lvov from Stasia Blumenfeld, with whom Count C. had left it in September before disappearing. The jacket had its own story—one can reconstruct certain personal destinies during the Occupation and the war from the history of objects that constantly changed hands and sometimes showed themselves to be more durable than their owners. Count C. turned out to be a spy, or he simply collaborated with the Germans. He was executed before the end of the war, but I didn't find that out until later, in Łódź, along with the story of the whole Blumenfeld family, of whom only the elder son, Janek, was still alive. Stasia Blumenfeld, who, during the September exodus, was Maria Dąbrowska's greatest passion—which I learned only from the posthumous edition of Dąbrowska's *Journals (Dzienniki)*—had been shot in Lvov in the prison on Łącki Street during the winter of 1941. Ineczek, Stasia's husband, waited for her for Christmas dinner on Gwiazdka Street. He survived the uprising and died or was killed soon after, but where and when I don't know. Their younger son was captured by the Germans near Czortkowo in the winter of 1942 and disappeared without a trace.

Janek Blumenfeld visited us in Zakopane in the summer of 1946. He came to say good-bye before going off on military exercises at Biały Dunajec, in the south of Poland. While there he was sent on a mission, as we learned many years later, to lure out of the forest his former comrades-in-arms from the Home Army underground. They must have been in one of the "subversionist bands," as they were then called. Janek either refused to obey the order or went into the forest and came back all by himself. He was promptly shot to serve as an example. The history of the destruction of the Blumenfeld family and Janek's story have yet to be written. Stasia's last letters from the Łącki prison are included in Anna Kowalska's book, *In Memory*. There is a photograph of Stasia in Dąbrowska's *Journals*. On Lidia's bureau there was an even more beautiful photograph of her wearing a headband. Stasia was one of the most fascinating women I have ever met. Lidia shared my feeling.

In the courtyard two salvos resounded. It struck me as ridiculous to die wearing that magnificent green count's jacket.

I left it behind. Later I bitterly regretted the decision. Jerzy Stempowski would never have approved of such pathetic and vain gestures. But I had not yet learned that even in the face of the final judgment one must respect things. The winter jacket stayed on Słupecka Street. Two more salvos followed. Anna and I ran out together holding hands, just as we were, without taking anything. They pushed us out to the left and then, with rifle-butt blows, toward the gate and the street. I shall never understand the rules underlying that selection. They pushed to the right, just in front of us, two older women from the third floor whom I knew because once they had given me some milk, and I can still see them, in the space of an instant, at the foot of the wall, their hands crossed on top of their heads.

In the street we joined the dense crowd being driven down Grójecka Street. From behind we were pushed by the soldiers' rifle butts, and from in front the Vlasovites bore down on us. They were drunk. They struck us with the backs of their hands or with whips; they dragged women into doorways or stripped them right on the sidewalks. They were after gold. I had two gold rings, which several months before the uprising I had obtained from Zygmunt B., to whom Lidia's parents were related. That last year we had lived primarily on the profits from the sale of jewelry and watches that he had turned over to me to sell. Zygmunt B.'s cousins had had a jewelry store before the war, and they had managed to hide some of their merchandise. From the sale of Swiss watches and fifty-gram cabled bracelets known as *cottes de mailles,* coats of mail, three families were able to live—and at least twenty people who were hiding on "the Aryan side." With Zymunt B.'s two rings and my wedding ring I was able to ransom Anna and myself just before we reached Zieleniak. From Słupecka to Zieleniak is a distance of not more than three kilometers, so our walk could not have lasted longer than three-quarters of an hour. It seemed an eternity.

Zieleniak, in the Ochota district, was the largest market square on the left bank of Warsaw. The Germans chose Zieleniak as the first point for confining the entire population of the southern districts of Warsaw, which they were progressively cleaning out. At least five or six thousand men, women, and children were camped there already. Zieleniak supplied all of Warsaw with flowers, vegetables, and fruits. Ordinarily there were rows of booths one after the other; not a trace of them remained. The most farsighted of those who had been there before us had made themselves primitive makeshift beds out of wooden planks and little rainproof shelters out of pieces of tar paper.

We stretched out on the bare ground. It had been softened by the bodies that had lain there before us. On either side of the square there were the remains of public toilets. But it was impossible to use them; an ever broader stream of urine and excrement poured out onto the ground. Two trucks with bread drove into the square as dusk fell. The Germans left them in the middle of the square. The people rushed to get the bread. The Germans fired two rounds, probably in the air. The people scattered in panic, but there remained behind three bodies lying by the trucks, shot or trampled, and the abandoned loaves of bread. A moment later two small boys ran to pick up the abandoned bread. The next day the same scene was repeated all over again. The people trampled one another and walked over the bodies of the fallen. This time the Germans didn't shoot. I didn't see it, but I was told that the Germans filmed the crowd rushing for the bread.

The nights were the worst. Soldiers alone and in twos went among the people stretched out on the ground, shining their flashlights in the faces and pulling out the young women. I smeared Anna's face, breasts, and legs with mud mixed with blood so that it stuck to her skin like a shell. During the first night they came near us twice but left her alone. The second afternoon Anna found her boyfriend in the square. I saw him only from a distance. He must have been three or four years older than she was; he was light blond and very tall. Wounded in the leg, he walked with a crutch made from a board. Anna went to see him and came back two hours later. She told me that he was her second man and that she had become engaged to him just before the uprising. If there are choices that seem ultimate, then they are made on just such a square, in the midst of five thousand bodies, on ground softened by sweat, blood, urine, and excrement. At that moment Anna chose salvation. She believed that I would get her out.

At noon on the third day Zieleniak slowly emptied. People were taken for the next convoy. We were in the last column marched to the Western Station. We were kept waiting on the platform. The locomotive was standing at the very end. Some men in our column ran down there and came back with water that was pouring from the engine. We had not moistened our lips for three days and were dying of thirst. At Zieleniak there were two broken pumps from which a few drops trickled. Anna did not have the strength to go for water. I had with me a dented tin cup I had picked up in the square, and I ran to the other end of the platform. Water was spurting from the engine. As from a faucet! From the cab of the locomotive someone not visible to me cried out, "Piotr, is that you?" "Piotr" was my alias in our group. He held out a hand to me, then his other, and with some effort pulled me up into the cab. There were two men in the cab, neither very young. One of them was German. It seemed to me I had never met them before. But the younger, the Pole, must have remembered me, perhaps from some gathering at Żółkiewski's on Tarczyńska Street. They passed me a canteen full of cold fruit compote. With chunks of real pears. In all my life, both before and after, I never had such a taste of paradise. They threw a railway man's overcoat on my shoulders, put a cap with a black eagle on a swastika on my head, and lowered me down to the platform with their arms. But to the platform on the other side of the tracks.

I started to run to Anna with the canteen. At just that moment the evacuation train came down the track. The sound of whistles, the barking of dogs, the cries of human voices could be heard. The next convoy was being loaded into the cars. I ran up to the train, but I was on the other side of the tracks. All of this did not last more than five or ten minutes. The train departed. With Anna. She remained alone. Without hope. For a long time I read Conrad with some resistance. But if something in my entire life had "a despairing look of betrayal," it was my running to get water at the far end of the platform and being left on the other side.

The locomotive at the far end had gone too. I was left alone on the empty platform. Fear gripped me. I was afraid that I would be instantly recognized wearing the coat of a German railway man. I was puffy-faced, dirty, with a three-day growth of beard. At the other end of the platform I found a stick with a metal point. With this discarded stick I began carefully, slowly, and methodically to spear the papers lying about the platform and to stack them by a flattened trash can. Dusk fell slowly. Over the city hung a dark cloud through which flames shot high time and time again. By their glow it was possible to see clearly the burned-out skeleton of the main Warsaw telephone exchange building. Three successive waves of Messerschmits made dives toward the Old Town. The wind kept blowing soot-blackened papers and rags. Some still smelled of pus and blood. I speared them stubbornly on my stick and carted them off to the same spot. I was alone on the empty platform. Warsaw kept on burning.

After an hour, or two, or three—time seemed to have congealed—when the platform was almost clean, a train full of soldiers came into the station. It didn't stay long. When it left, I jumped on the last car. No one paid any attention to me. No one asked me anything. What could be more normal than to see a German railway worker on a military convoy? I got off less than an hour later at Grodzisko.

That same evening I met someone I knew from trading money and gold. He had already started up business again. He took me home with him. I washed and we drank vodka all night. The dollar was up, but only coins were being bought; paper money could burn too easily.

The next day I went to Milanówek. The trains were running as if nothing had happened. I found Zygmunt B. He didn't have any news from Warsaw. Finally I succeeded in making a "contact." The convoys from Zieleniak went to Pruszków. It was a transit camp where the selections were made and convoys then left for the Reich. For the work camps, but some said they were going to Auschwitz. Each morning a team of doctors and nurses from the hospital at Milanówek went to Pruszków on special passes. I learned that they saved from the camp members of the Home Army who could be useful or who were well known. In the evening I went to the house of a young doctor, the head of the team. He could barely stand he was so tired. "It'll be done," he said. "We'll put an apron and a nurse's hat on her. Passes," he burst out laughing, "take all you want. Here is the list of the last convoy. But what's her name?" "Anna, Anka, a short blonde . . ." "But her last name . . ." I didn't know her last name. He looked at me as though I were mad. "Listen," he said, "There are hundreds of Annas and one out of two is blonde." He made a gesture of impatience. Only then did I realize that I knew nothing about Anna except that she had been in love twice and was in the Gray Ranks (Szare Szeregi). I had the impression that I remembered she had gray eyes, but I wasn't sure of that. We were together all the time, night and day, day and night, without a moment's interruption, and I never asked what her name was. Nor did she ask what mine was. Only first names. At that time nothing else was needed.

2.

Slowly the news from Warsaw began to arrive. But nothing about Lidia. I didn't know if she was alive, or who else was. They said that things were quiet in Bielany and that it had been full of Germans from the start, but it was precisely there, from the direction of Kampinos, that the partisans were to come from the woods to bring aid to Warsaw. The heaviest fighting had taken place in the Old Town; the center and Powiśle were still putting up stiff resistance. The Germans continued to control the major arteries. No help had come from London; the Soviets would not grant the use of their airfields to the Allied planes. There had been some airdrops to Warsaw, but these had stopped too. The uprising was in its death throes. One did not have to hear the news; it was enough to look at the sky. The black smoke above the city grew thicker and thicker and now blotted out the glare of the fires.

In train stations, beside former mailboxes, on every free patch of wall, scraps of paper announced that so and so was alive, was looking for such and such a person, and then names and addresses followed. One should ask here or there. And even more carefully inscribed little cards offered for sale a fur coat, cloth, a motorcycle, table service for twelve, a painting by Kossak, or a Persian rug. I remember that someone announced that he had an antique curved saber for sale. There were announcements for home-cooked dinners and for coffee shops, which sprang up like mushrooms after the rain, the most elegant one being in Milanówek, where they served an absolutely fabulous layered chocolate torte with almond paste. In these coffee shops, besides the "natives" from the suburban rail line, the adventurers and speculators, there appeared more and more frequently young men and women who wore the then-fashionable fancy breeches called "officers" tucked into their knee-high boots; they dressed in jackets like the count's jacket I had so recklessly left behind on Słupecka Street or in blazers. The young men let their mustaches and beards grow freely. That was the new postuprising fashion. It is perhaps not entirely accidental—and there is probably a general historical law operating here—that this style came back again in the second year of Solidarity, especially in the months preceding the imposition of martial law in December 1981.

These young people who lingered over a coffee or rowan-flavored vodka undoubtedly belonged to one of the many underground organizations, but this new sexual, commercial, and political life seemed to me repulsive in its normality. The weeks following the uprising have left few traces in human memory or in literature; it is perhaps Stanisław Dygat, in his *Farewells (Pożegnania)*, who has rendered most vividly and authentically the strange atmosphere of Milanówek and the tiny town of Podkowa Leśna.

At this moment, too, I learned that the People's Army had joined in the uprising, probably in the second week. If I had known while I was at Słupecka Street, I could have reached the outpost of the Home Army in the Ochota district. Now I felt nauseated, even though I had passed two days warming myself in the sun, half-naked, with one of Lidia's rediscovered little female cousins on the sandy beach outside Podkowa Leśna. I decided to go join the partisans and I didn't care which ones. It wasn't difficult to find them. "You go to the nearest forest," one of those young people in a hunting jacket said to me, "and you call out, 'Hoy, ho,' and immediately, from behind a bush, out will jump a guy with an automatic rifle." I wasn't sure if he was making fun of me, but it happened almost exactly as he said.

From friends I got some boots and a knapsack, in which I stuffed a change of underwear, heavy socks, and—the nights were starting to get cold—the German railway man's coat. It still proved to be useful to me, but for other reasons. I went off with one of Lidia's cousins in the direction of the Vistula and Góra Kalwaria. The same day, before nightfall, we chanced upon a partisan unit. We weren't asked many questions, only where we were coming from. "From Warsaw," we answered. That was sufficient. We were given haversacks, two grenades, and a carbine with a notched barrel, like the ones that poachers used in the old days. And a handful of cartridges.

We didn't ask many questions either. The unit was commanded by Captain Lanca, as we were told right away. The group was part of the Home Army, twice disbanded; the heart of the unit was a special section—but I learned about that and about its assignments later. After the uprising, a unit of the right-wing group, also disbanded, joined the Home Army. The guerilla band that I had chosen did not turn out to be the best, but it was too late to back out now. And there wasn't really anywhere else to go. I was, however, sufficiently cautious not to breathe a word about my belonging to the People's Army. Or, of course, about being a Jew. But I was not circumcised, in any case, and at the first well we splashed in the water naked and everyone showed off what he had to be proud of. My partisan adventure came to an end, though, much sooner than I expected and quite differently from what I imagined.

My German railway man's coat turned out to be an invaluable asset. There were two or three soldiers in the unit who had been wounded as the result of an accidental run-in with the gendarmes a few days before our arrival. One of them, seriously ill with complications from a shot in the hip, lay in a horse-drawn wagon, almost constantly delirious. There were two attendants whose sole function seemed to be to carry off the wounded on an improvised stretcher made of sticks and an old blanket. In the field pharmacy, as I soon found out, there were only three bandages, two bottles of denatured alcohol, each half-drunk, and several boxes of German condoms. The boys amused themselves by blowing them up and betting cigarette butts on which would burst first.

"You'll go to Zalesie," Lanca said to me. "It's some twenty kilometers from here. I'll give you a carriage and two men. Corporal Wrona knows the way. There's a doctor there, a gynecologist, I think but maybe he does surgery too." On a scrap of paper, he drew me a kind of map. "Just be careful. At the next corner there's the Gestapo. Don't make too much noise. Tell them there's someone sick at the station, or invent something. Bring the doctor back before dawn. Here, take this." He opened a chest with two padlocks and pulled out a thick leather belt. "These are from the airdrops," he said, laughing. "Not precisely for us, but we intercepted them." A row of twenty-dollar gold coins were stuck in the belt like cartridges. He pulled out two. "Give him these, and if he does his job, he'll get more." "And if he doesn't agree?" The captain looked at me as though I were an earthworm. "What does that mean: if he doesn't agree? Didn't they teach you anything at the railway, imbecile? You can bring him without teeth, provided he's still moving."

I went to find a gun and a Sten. But I had barely put my hands on the sten when a round went off; the homemade guns did not have a safety clip. Wrona went to complain to the captain. "He's going to mow us all down, that fucked-up railway man. If he's taking a Sten, I'm not going. That's certain death! I prefer to take on the Germans bare-handed." I turned the Sten over to Wrona.

Reaching Zalesie by evening, we stopped at the first little square. Some horse-drawn wagons requisitioned by the partisans, the *podwody,* were standing there. Two streets went off at right angles, bordered by rachitic trees and wooden houses with verandas and awnings with cut-out hearts. These same little houses in the same folk style could also be found in Józefów, where we had lived three or four months, from July to the beginning of October 1943, a year before the uprising. Our two addresses in Warsaw having, one after the other, become dangerous, it had seemed safer to leave the city for the summer. And that really was the right moment.

I remember the kiosk by the station at Józefów. Here there was a similar one, where ice cream and other things were sold. The one in Zalesie Górne was entirely covered, from top to bottom, with strange and ludicrous postcards. It may be because of that kiosk in Zalesie Górne that I took up my latest hobby, which I am still pursuing: collecting kitsch. Roman Karst, our next-door neighbor in Stony Brook, was scandalized by my taste for it. For years, on leaving our house, one went either to the left, "on the way to the Greek's," or to the right, along Quaker Path, "on the way to Roman's." The Greek restaurant that Roman and I liked so much burned down three years ago, and Roman is now dead.

Henryk Tomaszewski ran the ice-cream kiosk. We were sure that he was Jewish and that he thought, as we did, that Józefów was safer than the city. In fact Henryk was not Jewish, but his wife was. By running his little business, he was able to hide his wife and his entire family in Józefów. Alicja, his wife, whom we sometimes met, was very attractive at that time and did not at all have the Jewish "look."

At a time when we did not yet know her, she may have saved our lives. One day we were coming back from Warsaw in the early afternoon, walking along the deserted train tracks. Suddenly a young woman ran toward us and, gasping for breath, stammered, "Get out of here or climb back in the train immediately. Terrible things are happening here." Since morning, a roundup had been in progress in Józefów; the Gestapo had come with trucks and were going from house to house looking for Jews.

But except for that day, we experienced our most peaceful days of the entire Occupation in Józefów. My mother, whom

I hadn't seen since August 1939—when, upon our return from France, we had gone from Cracow to Bielsko so I could present Lidia to my parents—came from Cracow to spend a week with us. Once or twice Ryszard Matuszewski visited us. Not only had we gone directly to him and his wife in our flight from Lvov, but they had saved us many times. Nor were we the only ones whom Ryszard and Beata saved; the list of those who found refuge for a short or an extended time in their apartment in Żoliborz is long. Of our old friends, Włodek Pietrzak also visited us. He must already have been chief of staff with the radical right, but ideological differences, no matter how extreme, did not destroy old friendships and ties from university days, even in the worst years of the Occupation.

Włodek's blond wife, Iwa, was connected to the socialist underground. At that time, there were political differences in many marriages, even the most tightly knit. Iwa was courageous to the point of self-effacement. She pulled Jewish children out of the ghetto. And she helped us at the most difficult moment. After we came back from Józefów, my sister lived with us at Kamilla's. One day Lidia took her to a Dr. Loth, a famous orthopedist, who took one look at Lidia and my sister and refused to charge anything for his services. In helping us move my sister about Warsaw, blond Iwa acted as a guardian angel. On my sister's last night in Warsaw (it had grown too dangerous at Kamilla's, because I was now being hunted), Iwa took her to the Bieńkowskis, where she was put to bed on the kitchen table, under which lay the plates of the newspaper that Władek was publishing. The next day Iwa got my sister to the train station, from which she went back to Cracow without a hitch.

Zdzisław Jeziorański (the future Jan Nowak of Radio Free Europe) somehow managed to see us in Józefów after his first clandestine mission to Sweden. He was leaving shortly to serve as a courier to London. But I did not find that out until many years after the war. He offered us his help. But it seemed to us that we had all we needed: a little money, passable *Ausweise* and "authentic" *Kennkarten*—with, of course, false data—and two jars of lard left at the Matuszewskis' for the winter.

We didn't have any problems until the end of the summer. At the beginning of September, Józefów slowly began to empty out. The summer visitors, women and children whom the husbands and fathers came to see on Sundays, went back to Warsaw at the end of the holidays and the beginning of school. We really didn't have any place to go back to, so we decided to stay as long as possible. We had to extend our residency permits. An old man from the municipal office that dealt with such matters came to see us. I told him that Lidia had a lung ailment and that we had to stay for reasons of health. The old man stared at Lidia attentively and then said, "I don't know if you are sick, but you are a very pretty brunette." No sooner had the door closed behind him than Lidia started to pack our bags. "We're leaving immediately," she said. I tried to make her stay at least until the following morning, but she wouldn't hear of it. Like her father, she had never been attached to possessions, not even to mementos. A day or two after the arrival of the Germans in Lvov, Lidia's parents had left their apartment on Kadecka Street without taking a thing with them. We put what was absolutely indispensable in a basket and a knapsack so as not to attract attention, and that same evening we left for Warsaw. I think we ended up at Ryszard and Beata's, whose place was always our first and most infallible point of refuge. The next day I went nonetheless to pick up our things. "Last night they came to get you. . . ." The nice little old man from the municipal office was executed a few weeks later by the underground. He had been sentenced to death—we read in one of the underground bulletins—for blackmailing Jews and handing them over to the Germans.

I arrived at the doctor's villa a good half hour before the curfew. At first, the people didn't want to let me in, but when they saw my railway man's coat through the partly opened door secured by a chain, they finally agreed. The doctor had me sit down in the dining room. I was served tea with preserves—it must have been currants—and of course something stronger. "My neighbor makes it out of the finest potatoes. You can drink it—it's 100 percent pure." Children's voices could be heard behind the glass door. "My friend had an accident. He's at the station . . ." The doctor interrupted me. "At what station? The trains haven't been running for three weeks." I had got caught in my own story, and now I had to blurt the whole thing out. "The guy is seriously wounded. It's not safe to take him to the hospital. I have a carriage. You have to come, and right away." The doctor stood up and pointed to the door. "Back to the forest," he said. "You've gone mad, get out of here immediately." I put the twenty-dollar piece on the table. Right next to the carbide lamp, the eagle-side face up. The coin was brand-new and shone in the light as pure gold. I did business in those coins that last year at the bar At the Golden Orange, three houses from the brothel for German soldiers. There weren't any better deals than these gold coins; their value went up almost every week. For a gold twenty-dollar coin one could live for a month, and very well at that, and a full-grown cow wouldn't have cost more than two of those coins.

The doctor went up to me and weighed the coin in the palm of his hand. "I'd like to," he said, "but it's impossible." He made a vague gesture toward the window, undoubtedly in the direction of the German guard post, and toward the glass door, from behind which the children's voices could be heard. "There's no way. Here we're like a flea on a white sheet. We'd be informed against right away."

"You'll get another coin just like that, Doctor." He shrugged me off again.

I reached into the side pocket of my German railway man's coat and pulled out the pistol that Lanca had given me. "I'm giving you sixty seconds, you bastard, and then I'm blowing your brains out!"

He kept me in suspense for fifty seconds. "Give me my boots," he yelled through the door. "And two thermoses, one with vodka and one with tea!"

To this day I don't know if I would have fired. Back then I never knew either to the very last moment. The hand of the clock went incredibly slowly. Of course I did fire in September 1939. Something moved at the edge of the woods, or perhaps nothing at all. We were given the distance as 1,200. I didn't throw grenades; they were afraid to give them to me. In the regiment at Zambrów, I always dropped them at my own or my fellow soldiers' feet—fortunately they were only training grenades. In wartime it's easy to shoot. Everyone is always shooting. Anyway, in September 1939 the shooting was chiefly directed at us. But to fire at someone across a table covered with two glasses of half-drunk tea and a dish of currant preserves? At someone with whom you've just been drinking vodka? All that I remember is that his mouth kept moving like a fish's.

But I think that I would have fired. It is difficult not to fire when one has taken out the gun, released the safety clip, and aimed. I have often asked myself afterward, long afterward, chiefly when I wake up before dawn, whether it would have changed me if I had fired then. "A man who has never killed is a virgin." Those are the words of the terrorist Ch'en in Malraux's *Man's Fate*. In my *Shakespeare, Our Contemporary*, over thirty years ago, I wrote that that is the most terrifying sentence of the first half of the twentieth century. Murder is the loss of innocence for mankind, like the first sexual act in Genesis—knowledge unique, irreplaceable, and irreversible. "Adam knew Eve his wife; and she conceived, and bare Cain." Cain killed his brother, Abel. This equivalence of sexual knowledge with murder seduced me for years. Today it strikes me as a pathetic fallacy. A *cognitio* from the time of contempt (*le temps du mépris*). Malraux knew that. But could it be that I think this way because back then, at Zalesie, I did not fire? We slipped out the door just before the curfew. The doctor cared for the wounded man as though the man were his own son. He sat up with him all night long and took him to the hospital himself.

After this expedition to get the doctor, Lanca respected me and even came to like me after his own fashion. We were stationed not far from a village, at the very edge of the forest. The old women boiled the water and brought it to us in buckets. Like everyone else in the detachment I had lice. One could wash and do one's laundry, but no one wanted to; one threw one's dirty shirt and underpants at a peasant and took clean ones from him or, simpler still, off him. The peasant shirts, though, were often infested with lice too. In the evening, Lanca took me into his hut and we drank his moonshine. That's when I learned various things about him. He came from the east of Poland, and his father was a blacksmith. Lanca had never served in the army; as a child he had lost two fingers on his left hand. After the Soviets came, the smithy was confiscated and his father was deported in the winter of 1940. Lanca went into the German sector, to the General Government. Knowing something about horses and the blacksmith's trade, he joined the Gypsies. But in 1942 the Germans started rounding up Gypsies and sending them to Auschwitz. The rest of his stories were not very coherent, but what emerged from them clearly was that he went into the forest and organized his own band. He was a born leader, someone surrounded by a romantic aura. In the evenings the men used to recount how he had a wife or a mistress who followed the regiment in a carriage harnessed to four horses. Once only, at the edge of the village, I noticed a young woman in a sheepskin coat who appeared in the morning in a carriage with a single horse.

I never found out when or how Lanca had joined the Home Army and been made a captain or made himself one. The unit that he led operated in the triangle between Góra Kalwaria, Zegrzynek, and Warka, carrying out the sentences passed by the special underground courts. But that certainly was not all. Just before the uprising, the men were supposed to join the Kampinos group, which was to go to the aid of Warsaw, but on the way they came across the Germans. Lanca refused to go to Kampinos: "I won't let my men be ground up like mincemeat."

For his part, he asked me questions about everything. He was curious about the wide world. I mentioned that I had been to Paris. But he didn't really believe that I had worked for the railroad. He asked me to tell him about the Paris brothels. My experience had been quite limited, but I did what I could. His moonshine was strong. And he had bacon.

That very evening, when we had been drinking since noon, a *Volksdeutscher* couple were brought in. They were from Nadarzyn, where they had a little bar. They had given information to the Gestapo about the location of a cache of arms. During the operation, two Germans were killed; then hostages were taken and shot. That was before the uprising. But the sentence had just come from the commandant at Grodzisko. They took the man's gold watch on a thick chain and shot him behind the hut. The woman was much younger, stocky, with a big bust. "Which do you prefer?" Lanca asked her. "That we kill you, or that the boys bang you one after the other?" The woman just kept crossing herself. After about half an hour one of the men who had accompanied me to the doctor's came in the room. "Captain," he said clicking his heels together, "there's no place to stick it." We went outside. The woman was lying in a pool of blood. Lanca undid his belt and holster and tossed his pistol on the ground. "Knock that whore off!" We went back to finish our bottle.

A few years after October 1956—and after Różański was sentenced or perhaps after he was discreetly let go—it was said that Colonel Bristiger liked to amuse herself with the young officers from the Security Forces while prisoners were being tortured in the next room. It excited her a lot. When that was told me, she had already been kept out of sight for a year or two. She had been put in the department of "culture," as were most former employees of the Security Forces, and worked as an editor in a publishing house for young readers. Różański, too, became one of the directors of the publishing house PIW.

Lanca must have been planning something, because the activity in the unit was growing frenzied. During the day we cleaned our weapons; at night, we marched east. An operation was in the making. One evening, while we were bivouacking, two Hungarian officers appeared unexpectedly. The captain went off with them in a carriage and did not come back until the next day at noon. That night I heard rifle shots, but it was cold; I wrapped myself up more tightly in my railway man's coat, happy that no one woke us up. The whole operation took place at night. There were two lieutenants from a platoon of the National Armed Forces (NSZ) lying tied up in Lanca's hut. I never did find out how all that happened. The story was that they intended to assassinate the captain. But he must have known all about it in advance, since he and his men set a trap for them. He had a kind of personal bodyguard, whose presence went back to their first days in the underground. The NSZ men were disarmed during the night.

In fact, the whole struggle was over arms. Lanca had decided to cross the Vistula. I never knew his plans. Did he want to cross the front and rejoin the Second Division of the Polish Soviet-backed army or join the Home Army's Operation Tempest (Burza), or continue through the forest? The NSZ men had decided to leave their unit and go over to our side, and they insisted on sharing weapons. The howitzer and the two machine guns—one of which constantly jammed—came from the Home Army. But the NSZ men had automatic weapons: their own old rifles and the American guns that they had picked up from the airdrops. Lanca did not want to give them those American weapons. "They can go to hell, but bare-assed." He finally gave them something. The NSZ officers were untied and that same evening they left. Then it turned out that a dozen men from our unit had taken off with them.

There were perhaps 150 of us left, in four platoons. One platoon traveled by horse and by wagon; it transported the two machine guns, the howitzer, and the caches of ammunition. For two nights we advanced quite rapidly to the Vistula, carefully avoiding villages. We had to cross the river to the north of Góra Kalwaria. The wagons were to use the bridge, and the rest of us were to go in boats that would be waiting for us. The Hungarian division was supposed to open the way and cover us. Now I understood the reason for the visit from the Hungarian officers. Besides, the men had told me before that Lanca was trading briskly with the Hungarians. He bought horses and weapons from them in exchange for moonshine and gold—for those twenty-dollar gold pieces, two of which had been given to the doctor. In each of the leather belts there had been one hundred of them. With that money it would have been possible to buy the entire village.

We reached the Vistula by dusk. But as soon as we advanced across a large marshy field, we came under enemy fire. And from two sides—from the head of the bridge that the wagons were to cross and from the raised bank just before the bend in the river. We had fallen into an ambush. They were waiting for us. Either the Hungarians had betrayed us or the Germans didn't trust them and had their own men positioned there. At any rate, it wasn't an accident, because when we started to withdraw into the forest—and fortunately for us the meadow was overgrown with water willows—it turned out that our retreat was cut off. Shells started to explode low, right over our heads. We were caught in a noose.

The seventeenth or eighteenth of September 1939, when the Germans were already drawing close to Warsaw, I had come under mortar fire on the banks of the Vistula near Bielany. We were stationed in the apartment buildings at Żoliborz and from there we were to relieve an infantry company. I slid down the embankment and fell into a hole made by a heavy shell. That saved my life. I was covered with dirt two or three times, and the explosion caused the paralysis of a nerve (from which I still suffer) and the loss of feeling over a few centimeters on my left thigh. But that artillery barrage, when it seemed that the whole sky was being rent asunder, could not have lasted more than two or three minutes. At Góra Kalwaria, on the other hand, we sustained a fire of variable intensity, with short respites, for half the night, all the next day, and part of a second night. During the September campaign and with the partisans after the uprising, I had done little shooting; but I had been shot at often enough and savagely. I didn't lack experience in that department. The whine of "cupboards" is petrifying; artillery fire is psychologically depressing: one hears the shell arriving, and sometimes there is still time to jump into a hole or at least crouch down and put one's head between one's knees. But the most gruesome fire is that of machine guns, particularly when you are running under the shells. You hear the whistling when it is already too late, and you are caught in the thick fire as in a torrential downpour or hailstorm.

We tried to get out of the noose on all sides. Obviously there was no more hope of reaching the Vistula. The knot was drawing tighter and tighter. I remember that the next day, as I was lying in a little pine grove at dawn, crouched down like a hare in the field, a German patrol passed by a few steps from me. I saw their boots. We finally succeeded in getting out at two in the morning. With heavy losses. At the first stop, after covering five miles, we were missing nearly thirty men. Ten or so rejoined us later, but at least twenty were left behind forever at Góra Kalwaria.

To get as far away as possible, we continued by forced marches the rest of the night and all the next day. We stopped only at dusk, in a small woods from which we could go through the fields to the village where we had earlier been stationed. This time, Lanca sent only a few men toward the huts at the edge of the forest to get bread and lard. For three days we hadn't had anything hot to eat; we were forbidden to make a fire. Of that bread and lard there was only a small portion per person. Water was brought to us in buckets, but we didn't even have the strength to wash. We fell asleep standing up or wherever we dropped down.

Lanca put me on guard duty. The worst shift, from three till dawn. That's when one most wants to go to sleep. There was a haystack nearby. I crouched down for a moment, just for a moment. I woke up only when I was hit in the face and had my carbine snatched out of my hands. I don't remember much more. My belt was taken away and possibly my boots were taken off, because after I soaked my swollen feet, I couldn't find them. I slept night and day. I was awakened for the court-martial at dawn the following day. I don't remember much of that either. It must have lasted only a very short time. The court consisted of Lanca and two platoon commanders. I was asked why I had fallen asleep. What could I say? And besides, my head was spinning. I was condemned to death. The sentence was to be carried out at noon.

I kept on sleeping. Close to eleven o'clock—the sun was already high in the sky—Lanca came to see me and began to shake me. I didn't understand at first what it was all about, then I gradually realized that I could have a woman, a bottle of vodka, or a priest. Lanca knew the military customs. "That's the law," he said. "Your last hour, it's your destiny!" He started to shake me again, because I must have fallen back asleep in his arms. "What a hell of a world. So many of the boys have been killed, and I've got to kill you too, you bastard. But you see, it's the law—it's something sacred." I was woken up again by the stale odor of tobacco and vodka coming from his mouth. "Well, you're not going to have to complain about your last hour. I'll send you a woman, a quarter-bottle of vodka, and afterward a priest." I think I succeeded in persuading him that I just wanted to sleep. Or perhaps I simply fell asleep again.

From that point on what I remember is only through a fog. They sent for a paramedic; it seemed I was delirious. A thermometer was stuck in my bottom. I was running a fever of more than 104, as I was told later. A new court-martial was held, my sentence was revoked, a wagon was sent for me, and a peasant was told to take me to the hospital.

It must have been some twenty kilometers to the hospital since we didn't get there until almost evening. On the way I regained consciousness somewhat. The youngster transporting me alternately gave me vodka and water to drink. "The captain told me to tell you that he was going to put in for the Cross of Valor for you." In fact I got that cross, but after the war, for other bravery and from an altogether different quarter.

In the hospital I raved for two more days; on the third my fever abated. The doctors were unable to diagnose what I had. It was only when this raging fever that sapped my strength had attacked me twice again that I was told that it was a virulent and quite rare combination of malaria and typhus. It has a Latin name that I've forgotten. But I found all that out several weeks later in Cracow. In the hospital at Grodzisko no one had much time to pay attention to me. I was put in the corridor, but at least I had a bed to myself. The sick, suffering from every conceivable ailment, and the wounded kept arriving all the time. They were stretched out everywhere, on straw pallets, on torn mattresses, in every bit of available space. The smell was awful and there wasn't much of anything to eat. As soon as my temperature went down, I got out of the hospital.

I went to the station for the electric train line to Milanówek. The leaves were falling from the trees—I suddenly realized that it was autumn already. Someone in the car was reading a

German newspaper, and I noticed the date: 29 September. It didn't seem possible. I had lost my sense of time. It seemed to me that I had spent no more than two weeks in the forest with the partisans. I had been there more than three weeks. I suddenly realized that it was two months, almost to the day, since I had left Lidia to go as usual to Słupecka Street. That night, or at the latest the following night, I was to come back to Bielany. Those two months had taken place outside of time or in a different time.

That evening in Milanówek I hastened to Lidia's cousins. They hadn't had any news either from Lidia or about her. Bielany had been instantly cut off from the rest of the town. They confirmed once again that the Germans had occupied the district from the very start. It was thought that a relative calm prevailed there, although that wasn't absolutely certain. They had not heard of any deportations from that part of town. They had had a postcard from Lidia's parents, but it was dated from the month before. The following morning, I went to Podkowa Leśna and to Stawisko, to Jarosław Iwaszkiewicz's. The house was full of refugees from Warsaw. But there wasn't any news about our neighbors the Andrzejewskis or about the Zagórskis. And no one knew what was actually happening in Bielany. Żoliborz had fallen into German hands a long time ago. I learned from the playwright Ludwik Morstin and his family—who for some time now had been living in Stawisko, having been chased out of Pławowice—that Juliusz Kaden-Bandrowski had been killed by a bomb and that his two twin boys had lost their lives earlier. Halina Dobrowolska had taken the dying Karol Irzykowski to the hospital at Żyrardów. Among my friends, Włodzimierz Pietrzak had been killed in the Old Town, probably in the third week of the uprising, and his wife, Iwa, two days after, in the center of town.

I got some news sheets and the latest bulletins. Half of France had been liberated and fighting was raging in Belgium. Romania and Bulgaria had capitulated. As to the fate of the uprising, I had no need of news sheets. The lower half of the sky in the direction of Warsaw was red and black from dawn to night. The Red Army and Berling's Polish regiments had occupied Praga, but the uprising was all but over. The Old Town was a heap of ruins. Although there were isolated points of resistance in the center of town and in Mokotów, the last outpost in Czerniaków had fallen. The only connection between districts was through the sewers. The southern and eastern districts of Warsaw had been completely burned down. Convoys were leaving Pruszków for the Reich on a daily basis. But where to, exactly, was still unknown. Some said it was to Dachau; others claimed it was directly to the gas chambers, as with the Jews. The final capitulation of the uprising was expected from day to day.

I returned to Milanówek by foot the evening of my visit to Stawisko. I felt as though I had been cast adrift in an alien town, convinced that all the people whom I had known were dead and that I was alone. The capitulation of Warsaw was announced on the first of October. Convoys of the wounded arrived in Milanówek the same evening. All the inhabitants had to leave the city on foot, carrying whatever they could. I went to Stawisko three times. There were always new arrivals; it was astonishing how many the house could accommodate. And always new lists of those who had been killed. But no news about Lidia or the Andrzejewskis.

It was only a week later, on the sixth or seventh of October, that someone who had come from Stawisko let me know that Maria Andrzejewska had been there, that the whole group had left Bielany, and that Lidia was with them in Koczergi Dolne. I discovered that it was a village on the way to Wawrzyszew, three or four hours by foot from Milanówek. It was too late to leave that evening. The following day, halfway to Koczergi, about ten o'clock in the morning, I saw from a distance a man and four women. One of the women was pushing a baby carriage. The man looked familiar. But Jerzy recognized me first. "It must be Janek," he said to Lidia, "but why is he wearing a railway man's coat?"

They had left two days after the capitulation, when the forced evacuation had begun—Jerzy and Maria Andrzejewski, with eight-month-old Marcin in the baby carriage, and three Jewish women: Lidia, Marcin's nursemaid, and Danusia, who, having no place to go, had been taken in by the Zagórskis and had been living with them half a year.

They had left Bielany in the column of those being evacuated to the camp at Pruszków. But from the very start Lidia declared that she wouldn't go there. She knew, as her father had from the moment the Germans arrived in Lvov, that the worst was better than voluntarily letting oneself be penned up like animals. The first day, Lidia, followed by Jerzy and the three women with the baby in the carriage, left the column. At the edge of the forest, as Lidia told me later, there was a plaque with a death's head and the inscription *"Eingang auch für Deutsche verboten"*—entry forbidden to Germans also. Even before the uprising it must have been Partisan Land.

They walked two days before reaching the village of Koczergi, where they spent the following day. A detachment of the *Wehrmacht* from Bavaria apparently, was stationed there. When Lidia came out of the barn in her slip and with a net over her hair, the officer looked at her and exclaimed in surprise: *"Sie sind aber eine Mondaine"*—But you're a woman of the world. Up to that point he had not met such a woman in Koczergi Dolne, and it never occurred to him that fugitives from Warsaw could be sleeping in the barn. The German soldiers were helpful, perhaps even embarrassed. Lidia coughed horribly; the soldiers brought her hot milk.

That same evening our whole caravan reached Milanówek. On the way, a detachment of galloping cavalry passed in a thick cloud of dust and dirt. They had black greatcoats thrown over their shoulders and tall hats on their heads. Some even held large curved knives between their teeth. Women galloped after them in the same black greatcoats and wide Turkish-style pantaloons. Some of the riders held women on the saddles in front of them. It seemed to me for an instant that they had been transported live from Sienkiewicz's *With Fire and Sword* (*Ogniem i mieczem*), but they galloped on their Tartar horses not in the seventeenth century through the fields between Beresteczek and Zbaraż but on a country road, bordered by willows, between Koczergi Dolne and Podkowa Leśna. These were Don

Cossacks incorporated into Vlasov's regiments. They have remained fixed in my memory for almost half a century.

All the walls and fences in Milanówek were covered with notices in Polish and German stating the new regulations. Those evacuated from Warsaw had to register and were not free to leave their places of residence. They had to have special passes. Moreover, in the first weeks after the capitulation of Warsaw all trains leaving from Milanówek were *nur für Deutsche*. But Lidia and I climbed aboard one such a train full of soldiers headed for Cracow. We had no pass, of course, but I was still in my railway man's coat. Much as in Chesterton's *The Innocence of Father Brown*, where no one notices the postman at the time and place of the crime, it didn't occur to anyone to question the presence of a railway man at the train station or aboard the train. At the beginning of the war, right after the defeat of Warsaw, I swore to myself that I would never speak German; this was one of the rare resolutions that I have stuck to all my long life, and I would come to regret it bitterly only many years later.

I did not know how to speak three words of German correctly, but in that last year of the war, not only the "slaves" of the Third Reich but also its new warriors and its new functionaries spoke all the languages and all the dialects of conquered Europe. While we were waiting on the platform, I was asked for information about the departing trains, and I would spread my arms in a gesture of helplessness or I would say, *"Drei und zwanzig"* or whatever I was able to stammer. Lidia would almost roar with laughter. On the train, when tickets were checked, I would point to Lidia and say, *"Meine Frau."* That much I could say. The gendarmes never even thought to ask her for her ticket.

3.

I no longer remember where or with whom we lived in Cracow. Nor do I remember how we got word to Stróże of our arrival or sent our address. But scarcely a few days later, Wanda Garlicka, the daughter of the people with whom Lidia's parents had found shelter, arrived and took Lidia with her by train to Stróże.

A day or two after our arrival, we visited Krystyna Grzybowska, the wife of Konstanty, who was a professor of law at Jagiellonian University. Krystyna directed, or was a member of, the RGO, a committee that provided clothes and other aid for the people of Warsaw. It had a legal cover. Jerzy Zawieyski, too, was on the committee and he was undoubtedly the first to rush to our aid. We did not have a thing with us, only a sweater from Lidia's cousins and a change of shirts. Of course I still had my German railway man's coat, made of the finest wool. Lidia got a coat for winter, and I received a magnificent jacket and pants called "pumps" that buttoned below the knee and were fashionable before the war. We were also given linens and a bathrobe, and Lidia received two dresses, towels, and— what was most important to her—two large cakes of soap. As though we were victims of a fire. We left the committee with our hands full. We began to have things; it struck me as very strange.

But what was strangest of all was the Grzybowskis' apartment. Krystyna Grzybowska, born Estreicher, came from the Cracow haute bourgeoisie, from a family whose sons for at least three generations had all been professors. It was said of her father that when he was seven they put a rostrum in his nursery so that he would get used to lecturing. Such were the stages of initiation at the Estreichers'. The apartment was composed of seven or eight rooms in a suite, I think, so that from the entrance hall you went through three rooms to get to the salon. There we were offered coffee and dry cakes made of rye flour. The coffee was ersatz chicory, but served in old Meissen porcelain cups. The bulging silver sugar bowl, in rococo style, contained brown molasses; there was cream in a little pitcher, also silver—we hadn't seen any for years.

The salon was large and dark, the windows hung with double curtains. I was struck by the amount of furniture; in Warsaw, long before the uprising, apartments like that or salons like that no longer existed. Old-fashioned commodes, secretaries, little desks with multiple drawers all stood in a row; on the walls hung family portraits in heavy gilded frames, a Wyspiański, and two paintings by Malczewski. And everywhere books—in shelves, on tables and stands, and even on chairs. In the next room, through the glass door, one could see bookcases filled with books up to the ceiling. And in those old Cracow apartments, the ceilings were very high.

Suddenly I realized that I had been without a single book for a very long time, perhaps for the longest time in my life. In my earliest memories of childhood I always see myself with a book somewhere around. I have lost all my books so many times. In Paris when we left for Poland in the second half of July 1939, a month and a half before the war. Lidia's library from her school days and her first year at the university stayed in her parents' apartment in Kadecka Street, when we left it late one evening the day after the Germans entered Lvov. On Szreger Street in Warsaw, that last year before the uprising, I ended up having shelves with books. At that point they were selling books for almost nothing in the pushcarts on Marszałkowska Street and Nowy Świat Street. One day I bought the first, 1824 edition of Mickiewicz's *Poems* there. Everything was left behind on Szreger Street. In our apartment on Aleja Róż I had bookshelves up to the ceiling, loaded with books. When we left for the United States in the summer of 1966, I brought my own publications and some books with dedications. The rest were distributed among friends and people we didn't even know.

Before Lidia left for Stróże, we went to see my mother. My sister Lalutka had been living for several months with friends of my parents, the Sitkos, who, like them, had moved to Cracow toward the end of 1939, having been thrown out of Bielsko, which had been incorporated into the Reich along with all of Cieszyn Silesia. Mr. Sitko was a retired lieutenant; Mrs. Sitko, whose first name was Greta, was of German origin, but she never admitted it and did not sign the *Volksliste*. Their two daughters were classmates of my sister and her best friends. The Sitkos helped my parents at the most difficult moments and later my mother when she was all alone. Lalutka wasn't yet twenty years old, but I don't remember her physical appearance or my mother's features at the time. When she had come to see us in Warsaw the year before and then had stayed with us in Józefów during the summer, she was wearing a black veil. It was shortly after she became convinced that my father would not come back. My mother wrote me all about it in a letter to Warsaw. And she had to tell it all to me when she came to visit us wearing mourning. I forgot everything. At that point, in Warsaw, I was suffering from atrophy of the memory, and, after the uprising, in Cracow, there was atrophy of the feelings as well. It lasted a number of years. Only on my last visit to Poland, a few days before the proclamation of martial law, did that past return suddenly. I had long talks with my sister about our mother and father.

My mother was living by herself in a small, dark room that one entered directly from the porch, I remembered, and not from the stairway. It was in Józef Street, in the old Jewish district, but the ghetto did not extend that far. Before that, my parents lived with Lalutka on Smoleńsk Street. One morning my father went out and did not come back. He often went out in the morning to do the shopping. He went out as often as he had in Bielsko. I remember that he would bring home wonderful smoked meats—kosher, I suppose, because he usually brought the meat back on Fridays. I can still recall the white slices of turkey breast that I liked best and the freshly baked, crunchy rolls. From time to time the taste of these rolls wafts back to me. But then in Cracow he tried to earn some extra money to help my mother out. He was picked up at the café Europejska, which is in business to this day, next to the Hawełka restaurant. First he was put in the old Cracow prison on Montelupi Street, then transferred to Senacka Street, to the former Saint Michael prison. My sister and I went there in December 1981, along Planty Street. Senacka Street was quiet and deserted. The huge old brick building with its barred windows on the ground floor seem to be totally empty too. The plaque above the entrance read: Archaeological Museum of the City of Cracow.

My father had been sentenced by a German court to nine months in prison for subversive activity against the German state. "I remember the document," Lalutka told me, "it contained all the grounds of the sentence, since the Germans are so precise. It was in the house for a long time. But after Mother's death, I wasn't able to find it. I don't know what she did with it. It's too bad. Such an important document. And one of the rare traces left of Father."

Mother received permission to see him once or twice. She took his linen to be laundered and brought him packages of food. At the break of dawn she was waiting before the gates. Sometimes she managed to see my father when he was taken to work along with the other male prisoners. She hired a lawyer. He promised her that he would be able to set him free. They didn't know that he was a Jew. At the end of nine months— it must have been in August of the third year of the war—on the day he was supposed to get out, my mother went at dawn to the gates of the prison. All night long, she had prepared a meal of welcome. In the prison office they said that my father was no longer there. She could find out nothing else—neither when my father had been taken or where. It must have been discovered that he was Jewish. Either someone informed on him, or they saw him in the shower.

I didn't go to Cracow. My mother had written, I was told, saying that I shouldn't come. If I had come then, perhaps I would have been able to see him. Each time that he saw my mother, my father asked for news of me. If I had gone, perhaps I would have found a way. Sometimes people succeeded in buying prisoners from the Germans. I had friends in Cracow. I could have found a better lawyer. "You wouldn't have been able to help," my sister told me. "You sent money. Not much."

At the time of his arrest, my father was not yet sixty. He was thus fifteen years younger than I am now as I write these lines. I saw him for the last time at the end of July 1939, dur-ing the two days Lidia and I were in Bielsko on our way back from Paris to introduce Lidia to my parents. All that I have of my father is an old certificate of residence with his signature and two photographs. They were taken by Lidia's mother's brother when my parents, after having been thrown out of Bielsko, lived for about a year with Lidia's grandmother in a three-room apartment in Cracow. In these photographs Father is almost bald. But I remember, or perhaps it only seems that way, that before the war, in Bielsko, he shaved his head for the summer. In one photograph my father is wearing bifocals. Judging by these two photographs that have been preserved, I am getting more and more like my father. The fourth toe of his right foot was bent and slightly twisted upward, as if it had been broken. He complained often that shoes caused him pain at that spot. I have the same slightly bent toe on my right foot. Such marks of heredity are unexpected but infallible.

I remember so little, and then at the most unexpected moments my memory seems to come back. Writing about his childhood and early youth in his recently published memoirs, Ryszard Matuszewski recalls Złota Street in Warsaw, where as a young boy he lived with his mother. I used to visit him often after school. Złota was near Żelazna Street, which was lined with wholesale coal businesses; horse-drawn wagons driven by Jews in long black overcoats came and went. It was there that for a number of years my father owned one of those coal yards and did business. Suddenly my memory seems to have brought forth an image from my early childhood; I remember my father's hands covered with coal dust as he washed up after coming home for the evening.

In *Cinnamon Shops,* Bruno Schulz recalls "Father," a merchant by profession and the owner of a cotton-goods shop in Drohobycz. After many years someone remembered how old Jakub Schulz sat in front of his store on Sundays, when the shop was officially closed for business, and greeted his clients as they passed by. And I would give a great deal if I could see my father in front of his coal yard greeting his clients as they loaded heavy sacks with coal or coal dust onto carts pulled by skinny horses.

Photographs are more enduring than either the people or the objects they represent. In the second of these photographs, an enlargement of which now hangs in my room in Stony Brook, one can see lying on the dining-room table a small metal box that snapped open and shut in which my father kept his bifocals. In the same photograph there is visible in the background a large old-fashioned credenza. Mother is sitting at the table opposite Father. It must have been winter because she's wearing a heavy sweater and a shawl. There certainly wasn't any heat in Cracow that winter. My father is holding his arms outstretched in front of him with yarn wound around his hands. Mother is winding it into a ball. I saw almost exactly the same scene a few years ago at the La Mama Theatre in New York in a performance of *Uncle Vanya*. In the fourth act, Telegin, like Father, is holding his arms outstretched with the yarn around his hands, and the old nurse, Marina, winds it into a ball. Mother knitted sweaters for all of us. After the war broke out, I got a wonderful brown pullover from her for my birthday. And later, when my son, Michael, was born, she knit him little green pants for his first birthday.

Shortly after Lidia left Cracow for Stróże, I had a second bout of that paralyzing fever which had so unexpectedly saved my life in the forest. According to unwritten but everlasting law—since time immemorial right up to the partisans at Góra Kalwaria—the condemned must be fit as a fiddle and in full possession of all his mental and physical faculties for him to be sent to kingdom come. Shakespeare knew all about it. In *Measure for Measure,* when Bernadine, "a dissolute prisoner," is brought in, dead drunk, to be beheaded, the Duke stops the executioner: "A creature unprepared, unmeet for death, / And to transport him in the mind he is / Were damnable." I little thought then that I would have the occasion to invoke my own personal experience—and I think that perhaps I am the only one of the band of Shakespeare scholars to do so—thirty years later, when I wrote about *Measure for Measure.*

My sister was a messenger at the Lazare hospital and, thanks to her, I was taken to the section of internal medicine headed by Professor Miklaszewski. My mother, Krystyna Grzybowska, and the two Sitko girls visited me there regularly. They brought me food. Jerzy Zawieyski dropped in to see me two or three times. He must have known various things about me, because he called me his "Communist pal." Jerzy always had a somewhat jesuitic, sly way of using words and gestures. From these hospital visits of his there grew up between us a friendship—perhaps that is too strong a word—or an acquaintanceship and a mutual intellectual attraction that lasted all the years of the *Forge*. During my last visit to Warsaw I went to Zawieyski's grave in the quiet little cemetery in Laski. Barely a few steps away is the grave of Antoni Słonimski. The fate of Poles are strangely intertwined both in life and, long after, in death. Zawieyski had miscellaneous bits of information and various contacts. From him I learned that in Lublin there was coming out or about to come out a new literary weekly, *Rebirth* (*Odrodzenie*). And that Karol Kuryluk was the editor. And that Ważyk and Przyboś were on the board. I heard this news with cheeks flushed, and not only because of the fever.

Later I had a third attack of the same fever. I was delirious and ran a temperature of more than 104°; antibiotics were not yet known. But the fever abated, and they were already filling out the papers for me to leave the hospital when it came back again, this time with terrible bouts of coughing. By morning I was starting to choke, and I finally spit up a huge hideous mucus covered with blisters like a reptile's skin. It turned out that I had diphtheria that had not been diagnosed. Once again I had amazing luck not to have gone directly to the other world.

That wasn't the end of my illnesses. Before signing me out of the hospital, they took X rays and discovered a spot on my lungs. The doctor told me that I should go to the mountains as quickly as possible. That wasn't going to be easy, any more than it would be easy to stay in Cracow. I had neither the wherewithal nor a place to stay. I got a little money for the trip from the committee and was advised to go to Szczawnica because it was inexpensive and safe and a woman we knew ran a sort of boardinghouse there.

Throughout the entire time in Cracow I had not had any contact with my organization, but during my last week in the hospital someone from the People's Army found me and told me that the Soviet partisans were already active in the Czorsztyn and Nidzica districts and that, if I ran into them, I should refer to Zielony.

I left the hospital on 18 December. Before leaving for Szczawnica, I decided to go see Lidia in Stróże. Up until then we had never spent Christmas apart, nor would we ever again for almost half a century—it happened only that once. Stróże was already in the militarized zone and, even in the uniform of a German railway worker, I could not possibly get there without a special pass. It was issued in Gestapo headquarters. I was advised against going, because the Gestapo officer who handled these matters, known for his brutality, sometimes beat and kicked applicants for no apparent reason. But I didn't care. I had the papers signing me out of the hospital, under a false name of course, and a card granting me a leave. I handed these documents to the Gestapo man. He screamed horribly, but I didn't understand a single word. I think my complete ignorance of German helped me. Whenver he stopped screaming, I kept repeating, "Stróże, *meine junge Frau.*" I got the pass with the German "crow."

After Tarnów, only military convoys were able to continue. I climbed in an open boxcar and made myself comfortable on a tarpaulin that covered a small cannon. I got to Stróże without a hitch, even dozing a bit on the way. Almost all my exploits during the war and Occupation and my close calls and escapes had something about them of a grotesque Chaplin comedy, but perhaps there is a more general law operating here to the effect that being snatched from the jaws of death is in itself a kind of absurd farce. Lidia's parents and their hosts were very surprised to see me; for a week no one had come from Cracow to Stróże. The least surprised was Lidia. She was sure that I would come for Christmas. Even riding a cannon. Which proved to be the case.

Immediately after the arrival of the Germans in Lvov, Lidia's parents had left their apartment, abandoning everything. That had undoubtedly saved their lives. They stopped first at Zimna Wola, a few kilometers from the town. There, before our departure for Warsaw, I brought them the bare necessities, at least as much as I could carry, because I went on foot. Tadeusz Hollender brought Lidia's father the birth certificate of a Grzegorz Krochmalny, who had died, so that he could adopt a new identity. The papers were authentic; their owner had disappeared—that was all that was known. We saw Tadeusz Hollender for the last time in Warsaw, probably not long after our arrival, at a gathering, partly political, partly social, with much alcohol. Tadeusz was shot soon afterward in Pawiak prison.

Dolek—Mrs. Steinhaus's brother—and his mother were the first to leave Cracow and go to Stróże, thanks to their friends. Dolek then had Lidia's parents come. That was in the summer of 1942. They all stayed in the cabins provided for the agricultural workers in Berdechów, near Stróże. My father-in-law gave courses in Latin, Polish, and English as part of the program of underground education for the whole district. He signed his letters to friends: "Grzegorz Krochmalny. Solar Watchmaker." Dolek taught physics, history, and chemistry. When I arrived, my father-in-law and Dolek were sawing wood. Lidia's father was fifty-six or fifty-seven at the time. Her mother, who had green eyes under heavy eyebrows, looked astonishingly young. At forty-six she retained all her incredible beauty. She baked bread for everyone.

Neither Dolek nor Lidia's parents had any problems during their stay in Berdechów. The neighbors evidently knew that they were hiding there, but either they didn't suspect that they were Jewish or they didn't let on that they did. Lasko, a man of great courage, was the commander of the "blue" (Polish) police at Stróże. He worked very closely with the local headquarters of the Home Army. During the first years of the war, he got many local Jews across into Hungary, he saved many lives and protected the peasants from requisitions, and he gave advance notice of all German operations. Immediately after the liberation he was arrested; the peasants twice made petitions to get him freed, but nothing helped. He was deported in the autumn or summer of 1945. He did not come back until 1956. Lidia's father, in his memoirs, wrote about him in great detail.

I left Stróże a few days after Christmas. For several months, the front had remained stuck at the Vistula, but it was clear that the war would end and that the defeat of Germany was now a matter of weeks or, at most, months. But even at that moment, in the last days of December 1944, some two hundred kilometers from the Soviet positions, when half of prewar Poland was already occupied by the "Ruskis," our imagination proved a very imperfect and fallible instrument for foreseeing even the most immediate future. "After the war" remained beyond our comprehension, something that the imagination could not grasp. My father-in-law, Dolek, and Lidia still did not believe that the Allies would agree to give Poland to the Communists. Whereas I was waiting with great hope for the Poland that had started to take shape at Lublin.

I arrived in Cracow after the curfew. When I left the hospital a cheap room had been found for me not far from the train station—it must have been on Powiśle Street. On my way there, still wearing my railway man's coat, I ran into a German patrol coming in my direction. They turned into the street where I was living and stopped before the door of my building. They shone their flashlights, found the number, and went into the hall. It was only then that I realized that they had come for me. I heard their heavy footsteps on the stairs. That night in Cracow they were making sweeps to pick up people from Warsaw. Once again I made my escape. And once again that absurd farcical scene from a film was played out.

The next day I reached Szczawnica. I lived in a large, run-down wooden villa. Everywhere there were little balconies and overhanging porches with mountaineers' designs like cut-out lace. The facings of the steeply sloping roof were decorated with the same designs and elaborate interlacings. The villa must have known its glory days in the 1920s; it had been built in the so-called Zakopane style, which, in innumerable forms and more and more trashy imitations, had spread throughout all of central Poland up to the suburbs around Warsaw.

My "boardinghouse" in Szczawnica was half-empty. A few middle-aged ladies from Cracow and refugees from Silesia took their meals there or rented rooms. One of them, plumpish and—if I remember correctly—rather pretty, the wife of an art patron or a pharmacist from Cracow, with more than merely intellectual pretensions, undertook my education with great zeal. In the boardinghouse there were the vestiges of a library, and she brought books to my room for me to read, saying that one of them was perhaps not very suitable. Whenever possible she spoke with me about literature. She asked me what kind of work I did for the railroad and said that after the war I should further my education and perhaps even go to the university. I remember her wide-open mouth—like that of a giant fish—when, two or three years later, she saw me from the first row at one of my lectures in Cracow.

I spent, as I now calculate it, less than three full weeks in Szczawnica. But in my memory, my stay there lasted months. Perhaps because, for the first time since the beginning of the war, nothing happened to me. Of these weeks I have retained only a black-and-white memory: the white of the snow and the black of the etched line of the woods on the crest of the mountains, like dark lace against the sky. These were weeks of reprieve, a prolonged break. Almost no news of the world reached Szczawnica. Not even from the front, which was so close. And when I finally got near a malfunctioning radio, all that could be heard was a buzzing and humming.

As a rule I got up late. Before my departure, my doctor had advised me to stay in bed as long as possible and not to go out in the evening or when the wind was blowing. In the morning a girl came to the room to light a fire in the large wood-burning faience stove. With her, from the outside, came the morning chill and sometimes she would put her cold hands under the quilt to warm them against my body. She always brought two pitchers of water, one boiling hot, the other icy cold, and, on a large wooden tray, a huge chunk of black bread, sometimes still hot, with a cup of milk. When she left she took the chamber pot. The toilets—or, as they said, the "two zeros" (oo)—were somewhere at the end of the corridor, and perhaps only on the ground floor. The chamber pot was part of the equipment of each room and had its special place in the night table by the bed. One morning, as she brought the kindling, the girl shouted, even before she came in, "The Germans ran off during the night and the gendarmes left at dawn, and people say they've gone from Sącz too."

It was 16 January. At noon, I was told that the Ruskis, undoubtedly partisans, had been sighted in the direction of Czorsztyn and that they probably were stationed in the vast clearing that overlooked the sharp bend in the Dunajec. I ran off toward Czorsztyn without a moment's hesitation. I only put on my coat. But it was much further than I had thought. When I left the main road for the clearing through which the huge pine trunks were brought down to the river, night was already starting to fall. The days are short in January. The clearing turned into a path trampled by many feet. There was a deep frost and the snow crunched under my shoes. I thought that I had better stop when I saw right above me the flames of a camp fire.

4.

The days were equally short almost exactly four years and two months earlier when, in mid-1939, I had for the first time tried to join the Ruskis. I had crossed the no-man's-land near Małkinia, between the German and the Soviet zones of Occupation. And the first snow had already fallen.

After the capitulation of Warsaw, when we threw our carbines and bayonets onto the German trucks, I could easily— we were in the apartment buildings in Żoliborz—have taken off my uniform, kept only the belt, leggings, and boots, and returned to civilian life. I wasn't even a noncommissioned officer, I had only a single stripe, and it seemed to me that a simple soldier ran no risk and that it would be best to get back to Lvov. I had left Lidia with her parents at Kamień Dobosza, almost at the Hungarian border, but I was sure to find her in Lvov or, at least, to learn where she was. But everything, as it very soon turned out, was different than I thought. As soon as we threw down our arms, we were ordered to form columns and were marched through the town and out past Wilanów. It was only there, in the field, that we were allowed to stop. We were forced to march for three days, with brief halts, along the road to Lublin. On the way, we were intersected by columns of tanks and motorized units, covered with tarpaulins, on trucks. We passed the first night in the field, where blankets were given out, but not enough for everyone, and we spent the next two nights on the stone floors of churches. In the morning, we were brought cauldrons with something liquid and lukewarm, but again not enough for everyone. Sometimes the soldiers from the trucks threw us loaves of bread. We were constantly hungry. Then I noticed with astonishment that the intellectuals were better able to resist hunger and thirst than were the simple soldiers. The second day, when we passed a field of beets, the soldiers fell upon the discarded bulbs and ate them raw. Soon both sides of the highway were marked with blood-red excrement.

After Puławy, barracks with pallet beds were waiting for us. They were surrounded by barbed wire. We were in captivity in one of those transit camps, waiting to be sent to regular stalags in the Reich. We were always hungry. One of the barracks, bearing the symbol of the Red Cross, was supposed to serve as a temporary infirmary. I had a high fever, and when I grew delirious I was taken there. I was visited in the infirmary by a cousin who worked at the Agricultural Institute in Puławy. She had found out from the doctor that a poet from Warsaw had been hospitalized. She notified Wertenstein, my mother's brother. At the end of a week, or perhaps two weeks, Uncle Lutek came to get me in a car that he had rented at great cost, along with my great-uncle, Adam Lande, my grandmother's brother, who was a doctor. I was recovering from a serious case of pneumonia, I still had a temperature, and I was so weak that I could scarcely get up. The hospital doctor was a Jew, with the rank of major in the Polish army; two or three days later, German doctors were to take charge of this temporary field hospital. My doctor agreed to turn me over to my family. But he could turn me over only as a corpse. So he filled out a death certificate with a seal with the black swastika. Uncle Lutek took me back to Warsaw. For the weeks that followed, my only identity papers were a death certificate.

I do not remember where I lived in Warsaw then or if I lived somewhere else entirely. I certainly did not see either of the Matuszewskis; Ryszard had probably not returned yet from the war. I lived chiefly in Turczynek, the great house with the garden and the park, near Milanówek, that was the residence of the Meyers. Lutek's wife was from the Meyer family, which was involved in the Warsaw world of finance. Lutek's mother-in-law was the sister of Teodor Toeplitz, one of the celebrated militants of the cooperative movement who, at the beginning of the 1920s, was the cofounder of the housing cooperative of Warsaw. His son, Leon Toeplitz, was sentenced to many years in prison in the famous Communist trial involving military personnel that was known as *Wojskówka*. But there was also an Italian Toeplitz, from the Banca Commerciale Italiana, about whom it was said that he had financed Mussolini. Analogous divisions and twists of destiny could be found at the center of many wealthy intellectual Jewish families that had been Polonized for years and were even in part converted to Christianity.

I used to go to Turczynek with my grandmother or with Aunt Maryla when I was still at the gymnasium. At the train station, a coach with a coachman in livery would be waiting for us. I still remember his large, shiny metal buttons. At Turczynek, they raised horses; my cousin Wanda got to ride them. A white-gloved footman waited on table. I did not like visiting Turczynek, even though at Sunday supper they served delicious ice cream.

Before the war, my sister was brought to Turczynek because it was expected that the Germans would immediately invade Cieszyn Silesia. My grandmother moved to Turczynek in the first days of the war. That was where I must have seen her for the last time, because when I came to Cracow after the uprising and my partisan episode, she had been dead for a year or two. From this stay at Turczynek, I have not retained any recollection of her, and yet for years I had lived with her and Aunt Maryla when my parents moved from Warsaw to Bielsko. I only remember distinctly her grave in the Catholic cemetery in Cracow. I can see grandmother's grave, as my mother's grave is there too. My sister would not agree to erect a tombstone, because it would be too heavy for Mother. The wooden cross is worm-eaten, but there is a plaque and my sister takes care of this common grave for Mother and Grandmother.

My father does not have a grave. Neither does Uncle Lutek. But Aunt Maryla, my mother's younger sister, has one. She was known in the family as Marychna; as a child I called her Maja. She took care of me when my parents moved, and she taught me to draw and to paint, even on porcelain. Marychna herself was a very talented painter; the fragility and ornamentation of her line at first resembled art nouveau and then, later on, a stylization of the folk tradition not unlike that of the more famous Zofia Stryjeńska. I don't think she was in Warsaw at the time of my trip to Paris, as I don't remember saying good-bye to her, and she certainly was not in Warsaw when I came back from the war. By that time she was back in the United States (she had been there many times), where she taught painting and lectured on Polish folk art.

I don't remember whether any of her letters reached us in Lvov; we did get some letters from America, and she certainly wrote to me repeatedly after the war. Her letters were sad and then very bitter. I was her adopted and beloved son and she could not understand or forget that I had joined the party. And that was the period of my most rabid Communist activity. She wanted me to come to America. I turned a deaf ear and expressed my disappointment with her and, even more, with her enticements. She led a very hard life, often existing at the edge of poverty. Yet when our daughter, Teresa, was born, she sent a small gift, and in her will she left all her savings, one or two hundred dollars, to my children and to Uncle Lutek's children.

For long years I forgot Marychna, the same Marychna who had been like a mother to me. It was an atrophy of memory and of feeling on my part, as if all memories connected with my childhood spent with Marychna, had slowly evaporated, along with the memory of my sister and even of my parents. There must have been some deeply hidden causes that even now I am at loss to understand or explain. Perhaps there was some kernel of a feeling of guilt that has remained with me to this very day.

The memory of my Aunt Marychna returned to me only four years ago. I was in Los Angeles visiting Leonidas Ossetyński, whom I had been to see three or four times. He was exactly my age, but with his long, flowing beard he seemed a whole generation older, someone straight out of the turn of the century and the Young Poland movement. Moreover, he retained the distinctive accent of Vilno, his birthplace. Ossetyński had a house on a knoll just outside Hollywood, where he maintained a private theatrical studio mainly for very young girls. In Hollywood everybody wants to be in the theater and is ready to appear even for one spectator, even in a cheaply rented space at the back of some coffee shop. One entered Ossetyński's house by negotiating steep and winding stairs. I always gasped for breath, and I always got lost in that house of many additions, secret rooms, attics, corridors, and galleries that offered an unparelled view of the city below and Hollywood above. The house was overflowing with books and piles of newspapers and magazines; dresses, tights, and stockings lay strewn about everywhere. And many mirrors, often chipped and always smeared with lipstick. And above all a great many paintings. The house was full of them. On the walls, piled on the floors, in every corner, framed and unframed. Ossetyński was, in addition to everything else, an art dealer, and it was rumored that he took in paintings for "conservation" and rarely returned them to their rightful owners.

It was Ossetyński who told me all about the life of my aunt Maria Werten. That is how she was known in America, and that is how she always signed her paintings. She spent the last years of her life in Los Angeles. She was very sickly by then. In my family tuberculosis has been a hereditary disease on the maternal side. "Maria Werten," Ossetyński told me, "was an extraordinary person, admired by all. Especially by children, whom she taught drawing, of course for free. And their mothers too. She wanted to help and take care of everyone who needed help." Ossetyński had some paintings by her and a wall panel she did for a Polish restaurant that had burned down. He was going to dig them out and show them to me the next time, but when I saw him then he was already very sick and could not get out of bed. He told me where Aunt Marychna's grave was located—in Holy Cross cemetery, next to the Polish Church of Culver City, Los Angeles. There is a tombstone on the grave with a simple inscription: "Maria Werten. Poland 1888–Los Angeles 1949. Polish Folk Art Painter." The funeral took place on 9 December. Her friends must have raised the money for the tombstone.

The only painting of Marychna's that is left is a portrait of my sister Aniela when she was about eight. It hangs in her apartment in Cracow. It is singed in one corner; it must have been damaged during the bombing. One day Ossetyński's daughter brought me the panel done for the Polish restaurant in Los Angeles that burned down so that I could take a look at it. A couple of wooden planks depicting a series of Polish folk dances. In very vivid, beautiful colors. But the planks were too large to fit in my small apartment. I took photographs of them. She also gave me two Christmas cards painted by Marychna. Traces of a lost memory.

I do not remember either whether my sister was at Turczynek then. She attended the courses at Stawisko. But that must have been after my departure. Jarosław Iwaszkiewicz had organized a class for the three girls: his daughter Marysia; Basia Meysztowicz, who was the much younger sister of Ksawery Pruszyński's wife; and my sister. He taught them Polish, history, and Latin; and Lutek, mathematics and physics. But that lasted only two years, until the Germans, requisitioning Turczynek on the ground that its owners were Jews, threw the Meyers out and turned their house into a retreat for German officers. I only learned all of this a short time ago from my sister. For many years I was deaf to the history of my family.

I must have spent about three weeks at Turczynek then. I was still very weak, but I wanted at all cost to leave for Lvov. Besides, I wasn't held back in any way; and perhaps in fact they wanted to get rid of me as soon as possible. I learned that one could most easily cross to the other side near Małkinia and from there go directly to Białystok and Lvov. For the trip I was given a coat that came down to my knees. I still had my own pants and shoes from the army. They stuffed my knapsack with a loaf of bread, a piece of bacon, a jar of preserves, several lumps of sugar, a heavy sweater, a change of warm underwear, and long stockings that came up to the knees, which were worn before the war. That knapsack was very heavy.

I took a packed train from the Eastern Station in Warsaw and made the trip to Małkinia standing in the corridor. At the platform exit there was a German control point. I knew in advance that the Soviets didn't let anyone go in either direction. The Germans let everyone go through, but they beat Jews and took whatever they could from them. *"Jude!"* said a fat German pointing at me. I tried to explain something. *"Nicht,"* said a Pole in civilian dress, who served the German as a racial expert. "He speaks perfect Polish." Beyond the platform, one followed the highway and then a road through the mud in the direction of the forest. The Soviets were supposed to be past the forest.

What was there was a marshy clearing that until recently had undoubtedly been a tree nursery, but all the little trees had been pulled up along with their roots, leaving behind only deep holes. On this strip of land about five hundred meters in length, there were camped perhaps a thousand men and women. Many of the women had small children with them. I spent two days and nights there. I was warned not to try to cross over at night, because that was when both sides didn't hesitate to shoot. The first day I did not succeed in two attempts to get across.

At night little fires made from the remnants of roots and brush were lighted. In the morning, in a hut made of boards and pieces of tar paper, hot soup and pierogi with kasha were sold. For dollars or gold. In the evening, in another hut, on the edge of the stubble field, two women sold themselves. For a wedding ring or a pound of meat. They did it standing up because snow had fallen and the ground was wet. Sex was cheaper than bread. The second day, for a loaf of bread one had to give two wedding rings. The third day, before dawn, a dense crowd assembled and moved toward the Soviet side. Thirty, perhaps forty soldiers barred our way. They didn't shoot. They shouted: *"Davai nazad!"*—Get back. They pushed us back, but not with blows from their rifle butts, only with their guns held out flat in front of them. A woman in the crowd began to scream hysterically in Ukrainian, *"Khai zyvie Stalin!"*—Long live Stalin. Then everyone started to scream. The soldiers pushed harder and harder, but they still didn't strike anyone with the rifle butts. Someone began to sing the *Internationale* completely off-key. In total discord everyone pitched in. This time it was the crowd that pushed harder and harder against that handful of stupefied Soviet recruits. They were helpless. They had not been instructed to shoot. And at a certain moment the crowd, and I was swept up in it, seemed to engulf the soldiers and flow over them. I began to.run straight ahead of me. I was already on the other side. Then suddenly someone called out my name: "Janek!"

I had seen Wanda M. not more than two or three times before my departure for Paris. We liked each other a lot. And perhaps even more than that. There was a kind of tenderness between us. Wanda was one of the oldest girls among us, probably Włodek Pietrzak's age, eight years older than I was. She was, I think, the only one of our classmates in the Circle of Polonists who came from a working-class family. Short, pale, her hair combed smooth, never imposing on anyone, and always somehow a little unsure of herself, she was inflexible only when someone pestered her or something prompted her undisguised hatred and scorn for Fascists and anti-Semites. Slight and frail, she battled them during their "Days without a Jew." I knew that she belonged to the Communist Life, but I found out only after the war that she had been in the party for years and was very highly placed. And I found that out only by chance, since she never spoke about it.

I was walking with increasing difficulty and I fell twice. Wanda had a small knapsack. "Let's exchange," she said. "I'll carry yours for a while." We exchanged knapsacks. We had gone through the field a few hundred feet when suddenly a whole squadron of cavalry sprang out from behind the edge of the forest. Our column had long since broken up into smaller groups of people; the Cossacks on their Tartar horses also split into smaller units and started to chase us across the fields and to drive us, as though dogs rounding up hares, toward that no-man's-land again. I must have been hit by a rider or a horse because I was knocked down and remained dazed for quite a while.

When I came to, there was no one at all on the open field, right up to the forest. The cavalry had long since vanished, having driven back the refugees. I looked for Wanda, but she was nowhere. I was all by myself, but on the other, Soviet side. I dragged myself to the forest, then took the first road to the nearest village. I was chilled through and famished. The peasant I found in his hut didn't even have any milk. "They ate and drank everything. I don't even have anything to give the pig." He only gave me water to drink. I opened Wanda's knapsack. In mine I still had the leftover bread and bacon and the untouched lumps of sugar. In the knapsack belonging to party-member Wanda I found a skirt, a nightshirt, underpants, a lot of cotton, and three sanitary napkins.

Wanda showed up again in Lvov. She was paler than usual and seemed emaciated. She came to get her knapsack back. It contained only the sanitary napkins, nothing more. She tried to justify the deportations. She told me that they were tragic but necessary. That was all, and we parted. The last time I saw Wanda was a year before our departure for the States. It seemed then that Moczar was going to get all the power. The outbreak of the anti-Semitic campaign was imminent. Wanda looked still paler, if that was possible. She was wasting away, doing some insignificant job and trying to justify it all. And, I think, she was still in the party. Wishing me good-bye, she remarked, "I wasted my life, Janek."

I no longer remember how I got to Białystok. A peasant must have taken me to the town in his wagon, out of the goodness of his heart, because all I had to offer in exchange was Wanda's nightshirt. All of Białystok—the walls, the stores, many still nailed shut with boards, and even the fences—was pasted over with slogans in three languages—Polish, Yiddish, and Russian—in honor of the Red Army and of the liberation of Western Byelorussia. Even the rare window displays and all the store signs were drowning in red crepe paper. As if it had covered Białystok.

The streets were swarming. Like ants when the anthill is dug up people went bumping into one another, and like the blind they milled around in all directions. Many men were still in their military coats without insignia and often without the buttons with eagles. The women carried or dragged after them large bundles; others pulled children's prams loaded to overflowing with household goods. The Poles and—still, in that first November of the war—the Jews went from one Occupation zone to another, from the Soviet to the German and from the German to the Soviet, in search of their families and friends or simply in the hope of surviving. Białystok was one of the principal stopping points in this odyssey of refugees.

A great number of people were heading for the station. Hundreds, perhaps even thousands were camping out there. All the benches were taken; people were even sleeping on the platforms. The trains were supposed to be going to Vilno and Lvov. But one couldn't find out anything. From anyone. Three or four young women with small, slanted eyes and high cheekbones and wearing short padded cotton jackets with red arm bands—women probably sent from the depths of Russia—tried to alleviate this human misery. They took squalling babies in their arms and gave out hot tea. But they were helpless and didn't know anything either.

Repeatedly in the course of those hours I spent on the platform, trains arrived. The cars were empty. People flung themselves forward. But on the steps of each car there were NKVD soldiers with caps trimmed in fur and overcoats with blue rectangles. They didn't let anyone on board. *"Nyelzya,"* they yelled—not allowed. The trains left empty.

Toward evening I dragged myself back to the town. I didn't have any money, and I didn't have anything to eat or any place to sleep. My fever came back again. I sat down at the foot of a fence. It seemed to me that I would die soon. But when I opened my eyes for an instant, I saw on the fence a handwritten notice in big letters. "Władysław Broniewski, poet of the revolution, will read his poems at the Tailors' Union." I looked at the date, I counted the days, I miscalculated twice, but it was actually that very evening. I somehow discovered the way and dragged myself to the address in time. Władek was already there. He took me in his arms, and after that I don't remember much of anything. He led me to a room behind the auditorium, covered me with a pile of blankets, and gave me plenty of vodka.

I woke up only the next day, in a room black with smoke. "In three hours we're going to Lvov," Władek said. At the station we were taken into a waiting room where the seats of the chairs had been torn out. Snacks and vodka had already been set out on a table adorned with red crepe paper. Some kind of Soviet general was waiting for us; he had medals all over his chest. The train was totally empty and, as before, there were NKVD soldiers on the steps of the cars.

Besides Broniewski and me, there were a few other passengers in the sole occupied car on the train: Jerzy Kreczmar, whom I had known at the university, where he taught logic during my student days, and two middle-aged men and a woman whom I did not know. She was Lena Nizenstein, who had got out of prison in Brześć in September 1939. She had been sentenced to a long term and was still pale. The others were comrades from the central technical cell. They too must have spent many years in various prisons, because they kept talking about the experience during the long hours of the trip. Broniewski recited his poems, both old and new: "Head down, steps slow, / Out of German bondage goes the soldier."

We said good-bye at the station. I had only once before been to Lidia's parents' house in Lvov, but I remembered the address. Kadecka Street began at the corner of Pełczyńska Street, where the streetcar depot had earlier been. But by then it was the NKVD headquarters. Kadecka Street went up very steeply. It was evening and the snow had frozen. I still had Wanda's knapsack and even though it was empty I had great difficulty climbing up the street and kept slipping on the snow. Lidia's parents lived on the third floor. Lidia opened the door. She didn't recognize me. My hair had not yet grown back after the hospital and I weighed eighty-four pounds.

Two months later, of the occupants in that compartment of the empty train going from Białystok to Lvov, only Kreczmar and I were still at liberty. Broniewski, Lena Nizenstein, and the two men, who were in the party until its dissolution, were arrested in January. They were first jailed in Zamarstynów prison and then transferred to Lubyanka in Moscow, and when the Germans attacked Russia they were sent either to Siberia or beyond the Arctic Circle.

5.

On 16 January 1945, on that steep path in the vicinity of Czorsztyn, I also slipped on the frozen snow. When I finally saw the light of the camp fires, I ran as fast as I could. But I hadn't even had time to come out into the clearing when I received two sharp blows to the head and collapsed in the snow. Before I came to, someone picked me up and ripped the swastika off my coat. It hadn't occurred to me that before leaving for the woods in search of the partisans I should have taken it off my railway man's coat. I heard someone shout in Russian, "A German spy." I was punched in the face again and thrown in the snow like a sack. "Hand him over," someone yelled. "We'll hang the rascal." Scarcely a moment had passed before a noose made of thick rope was thrown over my neck and the other end was tossed over a branch above my head. They had already begun to pull it when the commandant, who must have been their superior in rank, because he was the only one with stripes on his coat, screamed: "A son of a bitch, but a man all the same! Give him a drink for the road." They passed me a flask, three-quarters full. I was suffocating, my eyes were popping out of my head, and it must have been pure alcohol half mixed with water. I took a big gulp, but it wasn't easy for me: I was standing on the tips of my toes so the noose wouldn't tighten around my neck. "Give him another snort," said the one with the stripes. "We'll hang the spy tomorrow." They loosened the cord; I didn't have to stand on the tips of my toes any longer. Then they even let me sit down. Now we all began drinking, passing the bottle around the campfire. I must have been quite far gone, but they were all drunk too when, half in broken Russian, half in Polish, I began to explain to them that I had a *putyovka,* a military travel pass, from Zielony to Sącz and that I had been in the party since 1942. "But where is your card?" They didn't even wait for my response. We began to kiss one another on both cheeks and drank another round *za pobyedu—* to victory.

When I sobered up in the morning, it was frightfully cold, although I had slept cuddled up between two big, strapping fellows. I finally woke up and only at that point did I realize that, although the rope was lying freely on the ground, I still had the noose around my neck. That morning we drank one last round. They gave me a flask with moonshine and a three-inch-thick slice of bacon for the road.

That day I left for Stróże. At the boardinghouse I had been given a child's sled, which I loaded with my knapsack and a bag into which I stuffed everything I had. It wasn't much, but when I started to pull, I saw that I had prospered, because the sled was frightfully heavy. I went down to Czorsztyn. From there a wagon took me to Sącz. The road was totally clogged. There were trucks with huge trailers and jeeps, one after the other. All the vehicles were heading west. I finally found a truck carrying requisitioned cattle that was going toward Gorlice. On the way the motor broke down, but I still had a little moonshine left in my flask and two lieutenants gave me a ride to Grzybów. From there a peasant took me almost to Berdechów.

The last four or five kilometers I pulled the sled again. Lidia saw me from the window, pulling that sled, in the same rail-way man's coat, although with the insignia ripped off. She was not at all astonished. She was sure that I would appear. After all, the liberation had taken place three days earlier. She had been expecting me since the day before.

The war had ended for us. We had waited for that day for years, but now the liberation seemed to come as a shock. We did not even know where we were going to live. It was less joyous than I had thought. Lidia's parents wanted me to stay at least a few days, but I wanted to find a ride and leave that very evening—to get to Cracow as soon as possible and be ready to start working for the new Poland. Lidia was appalled. There was no way she could come with me. I would return for her once I knew what was what. "Don't be in a hurry," she said. Our farewell was quite bitter; we did not know, she and I, that when I would come to get her it would be on the eve of our separation.

In Cracow I was immediately sent to the Hotel Francuski. That was where all the new authorities were located, as well as those from Lublin. I got my party card. "Look after it like the apple of your eye," said a young man in uniform, as he filled the card out slowly and with obvious difficulty. "The enemy is lying in wait." I remembered how I had taken the oath of loyalty to the People's Army.

I was allotted a room at the Hotel Francuski. Of those three or four days in Cracow right after the liberation, what I remember best is that hotel room. I never enjoyed taking a bath, but I still remember that first bath in a real bathtub full of hot water. Kamilla Olsienkiewicz came to my room to take a bath too. I don't know how she found me at the Hotel Francuski. She was going to Śląsk (Silesia) to organize libraries. She looked at me and started to take her stockings off. When we had lived with her during the second year of our stay in Warsaw, she had spent days on end in bed. There never was anything between us and nothing happened that day either. But I remember her bare legs like a frame from a film. Perhaps because they were the first bare legs of a young woman not my wife that I saw after the war.

I didn't stay a full three days in Cracow. But I still remember that the walls were covered with proclamations in honor of the Red Army and the liberation. "Fellow countrymen! Democratic teachers. And socialists. And even patriotic Catholics." Those were almost the same appeals I had written with Bieńkowski and Żółkiewski in my apartment on Słupecka Street on the day the uprising had broken out.

At noon on the third day I was taken to the military airfield. I had to fly to Łódź. Łódź and Warsaw had been liberated the same day as Cracow, precisely a week before. But the week seemed as packed with events as a year. The literary periodical *Rebirth* from Lublin had already been transferred to Cracow. The task of *Rebirth* was to win over to our side everyone who was not against us. It was to open its columns wide to writers, artists, and scholars. But our literary journal would be founded in the workers' city of Łódź. It would be militant. And a voice of the party. *Rebirth* could draw its strength from the past; our journal would forge the future.

I don't recall if the title the *Forge* was chosen in Lublin or only later in Łódź. If it was in Lublin, it was Władysław Bieńkowski who suggested it. He had styled himself a Jacobin of the Hugo Kołłątaj mold back in the distant days of the Warsaw Circle of Polonists. Żółkiewski was to be editor in chief of the *Forge*. I was to be his assistant editor.

At that point, on the plane to Łódź, it seemed to me that everything was still ahead of us. The plane was one of those little two-seaters colloquially known as "ears of corn" or, because of their terrible noisiness, "sewing machines." They could be heard miles away. They flew low but were quite safe. The pilot, a young man born at the foot of the Urals, had flown the same plane from Tomsk. The pilot's cabin in an "ear of corn" is open. "It'll rip your head off, comrade," he said. "You're a newspaper man. Maybe you'll need this." And he gave me his pilot's cap. It was made of leather, with earflaps, and lined with sheep's wool. It kept me delightfully warm, as in a cocoon. Three days later, I saw that I had lice again. But those were the last lice of the war.

In Łódź, immediately after the liberation, 8 Bandurski Street, a large apartment building at the corner of Piotrowska Street, was requisitioned for writers. The building was quite luxurious, and the top functionaries of the local *Arbeitsamt* must have been given apartments there. It was five-story building facing the street and a courtyard. When I arrived, it was almost empty. The caretaker showed me all the floors so that I could choose any apartment I wanted. I picked a three-room apartment facing the street on the third floor.

The previous tenants must have had to get out in a hurry, because their personal effects, papers, and photographs were scattered about all the rooms. There were dirty dishes in the kitchen sink. I went into the bedroom. Pushed together were two large double beds. With crocheted bed covers and with cushions embroidered with hearts and inscriptions in German. On one of the two night tables to either side of the beds there was a whip with metal balls on the end of the thongs. In the photograph suspended above the beds, a fat man held a young woman in a bridal gown in his arms.

A sudden rage overcame me. Against the Germans. But perhaps still more because I was absolutely alone in that post-

German conjugal bedroom. I opened the windows wide. The bedroom opened on the courtyard. First I threw out one of the night tables. Then I attacked the bed. It was heavy, but I managed. I got the mattress out, then I broke the frame, and without a second thought, I threw it all from the third floor into the courtyard. I threw the pillows and the bed covers and finally the wedding photograph. Night fell. A chill pervaded the room. I closed the window and lay down on the bed that I had kept. I had nothing to cover myself with; I had thrown out the quilts with the bed covers. I took my railway man's coat off the clothes hook.

Chronicle

I.

Less than a week later I returned to Cracow by car, guarded by the militia. The roads were still dangerous, but we reached our destination safely. I met Lidia at the Hotel Francuski, which had already been turned over to the party and the security apparatus. Right away, almost before entering the room or taking off her heavy coat—probably borrowed—Lidia said, "Stalin is a murderer." "Get out," I said, "you're not allowed to say things like that in my presence." Lidia did get out. And she didn't come back until a year or more after that, sometime in the late spring of 1946. Time went very fast then. And Lidia had not changed her opinion. Neither had I. It was impossible not to be swept up in the postwar euphoria and rabid enthusiasm for the party. "THREE TIMES YES!" The Home Army would have to come out of the forests and surrender or be wiped out. But I started to run high fevers. It was my lungs, most likely. Lidia wouldn't alter her views, but she did come back.

I should have known better by then. But what does knowing mean? In any case, you have to want to know. That kind of knowledge, or rather that kind of knowing, is never pure, and at that point it was even less pure than usual, clouded not only by fear but also by passions, amongst which the two most prominent were probably hatred and hope. A hope that had not yet been totally extinguished. Old Communists were coming back from "over there"— the Soviet Union—as were the surviving members of the countless families that had been almost totally wiped out by Stalin. During that first postwar winter I had a brief romance with Lucyna. It actually consisted of only two or three nights spent talking on a sofa with exposed springs in the office of a new publishing house where Lucyna worked at the time and was allowed to sleep. Having served two sentences in Polish jails, Lucyna's father had managed to escape to Russia via Germany, only to be imprisoned in Lubyanka during the first purge that followed the dissolution of the Polish Communist party in 1938. Her mother was sent to a camp in 1938. Her brother was sentenced too. Lucyna still hoped that he would come back. She spoke Polish with a heavy Russian accent. She did not stay long in the publishing house. She quickly rose in the party machinery and later may even have gone into the security apparatus. She had no doubts whatsoever. On that sofa with the exposed springs in a room dimly lighted by a single electric bulb, she would stubbornly repeat in her Russian-accented Polish that it couldn't be any other way.

At the same party publishing house I became friends with Kraus. He visited us several times in Łódź after Lidia came back. Lidia was fond of him. Kraus must already have been well past fifty; at least to us, he seemed to be a man getting on in years. While in Moscow, he had worked at the Marx-Engels Institute, or whatever it was called then. He knew the Communist "scriptures" by heart. He could cite chapter and verse, giving the exact page and date of the edition. He had been either sentenced to a short term in jail or exiled from Moscow. Kraus was a truly good and gentle man, devoid of anger despite stomach ulcers that gave him great pain. When I asked him whether Polish communism would be different, he merely gave a smile. It was a bitter smile, but only Lidia realized just how bitter. Kraus was soon moved from the publishing house to the Central Committee's Institute of Party History. By then he was in fact a sick old man and had little choice in the matter. And what else could he do except check Marxist citations? He died soon afterward.

I did not yet know Staszewski. Or perhaps we had met in passing at some theater opening night, because even then Stefan was drawn to writers and artists from a genuine need, and not only out of cultural snobbery. For a party activist and one at the top of the ladder (as the saying went then), Stefan had an astonishing interest in theater, or else it was part of his own calling as a politician. At the time he was deputy minister of agriculture in charge of the cultivation of potatoes. When we met, he had just returned from the district of Łowicz, where he was teaching the peasants new methods of potato growing. If they stubbornly stuck to the old ways of cultivation, he had them arrested en masse and beaten in jail for their own good. He was nicknamed "Bloody Stefan," and no potatoes at all came up that spring in the entire district. But the peasants learned their lesson and started to sell wheat to the state voluntarily.

He was infernally strong. He survived eight years in the mines at Kolyma, from which almost no one ever returned alive. I remember his hairy chest and his arms covered with red hair. I was both frightened and fascinated by him. He was a political beast—the only one, I think, with whom I ever became acquainted. He knew how to be a charming companion, especially during our evenings in Kazimierz over a bottle of vodka. He would open up on such occasions; he loved to have an audience. I was his audience. And he had stories to tell. Such as the following:

In a railway car carrying prisoners to the far north, on a journey from Moscow to Archangielsk that took an entire month, with all the windows tightly boarded up, every evening after the daily ration of hot water had been distributed, the men would tell their stories, often in the dark so as to save the only candle there was. One story a night, as in Boccaccio's *Decameron*. But these were stories of a different sort. One night it was the turn of the former head of the NKVD for a Ukrainian oblast. "One morning I went into my office as usual. It was a big room, a beautiful room, entirely wood-paneled. And what do I see? Behind my desk, in my leather armchair, there sits a uniformed fatso, a cap on his head. 'What are you doing there, you son of a bitch, you mother . . .' Without a word, he slowly raised himself up in my armchair and hurled the heavy bust of Lenin on my desk directly at my head. He hit me all right, because I came to all bandaged up on a cot in solitary confinement. In a prison that had been under my supervision . . ." At that point a voice came out of the darkness in the corner at the other end of the wagon. "Listen, comrade, I was the one who threw that bust of Lenin at you. That son of a bitch of a Lenin stood on the desk, on *my* desk, and nothing happened except it got slightly chipped. Then one day, I don't remember exactly when—I've lost all sense of time in prison—but it must have been at least three months ago, I walk through the door of my office, the office I liked so much, where a person could dream in peace about taking a little trip to the Crimea in the near future, and what do I see sitting in the armchair, in *my* armchair, but a huge hulk of a man, in a uniform, with a cap on his head. He stood up—he must have been seven feet tall— and didn't say a word but he really let me have it with that bust of Lenin. I still have the scar to prove it . . ." He must have displayed the scar, but nothing could be seen by the light of a flickering candle stump in the darkness thick with the smoke of cigarettes rolled in strips of old newspaper. "What would be the point of looking, anyhow," he ended his story. "Each and everyone of us has his own scar." And Stefan looked at me penetratingly with his bulging pale blue eyes that were almost glassy.

Once again my unreliable and overcharged memory plays tricks on me, mixing up different years, which then stick to one another like flies on flypaper. I must have heard that story out of a Soviet *Decameron* from Stefan during the "Polish October" of 1956, when, as first secretary of the Warsaw Committee, he was organizing the "defense" of Warsaw along with Gen. Wacław Komar. Or it might have been earlier, when Staszewski used to invite people over to have a drink with him late at night after the Central Committee's stormy meetings. Or maybe it was the night he let me read a numbered copy of Khruschev's "secret" speech at the Twentieth Congress of the Communist Party of the Soviet Union. Staszewski feared Moczar, but he despised Bierut. He was suspicious of Gomułka and did not want him back in power. He paid a high price for all that. First he was ousted from the Central Committee and then dismissed from all the positions he had ever held. The only thing he got was his retirement pension at a high party rank. Lidia remarked that he looked like a famished tiger in a cage. He lost his retinue: writers and actors less and less frequently accepted his dinner invitations. I, too, began to avoid him. And I did not go to see him on any of the three occasions I went back to Poland after emigrating. I was told that during martial law Staszewski did not miss any of the "national" funerals and regularly attended Sunday mass in the cathedral or at the Church of the Sisters of Visitation—on crutches; he had broken both his legs jumping off a moving train. Always impatient, he could never wait until the train came to a full stop. Staszewski is no longer alive; he died in the fall of 1989.

We acquire knowledge only when our own skin is at risk. The first wave of arrests was still far removed, but the next ones struck closer and closer to home until, after Gomułka's arrest and the arrangements for Spychalski's show trial, I was the only person from my cell in the People's Army during the Occupation left untouched—all the rest had already been taken off one by one. But it was only when the Jewish doctors were accused of trying to poison Stalin that I really began to fear for my own safety. People started talking, at first in whispers and then almost out loud, about the building of concentration camps for Jews near the Soviet border. That was in January 1953. Lidia and I were staying at a writers' retreat in Zakopane. Late in the evenings Władysław Wolski and Celina Bobińska, his wife, used to drop in on us. The room was small but there was no other safe place to go. Lidia would usually be in bed, curled up under the blanket. Wolski would bring his chair up to her bed and talk about the camps and about how the Jews had taken over the Polish party. And about how they all would be . . . It was like the croaking of a raven. We never did know whether Wolski was trying to warn us or to provoke us. In the first years after the war, or it may have been for only a few months, Wolski was the government's deputy in charge of repatriation and then the minister of public administration. He had his own intricate and long-established connections with the Central Committee. He hated Bierut and he loathed Berman. It was said he had been planning their ouster but miscalculated. He was expelled from all his government posts and later worked for years in the municipal library in Cracow. Celina was the daughter of Stanisław Bobiński, a long-time revolutionary activist who died during one of the first purges, and Helena Bobińska, the author of a children's book about Stalin that was printed in an edition of hundreds of thousands. "Whom did Soso [Stalin's nickname] make go boo-hoo?" (said Janusz Minkiewicz, in a witty transposition of its title). Celina, a historian, worked for a time at the Marx-Engels Institute in Moscow. We would run into each other at various conferences; she also worked with me on a new history of the Polish Enlightenment. We liked each other, but I always had some uncertainties about her. She never talked about her childhood or her years in Russia. All of them from the Comintern's "aristocracy"—Staszewski, Wolski, Helena and Celina Bobińska, their spouses, fathers, and brothers, linked for years by family, party, and sexual ties—had so many times gone through all the circles of hell and purgatory that they were no longer able to tell, not even for themselves, where loyalty ends and treason begins. Or, to paraphrase Conrad in the cruelest sense, they lived in times when treason put on the deceptive mask of loyalty.

Wolski had been seriously ill for a number of years; he limped and supported himself with a cane. With her black eyes and long legs, Celina retained her feminine charm and the figure of a young girl. But back then, at the writers' retreat in Zakopane, the short, wizened, already totally bald Wolski and the black-eyed Celina perched beside Lidia's bed reminded me of the dwarf and the witch bending over their prey in Goya's *Caprichos*.

A few years ago a young poet from Poland visited us at Stony Brook. He asked me about my reactions to Stalin's death. What did I think at the time? What did I write? And why? I answered his questions as best as I could. I was frightened when Stalin died. I thought that the whole world had collapsed. I was not the only one to be asked those questions. He told me that everyone, almost everyone, felt menaced, as if the ground had suddenly shifted under their feet. And that goes even for those who considered themselves free of the poison of Stalinism, not only then but before. "As if they had experienced," he quoted their words, "the death of God." With the exception of one Catholic weekly, which soon paid for its independence, the pages of all the Polish dailies, weeklies, and monthlies were filled from top to bottom with eulogies of Stalin written by the country's leading writers, scientists, and artists. There were few who held back; I could count them on the fingers of both hands. I did not belong to this select group, and thanks to Lidia my contribution to the idolatry was modest. The eulogies, both prose and verse, were put on display. The poems, in hitherto unknown meters of what Stempowski would have called the poetics of the funereal alexandrine, flaunted incredibly artful rhymes, as if the poets wished to cover their shame with a peacock's tail. But was it simply shame? I wonder. Certainly there was more to it than self-deception and bootlicking. And surely more than fear. Many of us had previously shown considerable courage during the Occupation and would again soon, quickly recovering our presence of mind and basic decency.

A rhinoceros's trumpeting came drifting through the window from outside. Never before had a rhinoceros's trumpeting been heard in the town. Then a rhinoceros was seen through the window. Rhinoceroses began to appear in the streets. One, two, three, a whole herd of them. A dentist opened the door to his office and started trumpeting like a rhino. The owner of a grocery store grew a horn on his forehead. Girls going to school with small knapsacks on their backs sprouted small horns on theirs. The town's leading newspaper was renamed *Rhinoceros Daily*. On the radio, only the trumpeting of rhinos could be heard.

In *A Short Dictionary of Surrealism,* compiled by Breton and Eluard in 1938, there is the following saying: "Elephants are contagious." It appealed to me. But in all my prewar innocence I could never have suspected that rhinoceroses, too, are contagious. In a brilliant essay published by the *New York Times* on the fiftieth anniversary of the outbreak of World War II and Hitler's attack on Poland, Stanley Hoffmann maintains that

Ionesco's *Rhinoceros* employs the most telling of all metaphors for the totalitarian plague. Not only did Ionesco hear the trumpeting of the rhinos, he also knew that rhinos are contagious. The Czechs must have known it too; on the third day of the huge rallies in Wenceslas Square in Prague in December 1989, they chanted, "Down with the dinosaurs."

A week or so after Stalin's death, I had a conversation with Janusz Minkiewicz. He had just returned from the writers' retreat in Zakopane, where he had been listening night after night to Radio Moscow broadcasts. His comment was: "Never before has Radio Moscow said so little about Stalin." Janusz was the oldest of my school friends and the most inveterately cynical of all. Not for a moment did he believe that he was a rhinoceros himself.

2.

I had been living with M. in Łódź, on Bandurski Street, for almost a year. I had met her in Warsaw a year or two before the uprising at a stupid little talk I gave for a group engaged in sabotage and direct action. Żółkiewski lectured there too, on the philosophical foundations of Marxism. It was all pure madness; those boys and girls, the oldest of whom were barely twenty, did not need lectures on the philosophical foundations of Marxism in order to throw grenades (which often did not go off, since the People's Army was not famous for its technological accomplishments). I don't remember who persuaded me to say something about Marxist aesthetics. Or perhaps it was even about the secular concept of the tragic, as I was writing or wanted to write something on the subject: Malraux versus Conrad. They listened to my lecture in a state of intense excitement and asked many pertinent questions. But my arguments that obedience to the process of history is more important than loyalty did not convince them. They had opted for loyalty and honor and for heroism.

I had two or three more lectures there after that. But M. was absent for the last one. So was her lover. He had been killed in action the week before. M. did not come to any of our meetings afterward. And she wouldn't leave her room. She spent days on end lying in bed. She wrote poetry in bed and slept with any young man who happened to come see her. Only once or twice a month would she take part in nighttime sabotage. It involved planting mines on the train tracks ahead of German military transports. That was her specialty in sabotage. But I learned about all that at a much later point. And also that M. was the first woman the young man—soon to die—had made love to ("And being enamored of your mortal face") and that he was the first man she had made love to. And that they slept together for the first and only time on the night before the fatal attack.

Romeo and Juliet, too, slept together for only one short summer night. Cressida and Troilus slept together for an even shorter, Trojan night. It was the first night of love for both Juliet and Cressida. At daybreak, with the morning fog still enveloping Verona, Romeo was forced to flee. At just such a daybreak, the old procurer Pandarus, who late at night had brought Troilus to Cressida's bed, was in a hurry to send her to the Greek camp as quickly as possible, to be exchanged for a captured Trojan commander. Juliet will stab herself with a dagger; Cressida will be a whore in the Greek camp. "My mind is now turned whore." It is the clown Thersites who puts those words into Cressida's mouth. But she would have not hesitated to speak them herself.

Romeo and Juliet and *Troilus and Cressida* are, after all, the same play. During the Nazi Occupation, years before *Shakespeare, Our Contemporary,* I started to read Shakespeare through the experiences of the war. In times of terror, human dramas—even the most common and universal—somehow become final and are purified of anything accidental. They are sharply defined to a striking degree, and their clarity is sometimes appalling. In a hostile world the lover is taken away after the first night of love. Whoring or suicide are the only choices. There was still a third way out: planting mines on the tracks ahead of military transports. Of all Shakespearean heroines, Cressida was closest to my heart for a long time. Twice I even called M. "Cressida."

It was well after midnight one night during the second or

third week after my return to Łódź that M. appeared at my apartment. She came with Helena, whom I also knew from those "ideological" lectures for our sabotage group in the People's Army. They probably came straight from the forest. Both of them wore black oilcloth coats taken from the Germans and carried *nagans*—Russian revolvers—and automatic guns. They left their pistols on the kitchen table and went to take a bath. It took quite a while. I telephoned Henryk. He had returned to Poland with the First Army and was perhaps already a colonel by then—promotions came fast. He was editing an army paper in Łódź that was then, I think, called *Fighting Poland* (*Polska Zbrojna*) because the names of prewar parties, organizations, and, of course, newspapers had been systematically stolen by the new regime ever since the days of the Lublin government (1944). Henryk brought several bottles of vodka. He put his *nagan* on the table, next to M.'s and Helena's automatic pistols, and we spent the night drinking vodka. In the morning Henryk took Helena to his place and M. stayed with me. Soon afterward Helena became the head of the Union of Fighting Youth (ZWM: Związek Walki Młodych) and a deputy to the Sejm. During the Polish October she made the decision to dissolve the union on her own authority. She was never forgiven for that.

M. and I lived in only one of the three rooms at a time, until it was no longer livable. M. was probably the laziest creature that ever lived. She was even lazy in lovemaking. Entering her was like entering the water, and she would rock gently underneath, like a moored boat. Laziness was a part of her sensual nature. Day after day she stayed in bed until late in the evening, just as she had done in Warsaw during the Occupation. We ate in bed and she wrote her poetry in bed and sometimes did translations for me or for herself. I am a messy person myself, but M. was unparalleled for disorder and domestic anarchy. It never occurred to her to clean the apartment or wash the dirty dishes. She washed and combed her hair only before making love. Each of the three rooms would last us no more than a week. When one room was no longer livable, we would lock it up and move to the next. After a month the entire apartment, including the kitchen, would be in a state of total chaos. Then we would move for a day or two to the guest rooms of the publishing house and send for some German women from the forced-labor camp—I don't know what it was called—to clean the apartment. The women were eager to get the job: it meant some small change, something to eat, and from time to time even the last of an unfinished bottle of vodka.

That first year after the war—when writers, suddenly privileged, were gathered up from all the ruins of the newly liberated country and began to trickle back slowly, drop by drop, from the deportations and camps—now seems to me unreal, despite the instantly restored normalcy. But it was a strange sort of normalcy that included those German women cleaning our three-room apartment littered with dirty dishes. Everything seemed not yet congealed, still in a continual wartime stasis, still in a state of flux and transience like that building on Bandurski Street where young women moved—sometimes even in the middle of night—from apartment to apartment and later were called "mandoliners" by the spiteful and envious wives. The most beautiful of them—and I think the youngest—was one with enormous blue eyes that seemed innocence incarnate when she opened them wide, as if eternally surprised by everything around her. Adolf Rudnicki called her "Sprig." Some dozen years later she stuck her head into a gas stove. Rescued, she lived on quite a while, without memory or feeling but retaining the same innocent smile and fed, as if an eternally young mummy, by a husband who was loyal to the end.

I remember the first summer after the war much better. In August we went to the seashore. Gdańsk was still in ruins. We lived right on the beach in Sopot, near the casino. It was a hot summer, the summer after the war that had not yet ended; the fighting continued unabated in the western provinces and in almost every major forest between the Vistula and Bug rivers. All of us were still unsated. And violent in our appetites. Many young girls came to Sopot. "New pieces," as they started to be called. They would be dragged out of the sand dunes two or three at a time and either thrown into the water or taken into the bushes right away. The girls did not resist. M., too, slept with other men.

The vaivode of the Gdańsk region was the famous Anatol, who was still "reigning" in Sopot. He was a Russified Pole and I do not know whether Anatol was his first or last name. When Adam Ważyk and I went to see him, he was sitting in a magnificent armchair that had probably been "appropriated" from some patrician Gdańsk home. It was entirely gilded, but its upholstery of gold cloth was tattered in many places, and the padding of horsehair was falling onto the floor in big tufts. Two military police officers, or they may have simply been women soldiers, were perched on Anatol's lap. Their unbuttoned tunics disclosed plump white breasts spilling out of black lace bras that, along with their black lace panties, were of the sort sold in the stalls near the casino. But as it turned out, the two Russian girl soldiers in unbuttoned tunics sitting on Anatol's lap did not in the least impair his efficiency in attending to business. Anatol gave Ważyk and me two large sheets with round stamps that entitled us to officers' dinners at the casino, with a quarter bottle of vodka or what was then called in Russian *sto gramov*.

I remember the casino quite well. Handwritten notices posted everywhere announced Tymoteusz Ortym's forthcoming appearance. During the Occupation Ortym had had no scruples about appearing for the *Wehrmacht*. In the packed auditorium Ważyk jumped up on a chair and screamed, "I won't allow it!" and reached for his seven-shooter. He still wore it in the holster that hung from long straps. I remember Ważyk in his captain's uniform chasing Ortym around the entire casino, brandishing his gun and shouting, "Throw the collaborator out." I don't quite know why, but implacable memory, obedient to its own cruel logic, calls up before my eyes at this very moment the picture of my last meeting with Ważyk. It was a Monday in 1981, the second day of martial law. I went to the publishing house on Wiejska Street. Its café was closed, but I thought I might get something to eat or at least meet some friendly face. All I saw was a long line of people waiting in front of a kiosk. Cigarettes—then rationed—were being sold:

eight Sporty or four Klubowe per customer. Ważyk was the last in line. It was cold. He was wearing a coat that was flapping in the wind, and he had a thick scarf wrapped around his neck. He had bags in both hands, or maybe a bag in one hand and a wicker basket in the other. There was an empty milk bottle in the basket. His immense glasses had misted over, and he was trembling from the cold. From the cold or from fear. He looked like an old man. His wife, Marysia—I remember her as the young fledgling actress, joyous and always hurrying somewhere, who married Ważyk in Łódź—had had her leg amputated at the knee years ago and wore an artificial limb. I never saw Ważyk again. He died during martial law in August 1982. A couple of months after his death Marysia found in a drawer a sheet of paper with a poem scribbled on it:

It will be like going from one room to another
like moving to another apartment
like a transfer to a neighboring town
like a journey across the ocean
like a flight to another planet
No, it's not true, there won't be any comparison
I was not given the fate of Odysseus or the fate of another
    great outcast

Probably it was the last poem Adam wrote. The handwriting betrays an uncertain, feeble hand. He did not show it to anyone, even to his wife. And nobody will ever know whom he had in mind when he wrote "the fate of another great outcast."

In the second or third week of that summer in Sopot the vaivode Anatol sent a messenger to me. The messenger turned out to be one of the two Russian "lap" girls, but this time a red slip was sticking out from under her skirt. Anatol was preparing an expedition to Wolin. Wolin was a small island, or rather a peninsula cut off from the shore by some sort of a canal, near Szczecin, right at the newly established border of the Recovered Territories. At the time it was a military port and the Soviets were still occupying it, not allowing Poles to set foot on the island. Anatol, in a sudden surge of patriotism, decided to "recover" Wolin from the Russians. Either he had sent a delegation to Marshal Vasilevsky or word had got to Moscow via Warsaw; in any case, Anatol received assurances that Wolin would be turned over to Poland, and the document was duly stamped with a round seal.

A whole column of "jeeps" set out to reclaim Wolin, headed by the newly appointed *starosta,* or official, in a Russian car bearing two flags: one red, the other white and red. The column was protected by a military guard, the militia, and security units, plus two wagons with the propaganda staff and leaflets and rolls of posters already somewhat out of date— "THREE TIMES YES!"—but taken along God knows why, since only Germans had stayed on there, or rather, as the rumor had it, young German women who were very pleased to have two hundred Soviet *komandirs* around and scared to death at the very mention of the *polnischer Banditen.* Anatol had persuaded me to join the "Wolin expedition" in the capacity of a press correspondent. "You'll describe it beautifully," he said.

Our column was stopped at the foot of a pontoon bridge to Wolin. *"Nyelzya."* We stood waiting there for another two hours until finally we heard: "The lieutenant general invites the Polish delegation to join him at his table." A table of enormous size had been set up in a hangar: besides us there were seated at least forty high-ranking officers so heavily bemedaled that there was no empty spot on their chests. In front of each of us stood a big glass, or rather a beer tankard, filled to the brim with liquid. I thought it was water. One of the generals at the opposite end of the table raised his glass and proposed a toast—"To the health of Comrade Stalin, the world's greatest leader . . ."—and he went on in this vein for quite a long time. Standing at attention we drank the health of Comrade Stalin. Bottoms up! Of course, how else? It was pure alcohol.

That wasn't the first time I had drunk pure alcohol. The first swig takes one's breath away, one's eyes seem to pop out, but a moment later, when that liquid fireball goes down into one's stomach and it is time to take another swig, one instinctively knows how to proceed: one has to keep regaining one's breath at short intervals. But here was a full glass and the toast to Stalin's health had to be drunk in one long swig. I survived the first round.

The orderlies filled the glasses to the brim again, pouring the pure alcohol from a gigantic bottle or watering can; I couldn't tell which, because my head had started to spin. The second toast was "To victory!" and "To the Soviets of the world!" and "To the world revolution!" Again we stood at attention. And again we drank bottoms up. It would be sinful not to drink such toast, but it was sheer torture. The orderlies filled the glasses again. To the brim. The third toast was "Long live everlasting friendship between the great Russian people and the heroic Polish people!" This time I managed to take two swigs. Then I blanked out.

I woke up in a barn, lying on some straw. It was even stuck in my hair. I was fully dressed, but someone had taken my boots off. It must have been around noontime, because the sun kept pouring in through the cracks between the planks. But it was noon the day after. Every member of the Polish delegation sent to recover the last scrap of seashore from the Soviets was lying on the straw in the big barn with his boots pulled off. Down to the last man: the *starosta,* the security agents, the propaganda, the radio, and the press, which I represented. Two guards with fixed bayonets were standing at the barn door. They would not let anyone out, even to go to the toilet. Once again it was *"Nyelzya!"* Finally after much threatening, begging, and entreating on the part of our chief of security, one of the guards went to the *nachalstvo.* He came back an hour later. "The *komandir* said that he won't talk with dumb pricks who don't even know how to drink. Get the hell out of here—in an hour's time there better not be any trace of you!" We got out of there in no time. But on the way back we kept both the red flag and the white and red flag tightly furled.

They say that as a consequence of this shameful failure the inestimable Anatol conducted a seminar on pure alcohol drinking for enterprising drunks. It must have been successful since the next Polish delegation actually did recover Wolin for the Polish People's Republic. But this time the expedition took place without my participation.

I did not know him before the war, nor did I meet him even in Lvov. I only knew that he was called *unus defensor Mariae* because he had prevented the new Communist authorities from removing a small altar with a statuette of the Virgin Mary that stood in front of the Ossolineum Foundation in Lvov. If I am not mistaken, he was in charge of it at the time. And he was on the editorial board of *New Horizons,* second in command after Wanda Wasilewska. So even then he must have had some support in Moscow. But I really heard about him for the first time only in Cracow, after the defeat of the Warsaw uprising, when Lidia and I arrived safely thanks to my German railway uniform. They said that he was looking for writers in the villages and country estates where refugees from Warsaw had fled and that he set them up in Lublin and took care of their needs. This was Maj. Jerzy Borejsza. And then he was simply known as the Boss, a name that stayed with him until his premature death. He was the head of the publishing cooperative Czytelnik (The Reader).

From the perspective of Cracow, which was still under German Occupation, the new Poland of the Lublin government was Czytelnik. Czytelnik was a state within a state or, more precisely, within a state of statelessness. Especially for writers. Of all the postwar hungers, the most acute for writers was the longing to see one's work in print. And rather than the "Hegelian sting" of history, it is this poisoning by despair that explains the writers' universal and irresistible fascination with the new faith.

Borejsza always wore a trench coat. Half-military, half-civilian, and always unbuttoned. From underneath, a shirt protruded, often unbuttoned as well, revealing his hairy chest. And always there was a cigarette stuck between his lips. I must have seen him often in Łódź, but I remember him best from a visit Lidia and I paid to his office in Warsaw. I think it was in the early spring of 1947, at the height of Borejsza's career, some three years before his downfall. It was literally a downfall: Borejsza had a stroke following a car accident when he was being driven from Jabłonna to Warsaw, and the accident was almost symbolically ominous since it happened at the point when his power started to wane. His decline was slow at first, and then faster and faster, as it would be in a Balzac novel—unfortunately never written—about the rise and fall of Major Borejsza.

During that visit to his offices Borejsza showed us, spread out on tables that had been extended to maximum size, the architectural plans and models for the future House of the Polish Word (Dom Słowa Polskiego). Borejsza took us to the construction site. All around there were still burned-out ruins. He walked about the excavations, taking broad strides, his wide trousers tucked into high boots. I doubt they had ever been polished—they were always caked with mud. He was showing us his site. As though he were a landowner or at least a landowner's overseer. Beaming with pride. He pointed out to us where the printing presses would be. "For months," Borejsza told us, "my men have been scouring the whole region from Szczecin to Zielona Góra and they use my trucks to bring back linotypes, whenever they can find them, and bales of paper and even lead for the type. The Patron congratulated me." In the party's upper echelons, Bierut was referred to only as the Patron.

At times it seemed to me that a child's soul was housed in that giant body of Borejsza's. He was childishly delighted if he could impress people, even Lidia and me, with the fact that number one telephoned him. Or that at any time he could reach for a special phone standing on his enormous desk and talk with Jakub Berman, number two in the party. But none of us ever had any way of knowing whether Berman or Bierut was actually at the other end of the special telephone line. Those phone conversations were probably a show. But they might have been real. No one knows.

Then there was Borkowski, a former count, who couldn't get a passport to go to Italy to attend to some family matters there. Borejsza arranged it all for him but first made him give a nobleman's word of honor that he would come back. Evidently there were unsatisfied yearnings within Borejsza, drawing him to the nobility. Even his assumed name—his real name was Goldberg—made it sound as though he were a nobleman from the former eastern provinces. Or else it could have been the name of some Lithuanian or Byelorussian demons. There were many demons lurking in Borejsza. The foremost was the demon of pride. In that new post-Yalta Congress Kingdom of Poland, Borejsza became the self-appointed prince of Czytelnik. And his realm stretched from Szczecin to Zielona Góra. When Tito, on his first postwar visit to Poland, presented Borejsza with a Yugoslav medal of some sort, Borejsza reciprocated the next day by sending several of his "adjutants" to Tito with Czytelnik's Golden Badge of Merit. Borejsza, too, had his distinctions and orders. Even if he didn't think up the idea himself, it was Borejsza who organized the Congress of Intellectuals for Peace in Wrocław in 1948. It was his greatest triumph. Over one hundred leading scientists and artists from all over the world came to Wrocław. Picasso and Jolliot-Curie were among them. Picasso said that the trip was his first by plane and that cubism was a discovery made possible by the airplane; the earth seen from above seems to be divided into squares. During one of the banquets Picasso stripped to the waist; I still remember his dark-brown muscular torso so like that of an Indian. For me it was Picasso as the naked satyr in one of his own drawings.

But during that congress the first signs of the cold war could be discerned. Fadeyev made a ferocious speech in which he called T. S. Eliot an "imperialist firebrand." The same day someone (was it Fadeyev?) gave a speech in which he called Sartre "a hyena with a typewriter." When Borejsza heard that, he turned pale but did not say a word. That evening Julian Huxley packed his suitcase and left the congress.

Nearly all of us were living off Czytelnik at the writers' house on Bandurski Street in Łódź. We would go to Czytelnik's warehouse to pick up pots and pans, sheets, and blankets. Teakettles and probably even chamber pots. It had been the warehouse for Siemens' department store and was filled with household goods. We took our meals at the Czytelnik cafeteria and had afternoon coffee in the corridors. Sometimes it was even real coffee. On the ground floor of the writers' house on

Bandurski Street there was a café. I don't remember whether the Pickwick restaurant also belonged to Czytelnik. That was where we spent many an evening, often late into the night, drinking vodka and eating pierogi, sometimes even a schnitzel. The *Forge* belonged to Czytelnik, of course; so did *Rebirth,* the second literary weekly, which was soon transferred from Lublin to Cracow.

I think it was Jerzy Borejsza's idea that from the very start there were to be two literary weeklies: the one "hard," almost party line, and militant; the other "soft," almost nonparty, and what was then called "broadly based." This kind of dance step with two types of literary periodicals lasted until martial law, undergoing successive waves of liquidation and apparent "revivals" under changed titles, new editors, and purged staff. Borejsza even organized his "own" bus line between Łódź and Warsaw. Had he lived in America, he would have become a second Hearst. Ksawery Pruszyński's book about Margrave Wielopolski was published at the height of Borejsza's activities. But in the recently constituted Polish People's Republic there was no place for a new Wielopolski, or a new Prince Konstanty for that matter. Soon there was no place for Borejsza either.

At that peace congress back in Wrocław someone called my attention to a slightly hunched-over man in a trench coat who sat in the rear of the auditorium and kept an eye on the members of the presidium on the platform. It was Jacek Różański. I was not aware that Różański had been nicknamed "Pony," because of his habit of creeping up behind prisoners under interrogation at the Rakowiecka prison and giving them a savage kick in the ankles. Nor had I any idea then or for a long time thereafter that Borejsza and Różański were brothers. In the smoothly operating system that was still working then, the former was in charge of culture, the latter of the state security apparatus. This osmotic and reciprocal infiltration of culture and security on all levels, starting with the district committees and going up to the Central Committee and the Politburo, was one of the most diabolical tricks devised by Stalinism, of which even Orwell had only vague forebodings, failing to grasp the full implications.

By the time Różański was removed from the directorate of state security because of Światło's disclosures and made the head of the Państwowy Instytut Wydawniczy, Borejsza had already died. But a year or two before his death the opening of the House of the Polish Word had been celebrated with much pomp, and the ceremony had been attended by the assorted government and party dignitaries and some writers especially invited for the occasion. Only Major Borejsza, who a few months earlier had been dismissed as the head of Czytelnik, was not among the invited. The official explanation was that the fragile state of his health following his stroke made his attendance impossible. Yet whenever I think about Borejsza, I can't help recalling Lukács's brilliant and irresistible theory of character types in Balzac's novels, where nothing is left to chance. In that as yet unwritten Balzac novel, Borejsza's car accident was something more than a matter of chance.

When Mikołajczyk fled Poland after the fraudulent elections and the dissolution of the Polish Peasant party (Polskie Stronnictwo Ludowe), Borejsza published his then notorious pamphlet "The Diva for One Season." And as for Borejsza, how many seasons did he manage to be the reigning diva? Four? Five? Six? Some forty years have passed, and I still think about Borejsza with undiminished admiration. And even a certain tenderness. He was a true visionary, one suited to those first years after the war, when our hopes, all our different hopes, had not yet been lost. In his principality of Czytelnik there was room for Ważyk and for Gałczynski, for Kruczkowski and for Żukrowski. The noose was tightening slowly but implacably, and forty years later it turns out that in the House of Writers there was room only for Żukrowski and Auderska. If it hadn't been for that car accident, Borejsza would probably have succeeded in bringing back to Poland half the emigrés from London, and, who knows, perhaps even the remains of Stanisław August Poniatowski—Poland's last king—would have been placed in the Wawel Castle.

Arnold Szyfman was another casualty of those years. Soon

after the war ended, Szyfman rebuilt the Polski Theater from ruins in record time. In my early childhood, when I was living with my parents on Oboźna Street, I used to watch—from the balcony of our fifth-floor apartment—the droshkies pulling up in the front of the Polski Theater at Plac Karasia. By January 1946, the rebuilding of the theater was completed. In 1948, under Szyfman's patronage (as he was very highly regarded at the time) and with the entire "leadership" present, the triumphal jubilee took place. But Szyfman had already been ousted from the theater's directorship, and his place was taken by his longstanding enemy, Leon Schiller. Szyfman then became the government's plenipotentiary responsible for rebuilding the Warsaw Opera. Although well past seventy, Szyfman was as stubborn and indefatigable as ever. I remember visiting him with Lidia on several occasions. In his sumptuous apartment, drawing boards laden with plans and plaster models of the opera house stood surrounded by stylish furniture beneath huge bronze chandeliers embellished with golden eagles from the time of the duchy of Warsaw. He already saw the Opera restored to its former splendor—one could see it in his dimmed eyes, hidden behind round glasses, which now and then would sparkle from excitement. His wife of two years, Marysia (who pronounced "r" gutturally, as the French do), a beautiful woman with the figure of a young girl, almost half a century younger than her husband, would serve red-beet borscht with pastry tartlets on Meissen porcelain.

And again everything unfolds as in that still unwritten Balzac novel. Marysia's first husband was a prewar officer. She came from a well-to-do family; her mother owned a beautiful villa by the sea. Marysia wanted to pursue her education, but because of either her class background or her husband's past she was not allowed to go to the university. She divorced her husband and married Szyfman. At the time we used to visit them, Marysia was in her second or third year in the English department at Warsaw University. Everyone said she was an exceptionally talented student, especially gifted at deciphering Old English texts.

This truly Balzacian novel has two different endings. Szyfman's very young wife, with whom he was passionately and devotedly in love, went to the United States on a scholarship. She soon got a job at the University of Michigan at Ann Arbor, where she continued to decipher and transcribe microfilms of the most difficult Old English texts. In due time she obtained a divorce from Szyfman (who had come to America to persuade her to stay with him), and then she married a young building contractor who promptly became a millionaire. They visited us not long ago and tried to convince us to buy some property in Florida. We didn't buy it.

The former Mrs. Szyfman and her American husband once invited me to a millionaire's club in New York. It was in the basement of a very elegant hotel. The waiters were in tuxedos but the food wasn't the best. I have never been in such a boring place, either before or after. Marysia was radiant. She was the only person I'd ever met who so frankly and with such naive pleasure enjoyed the first million. It's true that I have known few millionaires. Marysia was even prouder of the success of her entrepreneur than she had been of her old Meissen porcelain and huge bronze chandeliers many years before, in the period of Szyfman's glory.

Szyfman didn't enjoy it for long. He was not invited to the elaborate opening ceremonies for the Warsaw Opera, which were attended by assorted government and party dignitaries, artists, and writers, many of them displaying the Order of the Builder of the Polish People's Republic. Or maybe he was there, but not invited to sit with the presidium. And in the congratulatory speeches his name was not even mentioned. He was allowed to open the theater museum, but when he started to speak, the microphones were turned off. I think I remember seeing him sitting in the back row, holding himself straight as always, but his face behind the familiar round glasses was more drawn than usual. If I really did see him at the ceremony, it was for the last time. He died soon after that festive opening ceremony for the Warsaw Opera that he had built.

"*We've* dismissed *me* from the theater." I must have still been a member of the Advisory Council on Culture and Art when Schiller came in and said that. He was also a member of the council and I remember his apologizing for being late to a meeting that was already in progress. Or perhaps my memory is playing tricks, because that saying of Schiller's had been making the rounds in Warsaw for some time. *"We've* dismissed *me."* That is exactly what had happened. In an old prewar-Warsaw joke, the devils are torturing the damned in all the circles of hell. In the Polish circle, though, devils are not needed. If one sticks one's head out of the boiling tar, one's fellow damned immediately pull one back into the stinking concoction. *"We've* dismissed *me."* In the Polish circle of hell there is self-service.

And yet all we really wanted to do was to help the incomparable Leon Schiller. We had welcomed him with open arms when he returned from the German POW camp at Murnau and had hailed him as the greatest man in the Polish theater. We all kept repeating—and even Bierut and Berman joined the chorus—that only Leon Schiller was capable of creating a theater that would measure up to our times. The only trouble was what precisely should provide the measure. If he wanted to do a monumental staging of Mickiewicz's *Forefathers' Eve,* why, nothing could be better! But were the devils in it going to be allowed? There are devils in Pushkin, so surely it would be permissible for Mickiewicz's devils to torture Senator Novosiltsov. But were the angels going to be allowed? What about putting them in the stained-glass windows as an element of the stage design or making them part of a dream sequence? But what could we do with the scene in the Warsaw salon? "We're a lava field. . . ." It might be better to skip that scene entirely.

We certainly had to help Schiller. After all, we all wanted to see *Forefathers' Eve* staged. Even at the very top, the big Patron himself was in favor of letting the play be done. Włodzimierz Sokorski kept calling meetings and organizing special *Forefathers' Eve* committees. Schiller took part in all of them. His vision of *Forefathers' Eve* kept getting more and more progressive. *"We've* dismissed *me."* Schiller never got to stage *Forefathers' Eve.* Or Słowacki's *Samuel Zborowski* or Zygmunt Krasiński's *Un-Divine Comedy.* In the end what he did stage was Bogusławski's *Cracovians and Mountaineers*—his only major production in the postwar period. We certainly did help the incomparable Leon Schiller. We helped Mickiewicz and Krasiński too. I was especially eager to help. At a meeting of the Institute of Literary Research (part of the Polish Academy of Sciences), when the question came up about the difficulties with the publication of Krasiński's *Un-Divine Comedy,* and especially its ending, I proposed simply putting a question mark after the famous *Galilaee vicisti,* making it *Galilaee vicisti?* After I finished speaking, there was a moment of apprehension, quickly followed by an uncontrollable burst of laughter.

It was only after a number of years that I saw how efficiently and effortlessly that grinding machine had been crushing all opposition—from the very start, during the first five-year plan. Everybody got ground to a pulp: not only those who were turning the handle but also those who merely touched it or happened to get too close. Only one person somehow survived unscathed, and that was Sokorski, always kindly and well-meaning, with that half-idiotic smile permanently glued on his clean-shaven face. Before the war he had written a quasi-revolutionary, quasi-pornographic novel. And to the end he was pleased to cultivate both genres: on paper and in bed. It was said that he had almost become the commander in chief of the First Army, instead of Berling, before it went to the front. He was the permanent minister of culture under Bierut and under the second Gomułka government.

After the Protest of the Thirty-four in the fall of 1964, it was rumored that harsh sanctions would be taken against those recalcitrant authors who did not yield to either sweet words or blackmail and refused to withdraw their signatures from that first collective protest against censorship, which now seems mild and innocent but which then called forth a protest of more than six hundred writers "loyal" to the regime.

At just this point I saw Sokorski in the hall of a theater during intermission at the premiere of a new Polish play. "Those irresponsible idiots," Sokorski said right away, "have drawn up a whole resolution directed against all of you who signed the protest. I've just come back from the Building. (That was the Kafkaesque name used for the new Central Committee headquarters.) Your case has been put on the agenda. These fools have not cooled off yet and are still frothing at the mouth. None of you will be allowed to publish, and forget about trips abroad. But don't get too upset. The most important thing is to keep cool. They'll forget about it all in three months." "But Mr. Minister," asked Lidia, who was standing by my side and who wanted as usual to know everything, "have you read the resolution?" "Of course," replied Sokorski, "I wrote it myself." Then I recalled that Lidia's father had called all such people bandar-logs. After almost a half century, the only one to survive the meat grinder was Włodzio Sokorski. And there is nothing strange about that. Only the eternally smiling clown survives everything. Like the clown Pandarus in Shakespeare's *Troilus and Cressida:*

And Cupid grant all tongue-tied maids here
Bed, chamber, Pandar to provide this gear!

The grinding machine stopped only when it had ground itself up—as Przybos's daughter suggested to me.

4.

"I've been in an insane asylum," Ważyk kept repeating almost obsessionally. That was after his *Poem for Adults* had appeared in 1955.

Some eight years earlier—I'm not sure of the exact date; everything now seems to me to take place at the same time— I was having supper with Turowicz at the Kameralna restaurant in Warsaw. It was sometime after the Congress of Polish Writers. Recently, in the pages of the *Forge,* I had savagely attacked his weekly for the seven cardinal sins of Polish Catholicism's incorrigible obscurantism. But there was a mutual sympathy between Turowicz and me, a deep-seated attachment despite all ideological differences; we simply liked each other. Apparently we even resembled each other, in outer appearance only, of course. Ważyk, who happened also to be having supper at the Kameralna that evening, called Lidia over abruptly: "Tell Janek not to talk to the cardinal's spy."

"I've been in an insane asylum." That diagnosis, which was to become famous later, undoubtedly contains an attempt at self-justification but also a striking element of truth. The difference being that in that insane asylum—either without knowing it or without wanting to know it—we were all alternately or simultaneously patients, doctors, and orderlies. But when did that asylum begin to exist? For us? For me? Had it always been there? Or did it come into being while we were walking down Piotrkowska Street to the Czytelnik offices several blocks past Bandurski Street or while we were headed in the opposite direction, toward a meeting at the party's committee headquarters? Or when suddenly we were summoned to Warsaw and driven to the Building in a black Volga, had we unbeknownst even to ourselves crossed the threshold of the hospital, had the thickly padded doors opened and closed silently behind us? Were we there as the doctors, or as the patients?

I have great difficulty recognizing myself in those first two years after the war. And still more trouble judging myself. "The *Forge* is enchanted with itself!" That was the motto we put—with disarming humor—in the special April Fool's issue of our review. I was enchanted with myself, especially before Lidia joined me, and I remember that enchantment more than our arrogance, more than my own arrogance. It was a time when writing came easy, about anything and everything—first an article for the *Forge,* then a feuilleton for another magazine. Everything went right to the printer; it appeared the next day, at most in two or three days. In those days I could write faster by hand than I now can on an electric typewriter.

We were sure that we would change history by what we wrote. We were sure of history, as though it belonged to us. It was the same old "Hegelian sting," but we did not yet know that term and it was rather we who were biting history than the other way around. We were like mad dogs! Like the demiurges of postwar times. Enough to make one's head spin! It seemed that everything could be shaped at will as though it were clay to be molded. Robert Darnton writes in one of his essays that on the eve of the French Revolution and especially during its first years there was an incredible proliferation of writers and scribblers of every sort. Through the printed word, through each individual page, if not each single letter of the countless brochures and pamphlets, it seemed possible to change the course of history: to kill kings and then either further or destroy the revolution. Cabalists believed that HE whose name could not even be mentioned created the world from two letters of the Hebrew alphabet. Materialists believed in the power of SCRIPT, and with script in black letters on paper they wanted to change time itself: the names of the months, the reckoning of the years, the holidays, and the calendar itself. Even the names given to children. "Reality is slowly being transformed into the ideal." With one stroke of the pen. Not to mention tapping the keys of the typewriter. How could we resist such temptations? For us, Borejsza was the new Mephistopheles. And for a long time we did not know or did not want to know that Borejsza had the support of his half-brother Colonel Różański in the Security Forces. How could we at the *Forge* not suffer from vertigo?

"The First One Hundred Books" was the title of one of the most talked-about articles I wrote for the *Forge*. Those one hundred books were to be the first to appear after the war in Poland's devastated libraries. With what satisfaction I included *The Thousand and One Nights* and *Gulliver's Travels,* the Bible as well as *The Communist Manifesto* and *The Eighteenth Brumaire of Louis Bonaparte. Gulliver's Travels* and *The Eighteenth Brumaire* were and still are among my favorite books. Ważyk liked to say over and over again, "Janek is both good and bad, but the bad fades quickly and the good remains." My literary tastes, in any case, were always better than my political choices. And my style has always been superior to my thinking.

The Jan Kott of those years has not been forgotten. In May 1989, I was taken for a walk along the St.-Martin canal by Danielle Sallenave, a brilliant French novelist and philosopher of the school of Alain—he was one of my favorite authors in that last year in Paris before the war, and on our short honeymoon in Brittany I went to see him one night, after a quarrel with Lidia, walking several hours to the sound of barking dogs. Along the St.-Martin canal there are small stores, repair shops with old signposts, and sluices covered with green moss. It is one of the few remaining bits of nineteenth-century Paris; at every step you come across a picture out of Utrillo. Danielle brought along a young friend of hers who had just come from Poland. She looked me over distrustfully, then suddenly burst out laughing. "You're not so terrible as all that, although my father still remembers you with dread." The young woman's father had taught Polish literature in a provincial gymnasium and apparently used my edition of Bolesław Prus's *The Doll*.

In the second year after the war my two first booklets were "On Social Advances" and "Coal." The latter was the result of a trip to the coal basin organized for a group of party writers by the Department of Propaganda of the Central Committee. In innumerable Houses of Culture lined with portraits of dignitaries, we were treated to vodka and kielbasa by miners in gala uniforms and black kepis adorned with plumes. Once or twice we were taken down into the pits. "So the comrades can see for themselves how our foremen do their jobs." In my brochure there were two quotations—one by Engels, one by Lenin—short biographies of two Stakhanovite coal cutters who had gone from illiterate peasants to foremen, three diagrams showing the soaring curve of coal production, which I had laboriously copied, and a conclusion proving that the miners were turning the theories of Marxism-Leninism into revolutionary practice. The brochure enjoyed enormous success. In the course of a couple of weeks it went through two editions, on paper of very poor quality but in a printing of one hundred thousand copies all told.

For the first time after the war the British Council was getting ready to invite a Polish writer for a short stay in England. I don't know how it happened or through what channels the decision was reached, but in the end the British picked me. They said that it would be their pleasure to entertain, and share experiences with, a Polish expert on coal. On the evening of my arrival in London by plane, I was told to be down for breakfast at six the next morning because the train for Manchester left at seven. And the next day, right after a modest lunch, I was in the mine. I was quickly given a miner's hat and a protective coat and taken by three different elevators three thousand feet down to the gangway. The gangway grew narrower and narrower and I kept hitting my head against the vault. All I remember is the deafening sound of the pneumatic drills. It was late in the evening when I was taken back up to the surface. And the next day the same schedule was repeated in a different gangway. And day after day all over again for eight days. And only on Sunday was I taken to a gigantic exhibit—of mining equipment. My first trip to England I spent entirely underground. The English, with their distinctive but quite cruel sense of humor, obviously must have regarded this invitation to a Polish expert on coal as a practical joke. But it was an example of black humor. As a matter of fact, really black. And until fairly recently, whenever there was a family quarrel my son and daughter would recite in unison portions of my brochure on coal that had been printed in an edition of one hundred thousand.

5.

"We're digging our own graves," said Rudnicki. That must have been in Łódź in the second year of the *Forge;* we had been left alone for a moment after coming out of a meeting on Piotrkowska Street. That remark of Adolf's lay dormant and came back to me only after many years. At first I didn't grasp what he meant. Adolf had a different vision from that of the rest of us and a different conscience, probably because he was still living the destruction of the Jews—his people. At the time I was scarcely even aware that we were digging graves for others, and with ever-growing zeal.

We all had our own special aversions, some old, some new. There was no obstacle now to keep us from stamping out whatever we disliked. The no-hunting season on creatures of every sort had long since expired. And then, too, we had our own passions and old attachments from the prewar years. Some, like illicit affairs, were secret from the start; others were much too obvious to be kept hidden. And there were some that none of us could ever renounce. Jastrun, for example, could easily have renounced Słowacki, but he would never part with Norwid. In any case, Norwid was not on the list of dangerous authors; a "progressive" interpretation of his poetry was allowed, according to which he could be read as the Scriptures are in the cabala, using every other word or working backwards. But the situation was much worse with Rilke, who was Jastrun's great passion. Raising as high as he could his huge head worthy of the Roman emperors—placed, alas, on a body of not such imposing proportions—Jastrun would preach about the moral responsibilities of the poet. Ważyk could never have renounced Apollinaire—he would have preferred to slash his own arteries—but he now spent his time translating Pushkin's *Eugene Onegin,* a splendid accomplishment, incidentally, without a single masculine rhyme, just as he intended. Paweł Hertz would bury his face in his hands and say, "I have nothing to do with it!" He had been deported during the war to some place in Soviet Kazakhstan, and long after his return he kept on wearing his military outfit. He quickly exchanged his aping of Stefan George and his Parnassian veneer for xenophobia and Sarmatian airs. Now, in his opinion, nineteenth-century pastorals and idylls were the ideal models of what national poetry should be.

To a person, we all opted for realism. But what kind of realism? By that time we knew quite well, although we would never admit it to ourselves even in the dead of night, that socialist realism and Zdhanovism meant the death of all creativity. The problem was how to open the way to socialist realism—for after all, that was what we were doing—and yet at the same time somehow get free of it. In other words, how to put one's neck in a noose and convince others to do so— but prevent the noose from tightening. In *The Captive Mind* Miłosz, more effectively than anyone else either before or after, describes the games we played with the demon of double-thinking. It seems to me even now that when I woke up in the morning with Lidia by my side I sometimes had moments of clarity. But they would pass as quickly as a guilt-ridden dream that we forget upon awaking.

Critical realism was a term and a concept invented by Gorky and then continued by Lukács. I started to read Lukács before the war. But it was really only during the last year of the war that I read him seriously. From then on, for more than ten years, I remained under his spell. For better and for worse. Critical realism was for Lukács the highest achievement of bourgeois literature. And according to the "Marxist" theory of literary evolution, it should have been not only the precursor of but also the model for socialist realism. The crossbar was set high: Balzac, Stendhal, and then, perhaps a bit arbitrarily, Tolstoy. In naturalism, starting with Flaubert, before even getting to Zola, the movement of history began to evaporate from the novel, and all that later remained was a detailed examination of the human beast under a magnifying glass. From the mire of bourgeois decadence, Lukács saved only Thomas Mann, the last continuator of the great traditions of humanism. All of that suited me perfectly. I was fascinated by the idea of great turning points in history; during the war they alone offered hope.

But there were other reasons why I found that Lukács mirrored my own literary tastes—and not only my enthusiasms but perhaps even more my aversions. For quite some time Flaubert simply bored me, with the exception of *L'éducation sentimentale,* where the bitterness of unfulfilled love parallels the winds, or rather the stale air, of unfulfilled revolution. My apprenticeship with the surrealists preceded an apprenticeship with Lukács. The surrealists and Lukács had something in common: they both hated naturalistic description. These antitastes of mine were also shared by the Thomists, for whom nature's reflection must be illuminated by truth and grace. So anything but naturalism. And that is why it was Breton, hand in hand with Maritain, who led me to Lukács in a sort of *mariage à trois* not so exceptional, after all, for my generation. *The Eighteenth Brumaire* and *Les liaisons dangereuses* were the "fascinating" books of my youth. It would be difficult to say what Marx and Laclos have in common that could have fascinated me. They both must have seemed to me utterly lucid: sex on the one hand and naked force on the other, totally

stripped of illusions. The stratagems of desire and the stratagems of ideology were exposed as an endgame, but with this
difference: Laclos expressed secret admiration, Marx open contempt. I have always been attracted to mathematical formulas.
And abstraction. Even in the realm of the erotic imagination
and, need I say, above all in politics. Facts have never been my
strong point; in my lectures I would often get the dates mixed
up. Naturalistic novels have always bored me. What could be
more shallow than petty realism!

I considered Lukács's formulas strong medicine. "Typical
characters under typical circumstances" was the magic formula
Lukács discovered in a letter Engels sent in early April 1888
to the British novelist Margaret Harkness. To show how the
new bourgeoisie joined the ranks of the old aristocracy, Lukács
used the example of Lucien de Rubempré, with his seven new
suits and seven new vests, each more costly than the last, in
which he and others like him appeared in the salons of war
profiteers to offer millions for the hands of the daughters of
impoverished marquises and princes. Lukács is dry but makes
history transparent in texts. The drama of the protagonists is
the drama of history—sometimes even the tragedy of history.
That is what I learned from Lukács. I showed the workings
of the Grand Mechanism in Shakespeare's history plays. But
that was ten years later, after Stalin's death. From then on
my theory of the Grand Mechanism was cited for more than
a decade in almost all programs accompanying productions
of Shakespeare's royal tragedies in England and, to an even
greater extent, in Germany. In Peter Hall's famous production
of all six royal tragedies, which lasted one day and part of the
evening or two afternoons and evenings, the scenery remained
unchanged. The Usurper climbed the same stairs, and from
the throne at the top of those stairs the Anointed, wearing
the same crown, were toppled. The Grand Mechanism became
visible on stage.

I started to read Balzac seriously for the first time in Warsaw
during the Occupation and immediately after the war. And
what I liked most of all was the rustling of the duchesse de
Langeais's laces and the smell of decay in the pension run by

the widowed Madame Vauquer, where père Goriot lived and took his meals—I still can bring back that odor even today. I knew Stendhals' *The Red and the Black* and *The Charterhouse of Parma* almost by heart while I was still in Paris. "Typical characters under typical circumstances." The formula fitted Balzac perfectly, but what about Stendhal? For shooting his former mistress, Madame de Renal, Julien Sorel is sent to the guillotine on the eve of the July Revolution, and Mathilde de la Mole takes Julien's severed head and buries it in the family tomb just as her great-great-grandmother had done with the head of her lover, who was beheaded for his part in the wars of the Fronde.

"Typical characters." Lukács was a master not only of interpretation but also of dialectics. Balzac was a critical realist despite his allegiance to the throne and altar. Stendhal was a critical realist in a different way. "Typical characters." Lukács contrasts the boredom and pettiness of the characters and events of the Restoration with the models of greatness and courage that Julien Sorel finds in Napoleon and Mathilde de la Mole, unbridled in her passionate love and in her contempt for mediocrity, finds in Danton, to whom she compares Julien. And that is why Stendhal is a critical realist for Lukács.

The term *great realism* was, I believe, my invention. "Great" as opposed to "petty." And critical realism must be opposed to "uncritical realism." But what was this "uncritical" realism and where was it to be found? I think Lukács knew quite well what he was doing, what he was warning against, and what he desperately wanted to defend as long as he possibly could. I probably knew it, too, in my second system of thinking which Miłosz later called "Ketman"—the art of doublethink as practiced by the Muhammadan heretics in Persia.

As a last-ditch defense against the shallowness and pitiful schematism of socialist realism, Lukács held up Balzac, Stendhal, and Tolstoy as models. In my "great realism" I included Defoe (although for the time being I preferred not to mention his *Journal of the Plague Year*), Swift's *Gulliver's Travels,* and the eighteenth-century *conte philosophique*. In this case I was true both to my own taste and to the ideology. They were models of "the historical construction of destiny" and "historical paradigms." Robinson Crusoe, alone on his desert island, where not long ago cannibals conducted their feasts, keeps ledger books of capitalist economy; Swift mocks the court hierarchy and order that Gulliver witnesses on his journeys to the Lilliputians and Brobdingnagians; Voltaire's good-hearted Candide and pitiable Cunegonde, who is raped time and again, must experience one after the other all the plagues of slavery, feudal wars, and the superstitions of three religions: Christianity, Judaism, and Muhammadanism.

That was my School of Classics, which referred back to literary traditions earlier than Lukács's critical realism but more modern, in my opinion, in craft and techniques of narration. Soon after I added the encyclopedists and Diderot to my School of Classics. I translated Diderot's *Le rêve de d'Alembert* and *Paradoxe sur le comédien* and excerpts from the *Salons*. They were all presented as models of socialist realism. Almost ten years would have to pass before I realized that I was putting a noose around my own neck as well as putting others in a similar position, although I did all I could to keep the noose as loose as possible.

For the School of Classics I received some state award or order. I don't remember if it was the Gold Cross of Merit; the Medal of Labor, Second Class to be exact, I received at some later point, if I'm not mistaken. But neither Lukács's critical realism nor my great realism nor any construction of destiny could stop the arrival of socialist realism. And of the worst, most schematic variety. The first "production" novels started to appear, portraying heroic Stakhanovites surpassing work quotas many times over or young workers exposing class enemies without knowing any temptations of body or soul. It was more than I could stomach.

During the second or third year of the *Forge* I spent my vacation at the seashore once again. It must have been in Sopot as usual. The first evening I went to have a drink with R. He was one of the deputy ministers in charge of coal or raw materials, I don't remember which: there were so many of those deputy ministers. We had become slightly acquainted during the Occupation and then had met several times after that at conferences. He must have been of peasant background since his enthusiasm for the printed word was boundless. "We have a wonderful literature, full of optimism," he said. "It makes me feel good. And finally our life has been depicted as it is." "What are you talking about?" I was so upset I almost spilled my drink. "Those wretched novels make me sick to my stomach. But literature doesn't matter. What's important is that our industry is making great strides and coal production is breaking records." Now it was R.'s turn to almost spill his drink. "You're talking rubbish, man. The mine shafts are caving in one after the other, the machinery is only good for scrap iron . . ." "But our chemical industry," I interrupted. "And Nowa Huta . . ." "Our chemical industry is more dead than alive, and the steelworks at Nowa Huta will devour all our raw materials and pollute the whole district," said R. So we went on convincing each other that everything was fine except in the field in which each of us was, unfortunately, an expert. Deputy Minister R. did not finish his third drink. "I've got some reading to do," he said. He had a large briefcase. He opened it. Inside there was nothing but three new production novels.

I don't remember whether the conference in Nieborów on poetry took place before or after my conversation with R. in Sopot. Nieborów had remained a place beyond time: in the magnificent park not one of its century-old trees had been cut; the floors in the palace were still waxed and shiny as a mirror. Nieborów had belonged to the Radziwiłłs; after the war it was taken over by the Ministry of Culture. There were many Radziwiłłs left, but some of them had also been taken over by the system. One of the Radziwiłłs was the chief of protocol at the Ministry of Foreign Affairs, another worked at Książka i Wiedza, the leading Marxist publishing house in Poland, and another—Pani Izabela, charming, modest, always ready to help, with beautiful slanting dark eyes—was a secretary at the State Publishing House. Nieborów had belonged to her branch of the family and she was known as Balala to her intimate circle of friends. Paweł Hertz told me so, but I never dared call her that.

I was in Nieborów for the last time, also at some sort of

conference, with Zofia Nałkowska. It must have been a year or perhaps only a few months before her death. It was a mild, sunny autumn afternoon, and the leaves on the chestnut trees were already turning russet and yellow. "Never believe," Nałkowska said as I was seeing her off to the palace, "that an old woman doesn't need love."

But back in 1948 I was at Nieborów for the first time. Many young poets had come to the conference on the tasks of poetry. They kept to themselves and sat close together as if a storming platoon. I don't know who first called them the "pimply ones"—probably the indomitable Maryna Zagórska—but the label stuck. Woroszylski was their leader. And he was the one who first attacked Jastrun. He accused him of slighting Mayakovsky and ridiculing his technique of "tiers" as the universal recipe for socialist poetry. Woroszylski was then writing poetry in "tiers." There were accusations of petty bourgeois tastes and even suggestions of counterrevolution. Jastrun first turned pale, then grew red. When he was interrupted as he tried to explain something, he lost his temper and shouted, "Quiet down, you puppies!"

Jastrun returned to Łódź completely crushed. At that point we did not realize how fast the guard was being changed in the relay race to Zhdanovism and how fast the new team was taking up the baton, or rather the club. We were actually not so far away from a cultural revolution of the sort the Chinese would later experience; ours, of course, was in a different tradition, much gentler and never carried to its radical extreme. It was an attack on the *Forge,* but Jastrun thought it was an attack on him and his poetry. That was for him an incredibly touchy point. He could not tolerate the most harmless joke, the slightest criticism. Friends in Lvov during the war, we had become even closer in Warsaw, sharing the same fears and the same faint hopes during long walks before the curfew. Lidia and I were among the very few people to whom he could read his poetry. I was under its spell. But after the war, in Łódź, I detected a false note in his poetry as it grew increasingly pathetic. He seemed to view himself as a national bard like the Polish romantic poets of the nineteenth century. When

I told him that, Jastrun walked away without a word. "Janek is mean-spirited." That is what he kept saying and he really meant it. It cast a shadow over our friendship for a long time. After his death he appeared to me repeatedly in dreams. As if he were accusing me of something or wanted to tell me something. And he would say strange things to me in my dreams. "Why should I have to cuckoo again?" or some odd phrase like that or others that I was not able to remember. "Why should I have to cuckoo what has already been read before?" As though it were a message from the beyond that over there the only thing that exists is what has been read. But it was strange that that dream pursued me and each time robbed me of my peace of mind. Like a message meant to precede or follow death.

A year after that, or maybe it was later—all those postwar years become condensed for me like a barley soup so boiled down that only the barley remains—the Third Congress of Polish Writers took place in Warsaw. Shortly before that, during a closed party meeting, I was violently attacked. For the last time in my career, I was one of the delegates. I did not attend the Fourth Congress in Szczecin the following year, at which socialist realism was unanimously and universally acclaimed as the sole method of artistic creativity. I don't remember what I said at the Warsaw congress, but I know that at the end I defended Maria Dąbrowska as a classic writer who should be respected; there had been attacks made against her. I said that we should respect older writers like her even if they are not on our side.

That same day Woroszylski attacked me. In his speech he ridiculed as bourgeois superstition respect for writers who were class enemies. There was applause, at first only from the first rows, then from the entire auditorium. At this point Woroszylski pulled a letter out of his briefcase and read it aloud. It was a letter from me, but signed by my secretary. Woroszylski waved it in the air and talked about my conceit and about the canary in Mayakovsky's poem that sings shrilly in the bedrooms of new dignitaries and should be strangled as soon as possible. This time the whole audience applauded.

I turned pale and walked out. In the elevator I staggered and collapsed. A friend took me home.

I still had no reservations, or hardly any reservations, about anything that was going on. For the first year or two after the war and even well into third, none of us at the *Forge* raised any political objections. We all stood by the new order. Even at home I would repeat the famous statement, "One cannot make an omelet without breaking the eggs," as well as another saying, probably taken from one of Malraux's terrorists or political commissars: "You cannot make a revolution wearing silk gloves." Lidia would invariably leave the room, and Jastrun, if he happened to be present, would wave his hand and say, "Janek always talks pure rubbish until late at night."

At the *Forge* we stood by the new order out of either conviction or a deep-seated feeling of resignation not always recognized as such, but each of us brought along not only former tastes and predilections but also what proved more enduring— social habits and customs. We did not differ from the "pimply ones" in political commitment; I, for one, had monthly periods when I grew rabid, and for a long time thereafter I had recurrent bouts of "red fever." What distinguished us from the "pimply ones" was our prewar upbringing, while they had begun their conscious or barely conscious life during the war, the Occupation, the camps and deportations. Those of us who went to the forest had already finished university. We differed from them, too, in our abhorrence of denunciations and our absolute inability to repeat private conversations. We had a deeply ingrained respect for privacy, especially for the private life of friends. In those first postwar years a great wave of lying was bearing down, a mixture of peasant customs, petty-bourgeois hypocrisy, fulminations and castigation from on high, and Soviet puritanism masking total sexual anarchy as varnish covers unwashed floors.

But the Soviet mill was grinding up everybody one after the other. And it often separated the wheat from the chaff only at the very last minute. Sometimes it took a long time. It was in the years 1946–47 that the first group of young people was sent to the West on scholarships. A group of humanists about whose ideological commitment there were some doubts was sent to Paris. At any rate, their beliefs would not be damaged. They could at least learn the language. Only in the fifties were the most promising and ideologically sound sent to Moscow to study. The results defied all expectations. The young people returned from France nurtured on Sartre and full of contempt for the rotten West. They had joined the party while still in Paris. Those coming back from Moscow brought with them handcopied poems by Akhmatova, Mandelstam and hard-to-come-by editions of Yesenin and Pasternak. They had made friends among the Russian dissidents. And they were cured of communism once and for all. It was a remarkable vaccine. Woroszylski was one of those vaccinated for good. He was sent to Moscow in 1952 and returned in the summer of 1956. For years Wiktor and I have been friends. United by common experience. Like a heavy load we had carried together.

A year after the Warsaw congress, but still before the one in Szczecin, I was summoned to the Building. This time the noose was tightening slowly but inexorably around the *Forge*. The break with Tito had just taken place, although on his last visit, not so long before, he had been driven through the streets of Łódź amidst a sea of red flags fluttering in the wind, the honking of horns and the wailing of sirens from fire trucks and police cars stationed at every corner, and double rows of soldiers and security agents rounded up for the occasion from the entire vaivodship. Now all the newspapers were writing about the lack of vigilance in the party and about nationalist deviation. And it was about rightist deviation on the *Forge* that I was asked almost as soon as I entered the Building.

The conversation was conducted by three high-ranking officials, almost at the very top, including the secretary of the Central Committee and the chief of the propaganda section. Under three portraits: Lenin, Stalin, and Beirut. "You are suffering from a rightist deviation, comrade," said the secretary from the Central Committee.

I had been asked about such deviation once before, in 1945, almost immediately after the liberation. I was on my way to Stróże to pick up Lidia and take her to Cracow. I had been given a car and a chauffeur by Borejsza. We had taken some back road since the main route was jammed with military convoys, but not more than twenty kilometers from Warsaw our way was suddenly blocked by a truckload of soldiers. Naturally we had all our documents, duly stamped with round seals—all others were invalid—and our *putyovka*. The papers didn't do us any good; the soldiers hardly looked at them.

Just as they were ordering us to get out of the car, a jeep pulled up with three uniformed men in big fur hats. The blue rhomboids on their uniforms indicated that they were NKVD men. Later on I found out that they were from a *kontrrazvyedka*, a counterintelligence unit. A heated argument, punctuated by curses, erupted between the two groups. From what I could understand, they were arguing over our car. Who was going to take possession of it? The soldiers wouldn't give in. They were already sitting in it. But the tallest of the NKVD men, dark and handsome as a movie star in his magnificent fur hat— he must have been a Georgian—ordered the soldiers to give them the papers and the car keys. They divided everything up as they might have the spoils of war; the Georgian got us, the chauffeur, and the keys. The soldiers got the car, but since they couldn't start the motor without the keys they pushed it into a ditch. The handsome Georgian took us into a barn. I showed him my party membership card. "*Pravilno* [All in order]," he said, "*no kakoye u vas otklonieniye* [but what is your deviation]?" I knew all about deviations from my reading of *A Short Course about the WKP(b)* in preparation for that wretched examination back in Lvov. So I answered promptly, with surprising presence of mind. "*U mienya nikakogo otklonieniya nyet. Ya vsiegda po gieneralnoi linii.* [I don't have any deviations. I always follow the general line]." The Georgian looked at Lidia, who did not blanch for even a second. He rounded up the NKVD men, barked at the Red Army soldiers, and ordered them to haul our jeep out of the ditch.

The conversation at the Central Committee lasted considerably longer. "Your record during the Occupation is good," said the secretary. The verification of wartime activities had been almost completed. As a result, I had been promoted to the rank of second lieutenant and awarded the Cross of Valor, but to my astonishment and dismay I found out that all the time I had been included in the counterintelligence unit and that my chief was Marian Spychalski himself. I couldn't have dreamed of anything so frightening in my worst nightmare. I had met Spychalski only once, on Tarczyńska Street, and had had no idea what his position was. I was under the impression that he was only interested in the bimonthly that Hedda Bartoszek and I were editing. But recently rumors had been circulating that comrades who had spent the war in the Soviet Union were suspicious of those who had stayed behind in Poland and that Spychalski (at that time the minister of defense) was under serious investigation.

"We have a high opinion of you, comrade," said the man from the propaganda section. "Subjectively you're all right, but objectively there's . . . a rightist deviation." "Objectively," the secretary chimed in. And he became stiff and rigid. "You've got no backbone, either, . . . for party work." Then he became somewhat gentler. "What's your doctorate in, comrade?" "Romance languages," I answered. "I see," he said, "so you must know French." Now everyone was relaxed. "We need professors who belong to the party." He took a notebook and calendar out of his pocket. "Starting in September, you'll be given a professorship at the University of Wrocław." So I had become a professor because . . . of my rightist deviation. Only many years later did I realize that no other conversation ever had as much weight in the entire course of my long life. But only several weeks later, after settling in Wrocław, did I learn that my conversation in Warsaw meant the beginning of the liquidation of the *Forge*. Stefan Żółkiewski, its editor in chief, who was accused of being soft on rightist deviations and too concerned with intellectual subtleties, was replaced by Paweł Hofman from the Central Committee, a prewar Communist who had been on the central board of the old party. Paweł was a loner, a neurotic long enclosed within an impenetrable shell, one of the least typical characters in the unwritten novel of that period. Back then in Łódź he spent his nights playing Bach sonatas on the violin, only to appear at the editorial offices early in the morning before the cleaning women arrived. There he sat at his desk and scoured every article for the slightest deviation from the party line and the principles of socialist realism.

I don't know whether he quit the party after October, but he had no position whatsoever anymore and received the smallest possible retirement pension; he didn't write a single word thereafter and totally withdrew into himself. The last time I spoke to him was in America, when he came on a short visit to see his son. He warned his son not to go back to Poland when the changes came. He predicted a long bloody night for Russia, after which not a stone would be left standing. I think that even back then in Łódź he must have played Bach sonatas not only all night long but throughout the entire day too.

I was summoned to the Building many times after that conversation which brought about "my exile to the university." But I'll always remember when I went there for the last time. Once again the times are confused, but it was after my Shakespeare book, when I had already been teaching for many years at Warsaw University. Victor Erlich invited me to Yale as a visiting professor for a year. I had no trouble obtaining a leave from the university since my chairman, who picked as his graduate assistants the dullest of his followers, was delighted to have me off his hands for a year. Likewise, the ministry raised no objections, but I was told right away that I would have to have the approval of the Central Committee. I made applications, I telephoned repeatedly. There was no response—neither a yes nor a no. Almost a year passed. It was now May. Yale kept bombarding me with letters and then telegrams. They wanted to know whether I was coming. The American embassy intervened—to no avail. No decision had been reached. It would come in due time, I was told. But finally I had to know where I stood. So did Yale. Zenon Kliszko was the new number two since Gomułka's return to power. I had known him since the Occupation. I requested an appointment.

The conversation took place on the same floor as the conversation fifteen or so years earlier. In an office that was twice as big, with a double-padded door. The room seemed to be completely empty, as though it were unoccupied. Straight-backed chairs, a desk, and a table. Not a single armchair, not one sheet of paper on the table or desk. Kliszko had changed little since the war years. He was only a bit hunched over and seemed even thinner than before. He appeared not to see the person he was talking to; he spoke as though to himself, with the same nasal twang. He played chess with Gomułka or card games like war and sixty-six and dominos. And he drank only tea. He wrote poetry in his youth, or so they say. He considered himself an expert on Norwid. He would quote him in every speech he gave.

Our conversation started with Norwid too. Then Kliszko complained that Leszek Kołakowski had let us down by meeting in Laski with Cardinal Wyszyński, the primate of Poland. Kołakowski and Wyszyński sat on a bench and talked for an hour. "Kołakowski is a philosopher. What could he possibly talk about with a cardinal?" I kept trying to say that I had to let my students know whether I would be teaching my seminars the next year. But Kliszko didn't want to talk about that at all and said only, "We've got to think it over. We'll put it on the agenda." And he went back to Norwid and Kołakowski. Only as he was seeing me out the door did he look at me for the first time. "What are you writing about now, professor?" "About tragedy," I said. "About Polish tragedy." Kliszko turned red and I had the impression he wanted to nail me to the double-padded door with his gaze. "Calm down. Not about Polish tragedy but about Greek tragedy." Kliszko brightened. "A fitting subject!" he said approvingly.

The walk from the Building at the intersection of Aleje Jerozolimskie and Nowy Świat to my apartment on Aleja Róż took me no more than ten to twelve minutes at a leisurely pace. Lidia met me at the door and said, "We're going to America. There was a phone call a minute ago from the Central Committee. Next week you can go pick up our passports."

6.

I had met György Lukács for the first time during his visit to Warsaw in 1956, in early spring, I believe, since I remember that the evenings were still cold. Lukács was wearing an old-fashioned ankle-length fur coat and a felt hat. I was asked to look after him; several evenings I walked him back to his hotel through the streets of Warsaw, which in those years were still bustling with people. I recall two of the conversations I had with him. The first took place on the day that he got from his German publisher a book that ran to at least four hundred pages, the third or fourth volume of his works. I asked him how it was possible to produce such a large work year after year and sometimes twice in the same year. Lukács smiled and said, "My young friend, I have no inner life." The second of these conversations took place on the last evening of his stay in Warsaw. Bidding me good-bye at the entrance to the hotel, he said, "Throughout all of my long life, ever since the publication of my first book, I've been attacked by ortho-dox Marxists." He was just over seventy then. I remembered that in Mann's *Magic Mountain* Settembrini was said to be a portrait of the young Croce, and the Jesuit Naphta, securely entrenched in his syllogisms and invincible logic, was sup-posed to be a portrait of the young Lukács. I wanted to ask him about it, but I lacked the courage. "Many of my books," Lukács continued, "including even the most ambitious ones, I had to rewrite for each new edition. Which of course made them more and more obscure. Censors and scriptural com-mentators hate clarity. When my *Geschichte und Klassenbewussein* (*History and Class Consciousness*) came out in 1962, I had to en-gage in self-criticism on four different occasions. Maybe even five. Now I am an active or honorary member of many learned societies, and I am always invited to take my place with the presidium . . . and nobody treats me seriously anymore." Not long after that Warsaw visit—when, of course, he always sat with the presidium during the various official conferences—the Hungarian Revolution broke out and was crushed by the Soviet army; Lukács was arrested along with the entire govern-ment. Nagy and many others were executed. Lukács, too, had been marked for death but somehow was never actually sen-tenced. He was allowed to return to Budapest and his books. But then he was treated seriously.

Lukács was one of the first readers of *Shakespeare, Our Con-temporary* after it appeared in German translation. In a long letter full of high praise he pointed out that I had failed to recognize in Shakespeare the characteristic Renaissance belief in a better world and that my theory of the Grand Mechanism in history was a generalization based on the limited historical evidence of Stalinism. Undoubtedly Lukács was right to a large degree, but that was precisely what made Shakespeare our contemporary. In the French edition of *Shakespeare, Our Contemporary*—the only one with illustrations—the chapter "The Kings" was preceded by a documentary photograph of Stalin's funeral. His enormous coffin is borne on the shoulders of Malenkov, Molotov, Bulganin, Khrushchev, and Beria, all either in long coats or in military tunics, with huge fur caps on their heads. In the first week after Stalin's funeral, Beria was literally smothered by Malenkov (who threw himself at Beria during a Politburo meeting and strangled him with the help of some of the others) or, as a later official version reported, he was formally sentenced to death and executed only a month or more after that. All the rest of those mourners who carried Stalin's coffin to the Lenin mausoleum were shortly consigned to oblivion one after the other by Khrushchev. He himself was the last to go. But he was the first of Stalin's gravediggers. As the memory of the Grand Mechanism recedes farther and farther into the past, the horrifying ends of Shakespearean tyrants and their henchmen are also losing the contemporaneity that we had suddenly rediscovered there: Richard III in mud up to his waist, crying, "My kingdom for a horse": Macbeth, in Kurosawa's imagination pinned to the wall by arrows like a dying hedgehog; Polonius run through by Hamlet's dagger like a rat behind the arras. But just as I am writing these final sentences of my reminiscences, Shakespeare "our contemporary," implacable and cruel as ever, has returned once more, but this time not on the stage but on the television screen. The huge crowds in front of the Central Committee in Bucharest howl, "A rat! A rat!" when they see the helicopter with Ceausescu take off from the roof of the building. Ceausescu being pulled up by the neck like a rat from the bottom of a tank. And once again: "Dead, for a ducat, dead!" And once again Shakespeare, our contemporary.

In June 1956, thus not long after my last conversation

with Lukács, I went to Paris for a short visit. Warsaw was teeming with handwritten copies of the "secret" speech denouncing Stalin's crimes that Khrushchev delivered at the Twentieth Congress of the Communist party. A good friend of mine, Stanisław Gajewski, was Poland's ambassador to France at that time. *L'Express* was then the most popular magazine devoted to politics and literature. Once a week—I don't remember anymore whether it was on Tuesday or Wednesday—*L'Express* invited select politicians, writers, and often foreign visitors for *déjeuner* at the editorial offices. Gajewski and I were invited to one of these *déjeuners,* but he couldn't go and I went by myself.

Champagne and canapés were served, but the main attraction was Mauriac, whose regular column, "Le Bloc-Notes," on the last page of *L'Express* was the main attraction of the magazine. I had always been fascinated by pessimistic Catholicism, by the lack of belief in human nature it inherited from the Jansenists. That was what I found fascinating in Mauriac's novels. Mauriac was very interested in the visitor from the Communist half of Europe, and during almost the entire *déjeuner* he talked almost exclusively with me. As he was a brilliant conversationalist, I was truly delighted.

The next morning at seven I was awakened by the ringing of the telephone. It was Gajewski, "What have you done?" he yelled. "Get over here right away." The Russian ambassador had called him at five. "Who is that young writer who talked with Mauriac at *L'Express?*" he demanded. As soon as I got there, Gajewski handed me a copy of the magazine so freshly printed that it still smelled of ink. "I asked this young man from Poland how he would react if Radio Moscow announced that Khrushchev was a traitor and an American agent," Mauriac wrote in his column. "This young man," Mauriac continued, "was not taken aback in the least. 'I have seen so many things in my life that I wouldn't be in the least surprised.' "

7.

I came back from Paris full of anxiety as to what the consequences of my conversation with Mauriac might be. But no one even mentioned it. History had all of a sudden begun to accelerate rapidly. It was almost literally grabbing us by the throat. On the day of my return there was a strike at the Cegielski works in Poznań, followed by demonstrations throughout the city and a massacre of the workers. I remember that day quite well since immediately after my arrival I had to chair master's exams. The candidates did very well, but I had something on my mind other than asking examination questions. Cyrankiewicz had just made his long-to-be-remembered statement about the hand that has to be cut off.* Now I no longer know what frightened me the most: the shootings in Poznań or Cyrankiewicz's declaration. Lidia clenched her teeth and kept repeating that Cyrankiewicz's statement was shameful.

The weeks that preceded October have once again merged in my memory in a single accelerated time. Every evening and well into the night we listened to Radio Free Europe, which was being more violently jammed day by day. In *The Faith and the Fault*, Jacek Kuroń refers to the period as the "earthquake." This earthquake had begun with Światło's revelations about the use of torture during interrogations. I knew about the torture and executions, but there are different degrees of knowledge, or rather of its penetration into one's consciousness. And of its becoming firmly rooted in one's memory. There is the knowledge that is "jammed" internally like a constantly jammed radio, knowledge that no one wants to accept in all its most extreme consequences, knowledge that is rejected by that inner self-censoring which is much more drastic than the Freudian version.

In Wrocław, Stefan Łoś was a frequent visitor, first at Lidia's parents, then at our house. He had confidence in me. We had known each other since our scouting days. Łoś had spent several years in prison. He never talked about his imprisonment, and his eyes would dart wildly whenever I asked him about it. Only once did he mention the metal floor in the security prison in Wrocław; prisoners had to stand on it barefoot while

*At the time of the demonstrations in Poznań, in June 1956, Cyrankiewicz, then prime minister, said that anyone who raises his hand against the Fatherland deserves to have his hand cut off. [Ed.]

it was heated from underneath. In former days that was how bears were trained to dance. I pushed Łoś's story deep into the recesses of my memory.

It came back to me in those weeks before October. It came back to the surface every evening as I listened to Światło's revelations on Radio Free Europe. What until recently had only been whispered could now be heard said in a loud, clear voice. A voice on the radio heard at precisely the same time by tens of thousands. I was writing weekly theater reviews then. After years of inertia and apathy, I began to write again with the same passion that I had felt in my first year at the *Forge*. And at the end of September 1956, not quite six months after my meeting with Lukács and three months after the Poznań massacre, I went to Cracow to see the new production of *Hamlet*. *Shakespeare, Our Contemporary* had its beginnings in that Polish version of Elsinore, where "Denmark is a prison" and "walls have ears" but people don't. The title of my review was "*Hamlet* after the Twentieth Congress." But the renewal had started with the student theaters. "Strews Novelties with Blossoms Rare" was the title of another review of mine. It was a strange renewal. The performers in the little student theaters were making a discovery for the first time and with a sense of astonishment—astonishment at their own courage—and what they were discovering was that boys and girls have bodies. No one was yet talking about "socialism with a human face," as it would later be known during the Prague Spring under Dubček. But Ważyk had already shown its inhuman face in his *Poem for Adults*. Boredom was written all over that inhuman face. "It's all due to boredom, Your Honor" was the refrain of Agnieszka Osiecka's song from the musical at the STS (Student Satirical Theater). "The Poetics of Broken Color" was the title of my review. The songs were about poisoned joy.

Staszewski always went to the opening night of every program at the student theaters. Often there was some serious drinking at his apartment afterward. At the time he was the first secretary of the Warsaw Committee. Infighting at the highest party levels between the Puławy and Natolin factions had come out into the open. In the struggle for power Staszewski tried to win over to his side the party organizations in the factories, but also the cultural elite. I don't recall at what point the terms *cement* and *revisionist* started to be used. In this political newspeak, to call someone a revisionist was equivalent to a denounciation. More and more often "revisionists" meant "Jews." But for us at the *Cultural Review* (*Przegląd Kulturalny*) revisionism came to mean breaking free from ossified thinking. That is when we talked about going back to "the young Marx." We had already absorbed existentialism, and in this intellectual hodgepodge the young Marx seemed scarcely different from Sartre, and consciousness a matter of free choice for the individual as much as for whole social classes. I had never read the young Marx, but I had already begun to translate Sartre and then the early plays of Ionesco. And my own distinct voice was slowly beginning to evolve.

It was from Staszewski, I believe, that I first heard the term *them*. "Them" meant the party leadership and the Natolin group. But who precisely were "we"? All of Poland listened to Radio Free Europe then, but "we," too, listened night after night. It was around the same time, some weeks before the Polish October, that Ben started coming to Warsaw on a regular basis. Ben was the correspondent of *Le Monde,* and among all the foreign correspondents he had the reputation of being the best informed. And no wonder. He always stayed at the Bristol Hotel in Warsaw. Every day at noon, Edda Werfel, who was deputy editor of *Warsaw Life,* went to the Bristol to have a cup of coffee. She brought the latest news. In the evening or late at night I went to see Ben. Often I came straight from seeing Staszewski. "Tell Ben about the movements of the Soviet troops in the Ostrołęka region. It's not confirmed yet, but tell him." The next day, when he heard about the movements of the Soviet troops in the Ostrołęka region over Radio Free Europe, Staszewski believed what he had doubted the day before. "The news is true. I heard it on Radio Free Europe."

Now everybody was talking about Soviet intervention. And even today I couldn't say whether there was an underhanded fomenting of panic or genuine determination to resist. It was rumored that arms had been distributed to the workers at a car factory. We wanted to believe that was true. But no longer was the talk only about intervention. I remember a name-day party on 12 October. It was a larger gathering than usual; all the intellectual elite was there and all the wives. Staszewski of course was there. He kept talking about "a night of long knives" and warned those "in danger" not to sleep in their own beds. But Lidia calmly took me home.

After that, all that I remember of those days are the enormous crowds in the streets and the never-ending chanting for Gomułka and Cardinal Wyszyński: "Wiesław and Wyszyński!" "Wyszyński and Wiesław!" At the Warsaw Polytechnic and in the streets around it the rallies went on for over three days. I was scheduled to address the crowd on the second day. I couldn't get there. That was the first and last time I ever addressed thousands of people. I spoke in the Polytechnic's gigantic auditorium and what I said was transmitted to the streets through loudspeakers. After the Warsaw uprising of 1944, I had landed in the hospital in Cracow with diphtheria and pneumonia. Three days later, shortly before dawn, I had coughed up a membrane like reptile scales. At that meeting in October at the Polytechnic I had the impression I had coughed up that slimy membrane for good and all.

That same day, or perhaps it was the day after, I went out at night for a second time. Crowds were still swarming in the streets. For mid-October, the night was mild. Groups were being organized, and there were calls for a march on the Soviet embassy. My apartment on Aleja Róż was next to the headquarters of the Warsaw Committee—where Staszewski had his office. I saw trucks leaving the building one after the other. In one of them I thought I saw Putrament sitting next to the driver. He had a megaphone in one hand. The huge crowd from Aleje Ujazdowskie was spilling over into Aleja Róż. Putrament was shouting, "Why don't you go home to bed, you sons of bitches." It was Putrament all right—I recognized his booming voice. We were all afraid of a provocation; for years we had had the fear of everything spontaneous drummed into us. "Organization, comrades, organization is what counts!" But I had very mixed feelings as I watched those trucks from the committee telling Warsaw to go home to bed. Later on, those trucks came back to me in a dream. It was a dream that bordered on a nightmare. Only several months later did I realize that that mild night marked the beginning of the end of the Polish October. Gałczyński knew how to be a great poet:

All of Warsaw in a fog.
"When will it cease?"
Asks one passerby of another.
The same thing today, tomorrow, yesterday.

Soon thereafter, probably before the end of the November, Lidia and I went to Paris. At Sartre's invitation I put together an anthology of texts from the October events for a Polish issue of *Les Temps Modernes*. I also included my speech at the Polytechnic. I met Sartre's secretary, Marcel Péju, and a number of journalists and writers who belonged to Sartre's circle; most of them were my peers, but a few, were much younger. Our meeting spot was the Café de Flore, a favorite midday haunt of Sartre's. I was also invited to their homes. What has stayed in my memory from those visits to their apartments are the pictures and the empty frames hanging on the walls. Those empty frames had once contained portraits of Stalin. With the passage of time even the portraits of Lenin in many apartments were replaced by Mao Tse-tung in the familiar blue tunic buttoned up to the neck, as smily and as obese as representations of Buddha. Some years later, the same frame probably contained a picture of the bearded Che Guevara in a dark beret and military jacket, with a rifle in his hands. Above the desk in Marcel Péju's study there hung for years a small framed photograph of Mao, only not grinning. Marcel was on the board of directors of *Les Temps Modernes*. And perhaps it was even his idea to have the post-October Polish issue appear. He was less politically blind than my Warsaw friends and I were at that time, and even if at some point he had some illusions about Stalinism, he certainly had got rid of them. But for him the Polish October offered the promise of an approaching Dawn. That Polish issue opened with Ważyk's *Poem for Adults,* and Marcel's introduction was entitled "Socialism Awakened." The last sentence read: "Today the revolution in Poland melts the ice."

A year before, Marcel had met Ludmiła Murawska on a visit to Warsaw, married her almost immediately, and settled with her in Paris. Ludmiła, a painter by profession, was the only actress in Miron Białoszewski's "private theater on Tarczyńska Street," his one-room apartment. Ludmiła had not yet learned to speak French, and Marcel did not know Polish, but they communicated perfectly. Without words. Ludmiła must have learned from Białoszewski the art of silence that speaks. Whoever saw her once could never forget her deep-set eyes, dense as a mountain lake. They were opaque. As though present and empty at the same time. For me, secret affinities, which I am still unable to fathom, link Ludmiła from Miron's theater to the empty frames for portraits in Marcel Péju's apartment.

I no longer remember whether it was during that visit to Paris or the next one, less than a year later, that I met Jeziorański for the first time since the war. For many years, under the name of Jan Nowak, he had been head of the Polish desk at Radio Free Europe. He found me immediately. We met in Montmartre in a little smoke-filled bistro right by the "artists' entrance" to the Moulin Rouge. Jeziorański took me inside. B. was the star, or rather the starlet, of the latest show. I had seen her in Warsaw a couple of months earlier at a student cabaret. Naked and half-naked young women rushed by us, hurrying up and down the stairs, through the corridors, and along the narrow passageway behind the stage, giving off the sweet scent of cheap perfume mixed with sweat and whirling clouds of powder.

Slowly and methodically Nowak dusted the powder off the lapels of his jacket. He paid not the slightest attention to the girls, as though they did not exist, or rather as though they were only an annoying cloud of powder. B. looked even thinner and taller than she had in Warsaw—she was almost six feet tall. She took us to her dressing room and then left us alone there. On the mirror someone had drawn two pairs of lips in red lipstick. I don't know why Nowak chose that strange place for our conversations—perhaps for conspiratorial reasons, but certainly not for its ambiguous charms. He was the most austere of all my friends from the old Warsaw days, as he would also be later on.

On each of my subsequent trips abroad I called him collect —two or three times—at an agreed-on number from public telephone booths, never from the hotels where I was staying. Once I even went to see him in Munich. I told him in as much detail as I could what was going on in the party. Even now I am unable to explain exactly why I did that. No doubt I was fascinated by the risk, the element of play, and the new conspiratorial game, especially in Munich, where Nowak kept me hidden at the apartment of a priest he knew and allowed me to go out into the town only in the evenings. But that is not what was important. Nowak and I were separated by our political past and our outlook on the future. I was on the other side and would remain so for quite some time yet. But even then I could clearly see that in the threat posed by Moczar and the increasing sense of constriction, in the division into "them" and "the people," Radio Free Europe was an ally and a support.

I was tied to Nowak by long-standing bonds (although being "an old pal from the army," or "an old schoolmate" was never as sacred to me as it was for him), and I had complete confidence in his sense of discretion. And yet one day in Munich, in his study, I saw an elongated black object on his desk. I thought I heard it making a sound like the hum of a running tape. "You're recording me!" I yelled. He turned red and then suddenly went pale. "So that's how you've been programmed." Now I was the one who turned red with shame. The black object was simply an old camera.

8.

After my post-October return from Paris, time again began to speed up. But this time it was different. October, as I had seen it on Aleje Ujazdowskie from my street, ended even before it had begun. We were starting to be suffocated again. The Hungarian uprising had been crushed; Soviet tanks were still blocking all the squares in Budapest. *Quite Simply (Po Prostu)*, the most

"October" of all the journals and the first and the most impassioned and stubborn in demanding renewal, was closed down. Student demonstrations were met with truncheons. For three days the militia hunted down the students. For weeks several of my old friends tried unsuccessfully to get permission to start a new "European" journal. The former *Forge* had not existed for years, but we were still in the party. After the imposition of martial law in December 1981, Miłosz wrote that the worst crime committed against the people was to have deprived them of hope. If any of us had until recently still preserved some last vestige of hope, now it seemed that it had been taken away from us forever. In March 1957, Andrzejewski, Dygat, Hertz, Jastrun, Ważyk, Żuławski, and I decided as a group to quit the party. The farsighted Rudnicki had not paid his dues for years.

In the course of that one week we all returned our party cards one after the other. Jan Strzelecki was the secretary of the party organization at the Writers' Union. During the war and the Occupation Strzelecki had belonged to socialist youth organizations and had become a party member quite late. He always had doubts, but he believed in socialism almost to the very end. His sorrow was almost transparent. He told me to wait a little longer. Not to hurry. He talked in a very similar fashion on our last joint climbing expedition, when we were scaling Satan's Wall in the Tatras. Fog and then rain descended on us; the wall was slippery and inadequately layered. I wasn't able to get a footing. Jan had to make a sling with a spare rope. He always made a sling for the weakest.

After that week when he got back our party cards from us, he still spent a long time trying to figure out what to do with himself. He became associated with Janek Lipski, Jacek Kuroń, and Adam Michnik from the very beginning of the Workers' Defense Committee (KOR, Komitet Obrony Robotników). Later he became one of the Solidarity advisers. He was under surveillance during martial law.

Of those of us who gave in our party cards, Andrzejewski, Dygat, Jastrun, and Ważyk are no longer alive. Neither is Jan Strzelecki. He was murdered in Warsaw, his jaw and skull fractured by blows from a blunt instrument. The perpetrators were apprehended, but the murder was never fully explained. It took place after the lifting of martial law but before the round-table talks.

Strzelecki was a pure and splendid human being. Perhaps too pure for the country and the time in which he lived. Adam Michnik spoke at his funeral. In October 1956 Adam was ten years old.

Time passes rapidly. That is how a chronicle should end.

Santa Monica
New Year's Day 1990

Journey to the East

It was the best tea we had ever drunk. Almost transparent but very aromatic; after so many years, I still have its taste and smell in my mouth, like dried apricots, or rather the liquer made from dried apricots. It was Yunan, from the late autumn of 1944. "A bad year," said our host, "but one of the best harvests." Then we drank Szechwan from the winter of the preceding year—but that was after dinner—in little porcelain bowls so fragile that it seemed to us that they would break in our hands. That tea was dark and tart. "The winter was full of hopes and this late winter harvest is much appreciated by connoisseurs." On shelves and bookcases stood jars and pots, one beside the other, some very small, others immense, all with labels in black or red calligraphy. And all contained tea.

That was our first invitation to a Chinese home— the only one during our entire stay of almost two months in China. It was only shortly before our return that I realized how unusual that visit was. And what prior steps it had required and how many interventions from on high. It had entailed a special authorization, and probably from the very top, to invite foreigners to one's home. Even foreigners from a people's democracy, even from an official delegation. And for that permission it was necessary to make all the right moves weeks in advance. But Fu Tsong's parents had known for a long time that Smendzianka would be part of the delegation of artists and writers arriving from Poland on the occasion of the fifth anniversary of the Chinese Revolution. At the Chopin competition in Warsaw, their son had won first prize for the mazurkas and a scholarship to study for a year or two at the Warsaw Conservatory. Regina Smendzianka was one of her generation's most promising Polish interpreters of Chopin. She had already given many concerts, several times with Fu Tsong, I believe. They had become friends, and when she found she was to be part of the delegation to China, he had asked her to visit his parents in Peking. They invited her to dinner, but not wanting to go alone she brought me with her.

At the time Peking was closer to Warsaw than was Vienna or Berlin. West Berlin, that is, of course. China was closer than even Yugoslavia. We were already in the age of Khrushchev, a year or a year and a half after Stalin's death. People had begun to be let out of the prisons in Poland and the camps in the Soviet Union. Already there was talk even in the party, although still in whispers, about torture in the Security Forces. The word *thaw,* introduced by Ehrenburg, was gaining currency. China was opening up to delegations. But not only to delegations. To a new kind of hope. Maybe it wasn't even hope but a sudden return of faith.

Five years earlier, China had become newsworthy. My memory returns to those years with reluctance and aversion. "You remember so as to forget," Lidia told me time and time again. "But others will not let you forget." But that day I remember well. Peking had just been liberated; all the political activists in Warsaw were summoned to an official celebration at the Polytechnic. Everything was swimming in red: red banners, red arm bands, red cloth and papier-mâché covering the walls. And that red still seemed fresh. At the end there was the singing of the *Internationale.* Which went on and on. I can't carry a tune, but I screamed myself hoarse along with everyone else in the auditorium: "We have been naught, we shall be all. 'Tis the final conflict."

I don't know anymore where in Łódź we were summoned to when Berlin fell in May 1945, almost fifty years ago. I remember only that we hugged one another and that many were still wearing the striped garb of prisoners. And once again the *Internationale*—once, twice, and then all over again. The Polish flag was waving alongside the red flag on the Brandenburg

Gate. In Łódź there were only red flags. And over all the loud-speakers, Dąb-Kocioł, the vaivode (the old titles were still in use)—or perhaps he was already the president of the municipal council—proclaimed: "We have finally lived to see the day when the Polish soldier has become the gendarme of Europe."

That evening, at the headquarters of the party committee, there were lemonade bottles filled with vodka on tables covered with wrapping paper and red papier-mâché; mustard jars served as glasses. Thick-sliced pieces of sausage were spread out on the paper. There were two orchestras. I danced with, or rather I squeezed, a young girl. She told me her husband didn't come home nights. A friend tore me away from her. Almost by force, because I didn't want to let go of her. "Do you know whom you're dancing with?" I didn't have the slightest idea. "You must be out of your mind," he said. "That's Moczar's wife." At that point Moczar was the head of the Security Forces in Łódź. They worked mainly at night, a custom patterned after the NKVD. No wonder Moczar didn't come home until dawn.

I ran out into the pitch-black night without looking back. And I returned crestfallen to the empty Writers' House on Bandurski Street. Everyone else had celebrated the fall of Berlin until the following morning. A few months later, I came across the following passage in Stendhal's: "Upon entering a new city I always first pose three questions: What are the addresses of the twenty wealthiest merchants? What are the names of the ten most beautiful women? And what is the name of the man who can have me hanged without a trial?"

In Peking, at the home of Fu Tsong's parents, we also talked about Stendhal, even about his travels in Italy, but almost exclusively about music, Stendhal's fascination with Cimarosa. Fu Tsong's mother was undoubtedly a pianist too. Both his parents spoke French and English fluently. Fu Tsong's mother translated Balzac; his father, a professor, translated Shakespeare. But our conversation was just as much about politics. They detested Chiang Kai-shek. They call his era an occupation. They had had to go into hiding then. Now they were full of hope. They spoke of the teams of doctors who were being sent into the countryside for the first time, of the millions of manuals for teaching the illiterate to read and write, of the freedom that did not yet exist but that was on the way. At that point I did not yet know the expression *one hundred flowers,* but Fu Tsong's parents must have already heard of this new Chinese flower bed.

We returned late at night through a city that was completely deserted. Only rarely did we encounter bicyclists in their blue denim overalls with flashlights in their hands and white gauze masks over their mouths. What has stayed in my memory are the interminable streets like country roads where nothing arrests one's eye because clay walls stretch along both sides, behind which the shadows of dwellings are only occasionally visible. This return from the distant suburb through an empty Peking after conversation about music and hope brought back to me another return through a dark countryside and empty streets. Then, too, I had been drinking strong tea, with the only difference that it was served in a thick glass. But back then the roles were reversed, and I was the one who spoke of hope. My host had none.

It was in 1947, seven years before my trip to China. As on that trip, I was part of a delegation of writers and artists. This time to Moscow for the celebration on the thirtieth anniversary of the October Revolution. We were received by Russian writers, but Pasternak was absent. I asked about him; they said he was sick. I asked for his address; no one knew it. In Warsaw I had been given two messages to deliver to friends in Moscow. I found them. They said that they would take me to Pasternak. They told me to say, on a designated day, that I was sick with the flu; then I was to wait for them in the hotel. At midnight we reached Pasternak's dacha in Peredelkino. He was actually at work on a translation of Słowacki's *Mary Stuart.* He didn't speak Polish, but he understood it. He asked about his Polish friends and about the situation in Poland. I spoke about doctors in the countryside, about printings of poetry in the tens of thousands; I told him that we could write whatever we wanted. We drank stronger and stronger tea. Pasternak only smiled. "You are like birds singing, perched on branches.

Each bird sings his own song. Until one fine morning you all wake up in cages. Perhaps even golden cages. At the bottom of each cage there'll be a label. Under the first: 'Former Futurist'; under the second: 'Confirmed Symbolist'; under the third: 'Idealist'; under the fourth: 'Vulgar Materialist.' And above all of them: 'Enemies of the People!' " As a farewell present, Pasternak gave me his latest volume of poetry, *The Breadth of the Earth,* with the dedication "Best wishes for happiness." It was a thin volume of not more than sixty pages, printed on coarse paper, in a dark cardboard cover. In an edition of no more than five thousand copies. On my return from Moscow I noticed on the facade of the building housing the Writers' Union, at the end of Krakowskie Przedmieście, directly opposite the Zygmunt Column and the ruins of the not yet rebuilt castle, a huge streamer of red canvas with black lettering: "Writers Are the Engineers of Human Souls."

2.

On our way to Peking we stopped for twenty-four hours in Moscow. In the morning we went to Red Square and the mausoleum. Stalin was already there. I had seen him alive seven years earlier. It was at the Bolshoi, at a performance of *Swan Lake.* We were seated way up high with the delegates from the other fraternal republics. Stalin was seated with his marshals very close to the stage. Their medals glittered, but from the heights of the balcony, both Stalin and his generals looked like tiny figurines placed stiffly behind the red-plush railing, smaller even than the ballerinas on the huge stage, who after each pirouette froze stiffly in the tulle of their white tutus, which floated in the air for a prolonged moment.

It was Comrade Apletin who took us to that gala evening at the ballet. He was highly placed in the hierarchy and took special care of us. Żukrowski was also one of the members of that delegation of writers for the thirtieth anniversary of the October Revolution. He absolutely insisted on attending a mass in an Orthodox church. But Comrade Apletin, whom we called "Napletek" ("Foreskin"), knew only the St. Basil's Cathedral on Red Square, by the walls of the Kremlin. I wanted to see the stations of the new metro. The *Tribune of the People* wrote constantly of the marbles, mosaics, and statues in the Moscow metro. *"Ya khochu posmotret' na vash metropolit."* [I want to have a look at your metropolitan]. Comrade Apletin looked at me strangely. "You'll get an answer tomorrow." I was very much surprised it was such a complicated matter. The nearest metro station was two blocks away from our hotel. I did not get an answer the next day or the day after. "Wait a bit longer," said Comrade Apletin. "The answer will come." It did indeed. Three days later we left early in the morning in a special black Volga. Żukrowski came with us. In half an hour the houses disappeared and we were in the middle of fields on an empty highway. I didn't understand a thing. "They must be taking us to a secret station outside Moscow," Żukrowski said. "That's why we got those passes." Each of us had received three documents stamped with large round seals. Throughout the entire trip, Napletek did not utter a single word. After an hour we went off onto a side road bordered by alder and birch trees on which the last leaves were still fluttering. We drove through a gate and stopped in front of something resembling a large mansion, now quite dilapidated but still retaining vestiges of its former splendor. We were greeted by two black-cassocked Orthodox priests with immense beards almost to their waists. We were led through corridors and rooms—full of old men in black robes that flowed like women's dresses—into a huge salon, where we were received by the metropolitan and patriarch of all Russia, a gold chain with a gold cross hanging on his breast.

We were served sweet wine and sweet cakes with raisins. The conversation was as sugary as the wine and cakes. When Żukrowski suddenly asked, "What does Your Reverence think of churches being transformed into museums of atheism?" the metropolitan and patriarch of Holy Russia looked at us searchingly and I thought I saw something light up in his eyes, but perhaps it was only the reflection of the candles in the tall three-branched silver holders. He shook his white beard:

"Churches transformed into museums of atheism? I've never heard of anything like that. Perhaps in the past, in the 1920s."

We all kept silent for most of the return trip. It was only as we approached the city limits of Moscow that I said, "You Russians have a great source of consolation in your metropolitan." Comrade Napletek gave me a searching look, and in his eyes, too, sparks started to kindle. "In the Caucasus," he said, "there's an old Tartar saying. Just because two people sleep under the same quilt doesn't mean they have the same dreams." Long after our departure Apletin was a laughingstock everywhere in Moscow for taking two Polish writers who wanted to see the metro on a visit to the metropolitan.

I don't remember much more of my first trip to Moscow than those two visits, to the patriarch and to Pasternak. And Zofia Nałkowska's hats. Nałkowska had two specially made or bought for the trip, both with flowers, one with a veil and a large blue ribbon. In Moscow we were taken to model factories once or perhaps twice. If I remember correctly, they were chocolate and praline factories named after Feliks Dzierżyński. As we passed through a double row of women in head scarves and dirty white aprons, we heard them whispering, "The czarina has come."

The flight from Moscow to Peking in small propeller planes took almost forty-eight hours, and we stopped over for the night in Omsk or Tomsk. The hotel on the market square was quite bizarre. Something out of Gogol—and still of Gogol's time. The sofas, the bed covers, the curtains of purple velvet were covered with stains and cigarette burns, as if they hadn't been cleaned or replaced for years. And in each of the rooms there was an immense gold samovar. Mine was steaming when I opened the door. We were awakened at the break of day. The plane was waiting for us, but it wouldn't start for a long time. Then it started up, began to move, and a moment later came to a stop. We were told to get out. All around us, as far as the eye could see, was steppe, without a single tree, without any sign of human habitation. The pilot, wearing an immense sheepskin coat, crawled under the fuselage, then went back to the cabin and reemerged with a sledgehammer. He crawled under the wheels again and began to pound away rhythmically. The way peasants did decades ago, when their wagons broke down on the road. But the plane finally started.

It was still night when we flew over the Gobi Desert. It was covered with black craters and surrounded by a bright halo that seemed silvery, like the disk of the moon in photographs taken through huge telescopes. Many years later, I visited the Negev Desert. That desert has all the different colors: browns, violets, and every possible yellow. God could not show himself in the desert in a human form, but he could be a voice in a burning bush, an echo rebounding off the rose-colored columns of Solomon's porch. The Gobi is like the moon above an inhuman landscape.

But the airplane began its descent immediately thereafter. We were already in China. The earth looked like a garden. There wasn't an empty spot on it. It was divided into little rectangles, all of the same dimensions; they were sparkling. They must have been rice fields flooded with water.

That two-month stay in China was the most monotonous of all my travels. We lived in a newly built hotel for foreign guests. Each of us had a suite of two or three rooms. But it was impossible to seclude oneself, even in the bathroom: all the doors were without locks or keys. We were never alone; our guides accompanied us everywhere. They grabbed us by the arm, they constantly clung to us, as if they were perpetually afraid that we might stumble or get lost. This constant touching created a disagreeable sensation of claustrophobia, even in open squares.

Our guides and guardians, men and young women, were all dressed in blue denim tunics buttoned to the neck and pants of the same material and color. They all spoke a serviceable Russian; some knew a little English. But they never spoke to us individually; there were always at least two of them present at every conversation. Only one of our guides, probably the youngest—she still looked like a little girl, although all the women looked much younger than they actually were—stayed alone with us for a moment in the evening; she also stopped at the end of the corridor with M., who was the only painter in our group and always had a twinkle in his eyes. One morning she appeared in white tennis socks with colored stripes at the top. With the naive coquetry of a young girl,. she must have shortened her denim trousers by an inch or a half-inch. She disappeared that same afternoon and we never saw her again.

Every evening at our communal supper, we were asked whom we wanted to meet. We mentioned writers, artists, musicians. Our chief guardian would smile, nod assent, and methodically write down all our wishes in a thick notebook. But the next morning we were invariably taken to a kindergarten, a House of Culture, or a bicycle or thermos factory, I no longer remember which. Anyhow, they were all the same, as far as we were concerned. The ritual meeting in a "model" kindergarten, the Academy of Sciences, a shoe factory, or the House of Writers never varied. In auditoriums all hung with the same portraits, our delegation of "model" writers and artists sat on one side of a long table and on the other side sat five, sometimes seven, or even nine elderly gentlemen, very portly for Chinese, in the same tunics buttoned up to the neck, except that some tunics were better tailored and were made from tweed or other woolen cloth. Green tea was dispensed from huge thermoses.

"We have invited you so that we may learn from you because your revolution is older than ours." In response, the head of our delegation, accustomed to presiding over innumerable party meetings, would answer without ever changing either the order of his words or the tone in which he said them: "We, Chinese comrades, have come to learn how in five years you have liberated your heroic and industrious people from centuries of . . ." After which there was always applause, and the most portly of our hosts would rise to his feet: "Both we and you, our Polish comrades, must learn together from our comrades in the fraternal Soviet Union, the fatherland of the world proletariat. We now invite you to ask us questions, and we shall answer them as comrades speak to comrades, without concealing any of our mistakes."

Smendzianka was the first to speak: "How much does a pound of rice cost?" she asked. Our hosts huddled together and for a good two or three minutes whispered among themselves. All that reached us was "Shu, shu, shu . . ." Finally, an answer came from the thinnest one on the other side of the table: "Rice does not have one single price. Before the revolution the coolies in Shanghai . . ." What most amazed us was that we never got a simple answer even to the simplest questions; every question and every answer, whether it was in the model kindergarten or at the Academy of Sciences, was scrupulously recorded in thick notebooks by at least two Chinese, always thin.

In the evenings we were often joined for dinner by the French delegation. It was composed entirely of women. Very progressive women. They were particularly enthusiastic about the kindergartens. *"C'est extraordinaire,"* they would say, breathless with excitement. *"Ces pauvres Chinois ont des maternelles et des orphelinats."* But we Poles had had enough of both the orphanages and the meetings with thermoses full of tea. We wanted to see the town—alone. "What do you mean?" Our guardian reasoned with us in a gentle tone of voice, as if speaking to children. "After all, we've shown you the National Museum, the Imperial Palace, the Forbidden City, and the Empress's Garden." "But we just want to *walk* around the city." Our guide was simply astonished. Nevertheless, two days later we were unexpectedly allowed to get out of the cars. We were surrounded on all sides by little Chinese men and women, but we were finally taking a walk through the streets. Behind us, not more than twenty feet away, came the sad cavalcade of cars from which we had been released for an hour.

After a month in Peking we went on a trip throughout China. We visited a little mountain settlement a few thousand miles from Tibet. In this country, which for centuries has called itself the center of the world, thousands of miles is "close." We must have been at an altitude of almost ten thousand feet, because our breathing grew quicker and we could almost hear our hearts beating. The settlement was surrounded by the jungle. There was a school for boys and girls from a tribe that apparently did not yet know animal husbandry or metalworking. The girls did not attend the school of their own free will; the villagers tried to train young women caught in the jungle to be midwives. One of them sat at the table with us for supper. I shall never forget her eyes. There was no astonishment in them. There was nothing in them. They were deep blue and as moist as the eyes of a deer. But at the same time completely empty. Almost transparent, like two mountain lakes.

Then we traveled to the south, to Canton. I can still hear the clatter of wooden clogs that reached us on the highest floors of our hotel. It did not stop until after midnight; then it began resounding again before dawn, quieted down briefly during the sleepy and humid hours of the afternoon, and intensified once more with the light breeze from the sea. In Canton—I don't know how to put it any other way—we rediscovered the physicality that was hidden and dissimulated in the north. In Peking only the children possessed that physicality, laughing, running, and tumbling on every scrap of unoccupied earth, in bright red quilted jackets, caps with little bells, and little trousers with openings in the seats; the only living beings in a sea of blue denim buttoned to the neck, they would suddenly, in the midst of the general torpor of meetings that lasted hours, go racing off to chase a buzzing fly.

In the old town of Canton, one could smell the odor of frying oil and sharp spices, the houses spilled out into the little streets, or rather the street forced its way into the houses; there were basements, gates, wide-open windows, or houses without windows, made of packing crates, where in the evening by the flickering light of oil or kerosene lamps one could see huddled human bodies. Children and scrawny cats darted about everywhere. Fish were fried on little iron stoves or boiled in kettles.

Once, when we'd been taken on a morning walk by the seashore, two children ran up to us. The little boy must have been seven, the little girl perhaps nine, both in rags but very beautiful, with that delicate and almost crippled beauty of all the races of south Asia. They stretched out their hands to us. "Look at those begging children," said our guide. "In all of China you won't find such children anywhere else."

But of this journey to the East what I remember best is Shanghai. Along the entire length of the shore for miles and miles there were buildings of ten, twelve, and sometimes even fourteen stories one after the other, squeezed against one another like a clenched fist of cement, with entrances barred by grilles and grated windows, like gigantic bunkers. One could still read the half-effaced inscriptions and signboards of the English and American corporations, the Swiss and Dutch banks, the commercial companies and travel bureaus from all over the world. But on the other side of the road, everything was fragile and transparent: the bamboo scaffolding; bundles hanging on the ends of bamboo poles, swaying rhythmically like a pendulum; junks on the shimmering sea, with their little sails like white sheets stretched on slender bamboo masts.

We were staying in an old hotel in what was formerly the French sector. After the crushing of the Boxer Rebellion, Shanghai, like the territories in central Africa, was divided into autonomous sectors among the great colonial powers. The hotel where we were staying was the setting for much of Malraux's *Man's Fate*. At night I had the impression that I heard in the corridors the stealthy footsteps of the terrorist Ch'en, who believed that if everything is subject to destruction all that remains is to leave behind one a deep crater in the earth.

We were taken to a park in the former British settlement where the lawns were as thick and luxuriant as those at Oxford and where the bilingual sign on the gate still read: "Dogs and Chinese Not Allowed." In the Museum of the Revolution we looked at immense photographs—the length of the entire wall—of marching coolies: thousands of them, each behind his own fragile rickshaw, as if it were a bamboo tank. Instruments of torture, an ax, iron cages with spikes in the middle, chains. The faces of the murdered, beheaded, or hanged. It seemed to me that amongst them I had once again found Ch'en from Malraux's *Man's Fate* and Garin, the Bolshevik commissar from *The Conquerors*.

At an official reception given for us by the city, I met Chang. On the first day of our visit someone had told me about her. Shanghai had been taken less than a year before our arrival;

Chang's assignment was to "clean" the city. She was born in the second year of the Long March. And, with her mother, she had participated in the march to the very last day. People said that she had been admitted to the party at the age of five or seven. She was the youngest colonel—or perhaps it was general. But at that official reception she wore a soldier's blouse without insignia, except for the red star.

For a Chinese woman from the north, she was very tall. But she had practically no eyes. Only two slits, two slanted cuts. When they were opened, they condensed the light like two magnifying glasses. Her look was intense. We began to talk. From the start the conversation was intense. And from the first moment we felt a mutual attraction. "I'll come to see you," she said. She came to my hotel room late that night. She brought a bottle of Russian cognac and two glasses. She was probably the only woman in the whole town who could get away with something like that.

That young woman was undoubtedly curious about a man from a far-off world. Of that distant world she had seen only Moscow. But another sort of curiosity made her come to see me. She must have come well prepared for our conversation. I was much less well prepared. She knew everything about me, at any rate everything that she needed to know: that I had joined the party during the Occupation, that I had been a member of a delegation to Moscow. She thought I was much higher and much more deeply entrenched in the party than I actually was. She spoke broken Russian, and so did I, but we were able to understand each other easily.

The conversation began with Orwell. She had not read him; where and in what language could she have? But she had heard his name and knew the titles of his books. She asked me to tell her about *Animal Farm* and to summarize *1984*. That was just the preamble to our real conversation. It was only a year or two after this late-night meeting that I realized what Colonel Chang had actually been after, with her soldier's blouse unbuttoned and a glass of Russian cognac in her hand. She asked me about factions in the top party leadership. She was careful and never uttered the words *pro-Russian faction*. But that was what she wanted to find out about.

I, too, was careful in this conversation, or simply still naive, and I certainly knew far less than she did about the Soviet advisers in the army and in the Security Forces. But one has to pay even for half-truths in such conversations. She could not tell me that she didn't know the price of rice or how much rice a porter could buy after working a twelve-hour shift loading boats. I asked about the agricultural communes. "At the beginning it was a case of bending the stick too far"; Chang used exactly the same expression as the Polish party officials did. "Big landowners were tried in the villages and were usually stoned to death on the spot. We put an end to that. Now we put the rich peasants to work as swineherds." I also asked Chang about prostitution. Before the liberation, Shanghai was supposed to have had nine thousand, perhaps even twenty thousand bordellos. Until recently, double rows of teenage girls crammed the narrow streets leading down to the harbor. Sokorski returned from Shanghai two months before we left on our trip to China. He told us that he asked to be taken to a brothel. "All of them are currently being disinfected," he was told.

"We put two hundred prostitutes on a small barge," Chang said. "When it had drifted out to sea, the sailors unplugged two openings in the hold. Then they set off on a small skiff. Even before they got back to the port, the barge had gone to the bottom. That same evening all the bordellos shut down. The next day, many hours before dawn, the girls formed long lines in front of the offices that recruited workers for harvesting tea and carrying wicker baskets of silt to the rice paddies." After that there was nothing but prolonged silence. Perhaps Colonel Chang realized that she had said too much. She took her half-drunk bottle of cognac and left.

Shanghai was the last leg of our trip. A week later, we left Peking. We stopped for the first night in Ulan Bator. At the airport, camels were grazing in small herds of three or five right across from the hangars. On one side of the airport there was the steppe, on the other the city. A city of tents extending to the horizon. "At last we're back in Europe!" In that exclamation one could detect not only a bitter joke but also a deep expression of relief.

3.

About six months or perhaps a year after our return from China, Chou En-lai arrived in Warsaw. He talked of "a hundred flowers." At the time we, too, wrote about "a hundred flowers" and took them for a model. But before even a year had passed, of those hundred Chinese flowers there remained only one. It was just then (after a long hiatus) that I met Smendzianka in the street. "I have bad news," she said. "Fu Tsong hasn't heard anything from his parents for several weeks. He's afraid they've been arrested or"—here her voice dropped—"sent to work in an agricultural commune." The time of a hundred flowers was over. The Cultural Revolution had begun. A few weeks later, I ran into Smendzianka again. "The Chinese embassy insists that Fu Tsong return home immediately."

In Warsaw everyone adored Fu Tsong—fellow students and professors, women and men, Poles and foreigners. I met him at a party; he had fingers like ivory. Even one year of physical work would be the end of his career as a pianist. But what could he do? After all, Fu Tsong could not ask for political asylum in Poland. The Ministry of Culture and even the foreign department of the Central Committee tried to intervene. He still had a scholarship for one more year. At the embassy, the Chinese smiled, nodded their heads, agreed to all the arguments, and then declared that Fu Tsong must return home immediately. Pressure from the embassy increased. From that point on, two "guardians" never left Fu Tsong even for a moment.

Finally it was worked out with the embassy that Fu Tsong's concert in Poznań would be his last. The plane to Poznań was to leave at ten in the morning. Fifteen or twenty minutes earlier, a plane was to leave the same airport for London. Fu Tsong said good-bye to his "guardians" and got on the wrong plane. This was the first and perhaps the last time that the

British, Soviet, and Polish intelligence services—which as a rule sniffed at one another like ferocious dogs or, in the case of the Soviets and the Poles, watched one another closely—reached an understanding so as to usher to safety in the West a young Chinese with fingers like ivory chopsticks.

The news from China became more and more ominous. The Cultural Revolution was in full swing. Polish scholarship students coming back from China brought us firsthand information. They told me about the "water-drop" method. Professors, writers, and musicians who were accused of "aloofness from the working masses" would be visited by a member of the Red Guards at seven in the morning for a conversation. At the universities the person was usually the professor's own student. In a denim tunic, always of that same dark blue color and buttoned up to the neck, the young person—his or her tone extremely courteous—would lecture the old man or woman very gently but relentlessly about the errors that the victim had committed and the frank self-criticism that he or she should undertake. An hour later another Red Guard would appear dressed in exactly the same tunic buttoned to the neck and would equally gently and equally relentlessly lecture the victim about the errors that the victim had committed . . . An hour later a third would appear, then a fourth, then a fifth, and so on, late into the night. Day after day, week after week. The water-drop treatment led many to jump out windows in the third week, others to drown themselves in wells, as an old Chinese custom dictated. Obtaining poison was impossible. "Asia," said the young scholar who told me this story. "It couldn't happen here in Poland." I recalled our feeling of relief when, after leaving China, we landed in Ulan Bator.

The Marxist offensive against the universities began in Poland in 1949 or 1950, at first in the departments of philosophy and Polish literature. A two-day conference on "Marxist literary criticism" was organized at Warsaw University, and both the older professors and the young faculty members were invited to take part in an open and frank discussion. M., our protégée from the *Forge* in Łódź, undertook the organization and preparation of the conference. She had slightly prominent cheekbones, thick, moist lips that were always tightly pressed together, and smoothly combed hair. She wore blouses buttoned high at the neck and sometimes one of those old-fashioned white collars. At times she looked like a late-nineteenth-century feminist. We decided that I would make my presentation on the first day, after Roman Ingarden's talk.

The auditorium was full. Ingarden spoke very slowly, very calmly, and very clearly. He repeated his literary theory of the intentional and imaginary levels in a literary work. On the blackboard he drew a diagram with all the divisions and symbols. He covered the entire blackboard. Right down to the bottom corner. When he finished, there was some timid applause, mainly in the back of the auditorium. I waited a moment; then I stepped up onto the podium, next to the rostrum. I walked unhurriedly over to the blackboard and slowly and systematically began, with a big sponge, to wipe it clean from the first line at the top to the last one at the bottom. Until I had erased everything that Ingarden had written. Then just as slowly I walked back to the podium and said, "Now we can develop a scientific theory of literature, beginning at the very beginning." I was accorded thunderous applause, almost a standing ovation. After my presentation, M. came up to me. She kissed me with her moist lips. "You were magnificent! That was romantic irony in the grand manner." In fact M. had just begun studying romanticism. The secretary of the cultural section of the Central Committee also came up to me: "You've got a bright future ahead of you, comrade professor."

4.

Some thirty years later, the first, still not very large group of Chinese students arrived for doctoral studies at Stony Brook, where I was teaching. Their fields were chiefly computers and physics, but there was one doctoral candidate in comparative literature. She was extremely bright and gifted. In a few weeks she was conducting classes in linguistics and a tutorial for first-year students. In Peking she had been an assistant professor at the Institute of Foreign Literatures.

Mao rarely spoke. She was mistrustful or perhaps simply shy. She knew that I came from Poland and maybe that is why I was the first to whom she told her story. Her father was a historian who wrote about the French Revolution. During the Kuomintang, he had gone into hiding. Her mother was a sociologist and must have been a good scholar since she had been invited to Harvard twice. But she had never been allowed to go. During the Cultural Revolution the family had all been sent to work on farms: she, her mother, her father, and her brother. But each to an agricultural commune in a different part of China. Mao was nine at the time, her brother seven. For months they had no news of one another. For a long time they were not allowed to write letters. In any case, they didn't know one another's addresses. They all returned home some three years later.

"What was it like?" I asked. "It wasn't too bad," Mao said. "I did light work. Six hours a day. And in the afternoon I attended school for three more hours. But when I got back, I had a lot of catching up to do so I could get into the university."

Once I invited her to lunch at the cafeteria on campus. The food wasn't anything special, just roast chicken with rice. Mao ate very slowly. When she finished, there wasn't a single grain of rice on her plate. Then she carefully picked up all the crumbs of bread from the tablecloth and ate them. I pretended not to notice. But Mao turned her head away.

At more or less the same time, Fu Tsong went to China from England to see his mother. His father was no longer alive. I never found out whether his father died at the agricultural commune or after he returned home. One of our mutual friends wrote from London that Fu Tsong was taking his mother a supply of English tea.

Three Funerals

None of them was ever a close friend. I didn't even
know any of them very well. But all three have in
some way had an influence on my life, although not
while they were alive. It was their funerals that had
an influence on my life. And I remember their funerals more distinctly than I remember them.

Of the three, Andrzej Stawar I knew the least.
I had never talked with him for more than a few
minutes. And never about personal matters. In any
case, I don't remember any particular conversation
neither in Łódź nor, later, in Warsaw when we had all
moved back to the capital. We must have become acquainted in Łódź. Not at the *Forge,* because Stawar
never came to the editorial office. Nor at the Pickwick, where during the first two postwar years we
spent almost every night drinking vodka. Nor at
Czytelnik. Stawar didn't go there either. But in Warsaw, Stawar began dropping by from time to time
at the café of the publishing house on Foksal Street.
At noontime it was the gathering place for all the
fashionable writers and fashionable young women.
And a few wives. But that was at the end of the
fifties. By then Stawar had already been "rehabilitated" for several years. His books, both old and
new, were coming out. The literary weeklies were
publishing him on their front pages, and he had received one or two state prizes. But even at the PIW
café, I had never sat at the same table with him. Perhaps Stawar never actually sat down even in that café
but only just stepped in and stood near the door, by
the counter where the books and latest publications
were for sale. Yes, that is most probably where I remember him from. Certainly not from Łódź. But it

seems to me that he always looked the same, that he never changed, that he always wore the same trench coat, which was neither military nor Chinese. Or maybe it was an old-fashioned dark jacket buttoned up to the neck. His hair was always in a crew cut and he had a small, closely trimmed mustache, dark in color or perhaps slightly reddish. He wore, if I remember correctly, a flat cycling cap. He was different from all the rest. He did not belong to that literary café or to any other.

At one of the meetings of the editorial board of the *Forge* in Łódź, Żółkiewski said: "We've got to do something about Stawar." That must have been at the end of 1946 or the beginning of 1947. We all knew that something had to be done about Stawar. A year or two before, we had published him without running into any difficulties. But things were slowly worsening. For months he had been forbidden to publish. He wasn't able to earn a living. But that wasn't the worst. One could always find him some quick translation or hack job, if not under his own name, then under someone else's. He would get the money. But money wasn't the only problem. Before the war Stawar had published his translations of Sholokhov's *And Quiet Flows the Don* and Dostoevsky's *Poor Folk*. We all knew that we had to be careful with Dostoevsky because he still continued to be suspect. But Sholokhov was a classic writer and had to be reissued in a new edition. But how to get "them" to stomach the translator? Obviously, under another name. But everyone knew who was doing the translation.

"We have to do something about Stawar." Stawar was the *Lever (Dźwignia)*; Stawar was the *Literary Monthly (Miesięcznik Literacki)*. That was practically everything that had existed in Marxist criticism before us. Stawar was a legend, but that was a threat at the same time. Stawar was a Trotskyite. None of us could have uttered the word. It stuck in our throats. Even to hear it struck fear into our hearts. I remember how five years earlier in Lvov, in the autumn or winter of 1941, at the time of the first Soviets, I was working with a group of refugees from Warsaw to salvage the old court archives, which had been almost completely destroyed by the Soviet soldiers who had been quartered for a few weeks in the large building of what had formerly been a convent. They pulled the documents off the shelves and ripped them to shreds for use as paper for rolling cigarettes. Each of us got a daily allottment of more than fifty pounds of this trash to sort and classify. One day we found among the court records of a Communist trial a brochure by Trotsky. We were afraid to touch it. Report it, but to whom? To the NKVD? Terror. We looked at one another and without a word threw it into the fire.

"We must do something about Stawar," Żółkiewski had said. But what? It would always be possible to find some kind of work for Stawar, but what could we do about the *Literary Monthly* and the *Lever*? From the first issue of the *Forge,* we had been searching obstinately for what was then called the "red thread" in Polish literature and history. Beginning with the Warsaw Jacobins and Kołłątaj's *Forge.* That was where our journal got its name. It was suggested, I think, by Władysław Bieńkowski, who back then, in the thirties, in the Warsaw Circle of Polonists, styled himself a Warsaw Jacobin in his impassioned speeches; he was a born orator, standing there with his pockmarked face and banging the podium with his fist. The Jacobins were the easiest topic, in any event; no problems with the censors: the Jacobins meant the French Revolution and the patriotic enthusiasm of the Warsaw masses in 1794 during the Kościuszko uprising and the public hanging of Moscow's lackeys, the bishops and magnates. The Empress Catherine was not off-limits.

In the *Forge* we wrote respectful and enthusiastic articles about the Russian Decembrists of 1825 and their Polish friends, the revolutionary democrats, but of course we followed the line of Soviet "literary scholars" about those revolutionaries' aristocratic prejudices and utopian errors. We wrote about the "reds" in the first and in the second Polish insurrections (1830 and 1863), about Mochnacki, and about the Polish Communards and the first "Proletariat." Up to the revolution of 1905. After that the fog began, and farther on the abyss.

The *Lever* appeared between 1927 and 1928. I wasn't quite fourteen. I never had a copy of the *Lever* in my hands. Perhaps Broniewski showed me a copy once. His youthful poetry had appeared there. In the early 1930s (I was in the second or third year of law school), I followed Broniewski around like a puppy. Stawar was a party member at the time the *Lever* was publishing his articles. The architect and painter Mieczysław Szczuka also wrote for it. The constructivism of the artistic avant-garde still coexisted easily with visionary revolution and its great plans for the future. The *Literary Monthly* was the continuation of the *Lever*. Aleksander Wat was the editor in chief, but it was Stawar who gave the monthly its orientation and its importance. In addition to former contributors to the *Lever*, new writers joined the team; Leon Schiller and Władysław Daszewski were on the editorial board. The *Literary Monthly* appeared from 1929 to 1931. I didn't know it existed, but Miłosz, only three years my senior, already read the *Monthly* regularly. And he was fascinated by it. He mentions this in his conversations with Wat in Wat's *My Century* (*Mój wiek*). He was fascinated not by the literary works published in the *Literary Monthly*, nor by the Marxist criticism, but by the reportage on Polish misery. At our ages a difference of three years was considerable.

It was only in the winter of 1934 or the spring of 1935 that someone brought me some tattered old copies of the *Monthly*. I was living with my grandparents on Senatorska Street. I belonged to the Association of Democratic Polish Youth, but I had already begun to go Communist. It was Janusz Kowalewski who brought me the *Monthly;* he was one of my two "angels" in the party. The second was Witold Trylski, tall, broad-shouldered, and very dark. He looked like a Jew but wasn't. He taught courses at the polytechnic and was in charge of the clandestine Communist student organization. He always came wearing a heavy jacket and never wanted to take it off. In 1940, Janusz was arrested in Lvov the same night as Broniewski and Wat were and sent to the camps somewhere near the Arctic Circle. He returned to Italy with Anders's army via the Near East, and after the war he remained in the West as one of the most intransigent opponents of the Communist regime. Witold was hanged at dawn on 16 October 1942 with nine others on the same scaffold near the railroad crossing in the Wola district. It was the first mass execution in Warsaw. That morning eighty-nine people, Communists and non-Communists, were hanged in the suburbs of Warsaw. Janusz and Witold, my two party guardians from youth—how different their destinies were. Destiny is stronger than character. For if Janusz had remained in occupied Warsaw and Witold had reached London after the camps and Italy, their fates would have been reversed.

It was Janusz and Witold who persuaded me to install the mail drop in my grandparents' apartment. At the designated password I was to receive and deliver letters and packages. The place was well chosen: since my grandfather was a gynecologist, someone was constantly at the door ringing the bell during his office hours. But my grandmother began to be suspicious of my "guests." "Who are these strange people asking for you at all hours? What sort of students are they?"

Not only did I not belong to the Communist party, I didn't even belong to the university Life; the people in that cell considered me too weak ideologically. "Sign up for MOPR (the International Organization for Aid to Political Prisoners) and you'll be a fellow traveler. That will be better for you and for us."

Not one member of the *Forge*'s editorial board had been a member of the party before the war. We had at most been members of the Polish Workers party during the Occupation. I now think that the selection of the board members was made consciously. The party, accused of being "infiltrated by agents," was dissolved by the Comintern in 1938. The Communists who had tried to oppose this resolution were condemned as Trotskyites. Perhaps the founders wanted the *Forge* to start from scratch without any prior baggage. And perhaps that was the source of our enthusiasm and our arrogance in those first postwar years. It seemed to us that we had become Marxists by our own choice and of our own free will. In fact, we had become "Marxists" with the blessing of Borejsza and Jakub Berman. I think that Stawar must have had a good deal of contempt for our brand of "Marxism." And not only Stawar.

Borejsza called the *Forge* "the great tribune of the progressive intelligentsia." But Żółkiewski and the smart ones among us realized quickly that the legend of the *Literary Monthly* was still alive. The *Lever* and the *Monthly* meant Stawar. "We have to do something about Stawar." We decided to take his case to Berman.

Comrade Berman was then number two. Among other things, culture and security were in his hands. This overlapping of functions, which only looks strange on the surface, is characteristic of the system. It was Orwell, I think, who first commented on this phenomenon. Berman had been warned of our visit. The security officers passed us down the line from one agent to another, ushering us through five or six empty rooms in succession. The felt-padded doors closed noiselessly behind us. In the final room, almost as empty as the others, Berman was seated behind an enormous desk, under a portrait of Stalin. "Sit down, comrades."

He was called Jakub of the Golden Voice. Berman could mesmerize with his voice. He knew it. The almost velvet tones of his voice were like those of a great tenor. But now we saw another Berman. He got up, grew red in the face, banged his fist down on the table, and almost went hoarse from screaming: "Let him get down on his knees and take back all the lies he has spread about us."

Stawar was not "pardoned" until 1955. By then the *Forge* had already been out of business for five years. It had been disbanded for a lack of vigilance. In 1949 Gomułka had been removed from power and shortly thereafter put in jail. His trial was three years in the making. The noose tightened until Stalin's death in March 1953; at the end of that memorable year, a slight thaw set in. At first in security and in culture. Tortured prisoners began to be released; the literary reviews and their editorial boards changed. Iwaszkiewicz took Ważyk's place as the editor in chief of *Creativity (Twórczość)*. At one of the first meetings of the new editorial board, it asked Stawar for a contribution. But Berman's approval was still necessary.

Many years later, the unforgettable Roman Karst, during one of our evening walks in Stony Brook, told me about that meeting of the staff at *Creativity:* " 'Roman, you are his comrade from the party," said Jarosław Iwaszkiewicz. "Go to Mr. Berman and tell him why we want to publish Stawar.' " "Berman seemed to have gone completely downhill." Roman continued his story. "There was nothing left of his former dynamism. He thundered for a moment but then sat there all hunched up behind his desk under a huge portrait of Stalin. 'Publish him if you want, let him write about Sholokhov, but in the first article, he's got to practice self-criticism.' " A few months later a long essay by Stawar on Sholokhov appeared in *Creativity,* but without a single word of self-criticism.

In 1957 Stawar published his *Literary Essays* and then, in the following three years, his studies of Boy-Żeleński, Gałczyński, and Sienkiewicz. Those were good years for Stawar, but he was becoming increasingly ill. He spent entire months at the writers' retreat in Zakopane. At the end of 1960 he was allowed to travel to the West for treatment. A few months later, word reached Warsaw that he had gone to live in Maisons-Lafitte, the home of Jerzy Giedroyć's émigré monthly, *Kultura,* and that he was writing a new book.

Stawar died in the first week of August 1961. The next day, a plane brought the urn with his ashes back to Poland after a short ceremony at the crematorium. The whole hurried affair was organized by Putrament, the secretary of the party at the Writers' Union. Three young writers picked up the urn at the airport. Years later, one of them told me that they had had trouble locating the urn. Finally, in the storage area for unclaimed packages, they found a small box marked "Duty-Free." The urn was inside. They took it directly to the cemetery, holding the urn on their knees as the car was so small. The funeral took place at state expense, complete with a military band, color guards, party and state delegates, and burial in the area reserved for the meritorious in Powązki cemetery. Putrament was the main speaker at the grave site. He spoke of Comrade Stawar the model Marxist writer and activist, faithful to the party to the very end.

Many writers had come to the funeral. It was a muggy day and we were sweating profusely. But I think it wasn't just from the heat. M. leaned over toward me: "Putrament stole his body, but Giedroyć took his soul." Did Putrament know? We knew. The whole funeral was like a nightmare from which we could not wake up.

Several months after Stawar's death, the Literary Institute of Paris, *Kultura,* published his *Last Writings.* The book contained self-criticism, but not the kind that Berman had wanted. In *My Century* Aleksander Wat writes that he received a letter Stawar wrote shortly before his death. He said that he left Poland to be able to publish the book. In the book he assembled articles that had been published in the underground after the Polish Communist party was dissolved in 1938 on Stalin's orders. Stawar defended the dismantled party. This voice had had to wait almost a quarter of a century to appear again in an émigré publication that was part of a dissident tradition already over a century old.

I last saw Jerzy Stempowski in Paris in the summer of 1968. He was already barely audible, speaking almost in a whisper. He had gone to see Stawar in the hospital in Paris every day until the end. Stawar had a prolonged and difficult death. After the end, Stempowski put the dentures back in Stawar's mouth. He considered this a last service that would make Stawar more dignified. I think that this image of an "unhurried passerby," as Stempowski called himself, inserting dentures in the mouth of the dead emigré is worth remembering and preserving in the bitter history of Polish exiles.

2.

His first name was Szczęsny—"Lucky" in English. A nice pseudonym at the time of the German Occupation, but that was his real name. Szczęsny Dobrowolski's funeral took place three or four weeks after Stawar's, in August 1961 or perhaps at the beginning of September, in the same area for the meritorious in the military section of the cemetery. With standard bearers and an honor guard.

About a year and a half before the uprising, Szczęsny and I met once or twice a week at the vulcanizer's workshop on

Żurawia Street. We always met at the same time, 11:45 a.m., in the same apartment building, the fourth or fifth house from Marszałkowska Street, on the side with odd numbers. The vulcanizer was an old member of the Polish Communist party who had been through a lot, not only spending some time in prison but also being accused of betraying his closest friends, which kept him from joining the new party. He had received so many hard knocks that he resolved: never again. But he remained a sympathizer. He gave us a place to meet and storage space behind his workshop where we could keep, before further distribution, half the printing of the bimonthly *Young Democracy*. There must have been two or three hundred copies, in small, octavo format. And sometimes other fliers and underground bulletins.

There were six or seven of us in that cell of the People's Army, including Leszek, who had recruited me for the work and witnessed my oath; Hedda, our liaison; and Szczęsny, who was responsible for us politically. Hedda had large blue eyes; they grew round when she raised her eyebrows slightly. They changed color, too: sometimes they were completely transparent. Szczęsny, perhaps three or four years my senior, was tall, very thin, and even then slightly stooped. Constantly in a hurry, he walked fast; I could never keep up with him. He wrote editorials for our paper, always on what was to come. After the great victory, of course.

The vulcanizer got to like me. He looked like an old man, but he couldn't have been more than fifty at the time. He was almost crippled, and his mustache was streaked with gray. Sometimes we were left alone. "With you," he would say, "I can talk, but that tall guy"—he was thinking of Szczęsny—"is stubborn as a mule. It's only the future generations he cares about. Let those future generations take care of themselves— I've been slaving for them all my life." But he helped us as much as he could.

Hedda was indefatigable. We each had a life of our own. A job, studies, a family. Hedda worked around the clock, from dawn until curfew. In the bag she always carried with her she kept a toothbrush, a change of underwear, and a jacket or a raincoat. She did not need much else. She slept wherever she could. Her husband, Bartoszek, had been killed in an attack on the Społem bank in the spring of 1943. At that point I barely knew Hedda. She never spoke about it later on. She never talked about personal matters. There wasn't enough time for that.

One always came to the meeting at exactly the fixed time, down to the very minute, because one never could tell. But once—it was in October or November—I was fifteen minutes late. I no longer remember why. I was coming from Bielany, and there must have been a breakdown on the trolley line. When I turned off Marszałkowska onto Żurawia, it was already close to noon. A black limousine like those used by the Gestapo was standing in front of the gate to the vulcanizer's. I walked by the gate and crossed to the other side of the street. I kept retracing the rectangle made by the four intersecting streets. I took the second street that went back to Marszałkowska and then to Żurawia. They must have caught Hedda. We always stayed at the vulcanizer's as short a time as possible. Sometimes only five minutes. To leave an article, take a leaflet. If I had come on time, perhaps we would have gotten away in time. Those were not the best moments of my life. The Gestapo, I felt sure, must have arrested Hedda because I was late.

At the corner of Mokotowska, as I was making my second circuit, Hedda threw her arms around my neck. She was deathly pale. She had been desperately walking the same rectangle, but on the opposite side. She had come to the workshop ten minutes too early and had waited for me until ten minutes to twelve. She had some other urgent "mail" to deliver nearby. When she came back fifteen minutes later, the black car was standing in front of the gate. She was sure that they had caught me because of her. If only she had waited five minutes more, perhaps both of us might have succeeded in getting away. The Gestapo had arrived—someone must have turned the place in—at five minutes to twelve.

That wasn't the first or the last time that we managed to slip out of a trap. But not all of us were so fortunate. The vulcanizer was shot or tortured to death at Gestapo headquarters on Aleja

Szucha that same week. The workshop was sealed. Nearly half an issue of the journal and a pile of leaflets had been left behind in storage. We could not stand to lose so much material. We reported what had happened to the center. A couple of days later two boys from the sabotage section—they attended the lectures on Marxist philosophy—came on bicycles just before the curfew, broke down the sealed door, and cleaned out the place down to the last scrap of paper. One of the two was Szczęsny. That's how I found out that he was also in another section of the underground.

Hedda was arrested five years later. And Szczęsny a few weeks after her. In countries like ours history moves swiftly. Or rather it repeats itself swiftly. After Gomułka and General Spychalski had been sent to prison, the trials of ever-lower-ranking members of the People's Army and the party during the Occupation went ahead apace. Or perhaps Hedda and Szczęsny were arrested even before Gomułka and Spychalski were put in jail? We were living in Wrocław at the time, and that summer or autumn the municipal authorities assigned me a house, or rather half a house with a garden, in a beautiful neighborhood, near Parkowa Street. In recognition of my being a writer or perhaps my being a professor. And, certainly, a party member. The previous year we had lived with my wife's parents. Shortly before we moved to our own house, the mailman—he was an old mailman from Lvov who had brought the mail to the family before the war—said to my father-in-law, "Professor, all the young gentleman's mail is being taken directly to the security police." When Lidia repeated that to me, I said that the mailman was a reactionary and that I didn't believe him. Hedda's arrest was not, of course, the first that I knew of, but it was the first arrest of someone from our group—the six- or seven-member cell of the People's Army formed during the Occupation.

A week or two after Hedda's arrest, I went to Warsaw. From the local party headquarters, I had made an appointment with Colonel Bristiger by a special telephone called "vu-che" in Russian. She was—I believe—a deputy minister or a director in a special department in the Ministry of Security. She was from Lvov and had apparently showed great promise as a historian of the early Middle Ages. She had spent many years in prison and now occupied a very high position in the Communist party of the Western Ukraine and in the central committee of the International Organization for Aid to Political Prisoners. A heavyset middle-aged woman, she must have been ten years older than I was; she had large, moist eyes, which at times seemed to catch fire, and thick, fleshy lips. She was interested in literature. Or rather, because of her line of work, she was interested in writers. In writers who lived in Poland and especially in writers who had lived in, or emigrated to, the West.

She greeted me cordially. Even warmly. The cordiality disconcerted me. We knew each other only from a few discussions and conferences. She knew why I had come and of course everything about me. I told her about the ever-present toothbrush in Hedda's bag and about our meeting place on Żurawia Street. "We appreciate your concern, comrade professor. I shall take charge of the Bartoszek case personally. Everything will be gone into thoroughly. If the accusations are groundless, she will be released immediately. I give you my word. Come see me personally"—she glanced at her calendar—"next Friday. We're here till late at night working."

I went to see her the following week. She was even warmer than before. Almost compassionate. "You were mistaken, professor. Hedda was an enemy agent long before you first met her. On the very night that Comrade Bartoszek died fighting heroically, there was an orgy in the brothel on Złota Street. Hedda took part in it, with at least five officers from the Gestapo. Here is her confession, which she signed herself. Go to the secretariat next door, get her dossier, and read it. But next time don't be so quick to risk your neck for someone else. Her present husband, Comrade A. from the Central Committee, has not intervened. Take him as an example." I didn't go to the secretariat. That evening I left for Wrocław.

I knew that Hedda had stayed in the apparatus after the war. She was in the chief command of the newly organized scouts, in some international women's associations, and in who knows what else. During all those turbulent years I saw her only a few times. And that was in passing. But I heard various things from different sources. She knew foreign languages, traveled to the West frequently, and, I assume, worked in our intelligence or in something closely related. Never for an instant did I believe in that orgy on Złota Street or in the American intelligence story. But all the time on that crowded night train from Warsaw to Wrocław, I kept thinking that there must be something—otherwise why would they have taken her to the security prison on Rakowiecka Street? In intelligence nothing is free; information must be exchanged or paid for in one way or another. Hedda liked men. Maybe she had a lover on the other side; maybe she went too far in something she said or had talked at the wrong time.

I learned of the arrest of Szczęsny from the newspapers. It was immediately made public that he had been recruited as a spy during the Occupation. This time I did not intervene. By the end of the year, I was the only one of our vulcanizer's group except Leszek who remained free. But Leszek had joined the Democratic party immediately after the war.

They lèt Hedda out in the early or late spring of 1954. She was one of the first prisoners to be released. After five years in prison. We were living in Warsaw again by then. I went to see her the day after she was released. She looked quite well, although her face seemed somewhat bloated. She still had those enormous transparent blue eyes of hers. But they were completely dead. I cried out: "You are innocent, innocent! Now *they* are behind bars. Różański was turned over to the prosecutor a week ago." I tried to embrace her, but Hedda pushed me away gently. She looked at the wall above my head. "I am guilty," she said quietly, in a completely natural voice. As in a conversation among friends. "We are all guilty, Janek. I was recruited in Spain in 1935. Go to the room next door and write your biography. Starting with your birth. Here is paper and pencil. Pens are not allowed. And when you've finished, give it to me, go back to the room next door, and write it all over again from the beginning. But remember to number the pages." A week later she was sent off to an asylum. She came back after a few months. She began to work again. Then she gave birth to a daughter. I saw her occasionally. There was a gentle touch of melancholy about her. She always seemed to be somewhere else, but she still had those eyes of hers, translucent as water. And she stayed in the apparatus.

Szczęsny was also released at that time. Rehabilitated, he returned to his former position, except now he was a deputy editor not of the party paper but of *Warsaw Life*. From time to time I read his editorials about "the former period of errors and distortions," about the new leadership, about exceeding the planned quotas . . . Apparently he drank a lot.

For a long time I didn't see him. We did not meet again for two or three years, until 1956 or 1957. In a government clinic. Besides the *nomenklatura,* laureates of state awards, "protected" newspaper people, and distinguished artists, actors, writers, and scholars were entitled to use the clinic. Compared to other Polish hospitals, the government clinic was luxuriously equipped, but it did not enjoy the best reputation among doctors. I was taken to my room by the head nurse. An exceptionally ugly older woman. "Comrade professor," she addressed me, "you of course know what sort of hospital you are in. Half our patients are buried in the Powązki cemetery, in the plots for the meritorious."

I had come to the clinic for appendicitis, but I caught pneumonia there and was not able to leave for three weeks. When I began taking walks in the corridors, I met Szczęsny. It turned out that our rooms were on the same floor. He was being treated for duodenal ulcers and other stomach problems. Typical prison illnesses. He had aged enormously and was all hunched over, and, wearing those striped clinic pajamas in the dark corridor, he looked as if he had just got out of a concentration camp. He walked very strangely. I knew that he had been tortured—longer than anyone else. At first he had confessed to everything and immediately signed whatever they wanted because he was told that it was for the good of the party. But after two or three months he came to the conclusion that something terrible had happened and that he had fallen into the hands of Fascists; he retracted all his confessions. That's when they tortured him for months. He was let out, as Hedda had been, after five years.

Two or three times at the clinic we drank a bottle of Georgian cognac together on the sly, even though it wasn't the best thing either for his health or for mine. We never spoke about the past. What good would it have done? One day he said to me, "What's the point of saying anything, old pal? We know it all by heart." But he was wrong. I didn't yet know it all.

Szczęsny's funeral took place about five years after our meeting in the clinic. The military honor guard fired a salute. His medals and decorations—of which there were many, both civilian and military—were carried on a cushion. The government and the party sent funeral wreaths so heavy that two people could barely carry them. Speeches were given by two obese comrades from the Central Committee, both reading from notes, and then by the editor in chief of *Warsaw Life*. They all spoke of Comrade Szczęsny's uncompromising stance and his beautiful life.

Over one hundred people accompanied Szczęsny on his last journey: old comrades; new comrades; those who had already managed to quit the party or who had been thrown out of it; the plainclothes security police and their victims; the interrogators and public prosecutors and their rehabilitated prisoners, who had served their five or eight years behind bars. After all, this was 1961; Gomułka had been returned to power, the Polish October had long passed, and the zealots from the period of "distortions and the cult of personality" had returned to the security and the party apparatus. At the funeral the torturers and the tortured jointly rendered final honors to Szczęsny. This seemed perfectly natural, normal, and ordinary to everyone. And that was what was truly appalling.

M. drove me back to town in his black Volga. We didn't exchange a single word during the entire drive from the cemetery. It was only when we got to my place that he said, "Straight out of Shakespeare, eh?"

3.

That same autumn, during a search, Holland jumped or was pushed out the window of his room on the sixth or eighth floor of his apartment building on Nowotko Street, just at the corner of Świerczewski Street. His funeral also took place in Powązki, though not in the plots for the meritorious but in the new part of the cemetery, where the graves seem to be dug in the open field.

The last time we were together for an extended period was in the same government clinic, when Szczęsny and I were there for treatment. Henio had a gallstone; I don't know whether he thought of it himself or whether his doctors advised him to, but twice a day, in the morning and in the afternoon, he would jump step by step, two feet at a time, down the clinic stairs. The clinic was five stories high, and Henio Holland hopped from the top floor to the bottom. He provided great amusement for everyone, and the healthier patients gathered to watch the show. But that didn't bother Henio; he always enjoyed being the center of attention: "Have you given birth to that stone yet, Mr. Holland?"

I had known him for a long time. He belonged to the first postwar rosters of the Communist Youth Association and he had hung around the *Forge* and the Pickwick in Łódź. He went as a reporter to the Recovered Territories and even to Germany. I see him in his uniform, half-military, half-civilian, always too big for him, with torn pockets. He was always boasting of his military and sexual conquests. But he wasn't offended when we refused to believe him. The good soldier Schweik. Apparently that pose suited him. But in fact, when he was in the army he conducted himself with great courage at the front.

After that I remember him from the "Astoria," the writers' retreat in Zakopane. We must have spent two seasons there together. Breakfasts weren't the most joyous moments of the day, especially when it had been raining for weeks, as was often the case in the mountains. After a night spend drinking, usually followed by too little sleep, the boarders would come down to breakfast, as though about to face God's judgment, with slow steps and pained expressions. "Well, what's your complaint today, pal—physical, psychic, or erotic?" But one morning Henio came down smiling and cheerful as never before. The previous evening he had not come to supper, and he always ate for two.

"What happened to you, Henio?" we asked.

"Two female students asked me to supper."

"You ought to be ashamed of yourself, Henio, taking advantage of penniless girls!"

"Penniless is hardly what they were," he said, pouting. "I followed them along Krupówki Street to a bookstore; they went in and bought some books." Henio literally trembled with astonishment. "Books! They had no idea what to do with their money. I invited them to have coffee with me, and the girls got loose and took me to supper."

From then on "got loose" entered our vocabulary. "What young thing got loose for you today, Henio?"

No, it was difficult to treat Henio seriously. It occasionally happens that a theater director by mistake, out of malice, or for unknown reasons casts a comic actor in a tragic role. Sometimes the results are astonishing, as when Woszczerowicz, one of the greatest Polish comic actors, played the role of Richard III. But history? History seems to be infallible in its casting of comic and tragic parts. Of all my friends and acquaintances, Henryk Holland was the least destined to play the role of a tragic hero. And yet he was treated seriously. For several hours his badly mangled body lay on the sidewalk of Nowotko Street near Świerczewski Street, guarded by an undercover agent and two uniformed policemen. Perhaps History knew what it was doing when it cast Henryk in the role of its unknown hero. He was hated by the apparatus and the security.

The mystery of his death has never been satisfactorily cleared up. At a certain point all attempts to explain it have run into a stone wall or become mired in contradictions. Only one thing is certain: Holland's arrest was connected with revelations and leaks from the Twentieth Congress in February 1956. Rumors were then circulating in Warsaw of Khrushchev's drunken outpourings about Beria's liquidation in the Kremlin. How on the very evening after Stalin's funeral, Beria locked himself and his staff in KGB headquarters, which were guarded by tanks from the Special Forces. The Politburo, with Khrushchev and Malenkov at its head, locked itself in the Kremlin, which was guarded by the armored divisions hastily dispatched to Moscow by Marshal Zhukov. The conversations between the masters of Russia were conducted exclusively over special government telephone lines. Khrushchev knew perfectly well that the whole Kremlin had been wiretapped by Beria, so he communicated with his comrades on little scraps of paper that they burned immediately afterward. Both sides were petrified.

"At that moment," Khrushchev ranted, "I thought of a stratagem. We called a solemn session of the Politburo and elected Beria to the post of first secretary. Unanimously! We sent that upright Voroshilov to inform Beria and bring him to us. Beria thought he knew everything because he had had the room bugged, and the old fox fell into the trap. When he came in and sat down at the table, first Malenkov, all two hundred pounds of him, jumped on Beria and started to smother him. Then we all joined in and strangled the viper together." Khrushchev chuckled. "The trial took place and he was formally sentenced to death . . . long after he was in the other world."

The official communiqué about Beria's trial was released much later. According to that report, Beria was executed after a trial that took place three months after Stalin's funeral. Before the execution he had even asked for mercy!

Holland met with W., a correspondent for *Le Monde,* at the Dom Chłopa Hotel in Warsaw. It was well known that for foreign guests, hard-currency whores, and all sorts of local big shots this new hotel had specially reserved rooms equipped with superb listening devices. Holland liked to impress people with firsthand information. And that is what probably cost him his life. The conversation was recorded.

He was arrested the following day and taken to the prison on Daniłowiczowska Street, whose basement had served as security headquarters even before the war. A prosecutor issued a warrant for a search of his apartment. This was the epoch of "legality"; the search had to take place in the presence of the defendant. The next day Holland was taken to his one-room apartment. According to the official version, during the search he jumped out the window onto the sidewalk on Nowotko Street, right next to Dzierżyński Square, as it was then and for a long afterward called. The names of streets and squares in Warsaw have often acquired strange and unexpected connotations. Nowotko was parachuted into Poland not far from Warsaw shortly after Hitler's invasion of Russia in 1941. He was supposed to rebuild the Communist party and be its first secretary. He did become first secretary, but only very briefly. He was shot by one of his closest comrades, who was also parachuted into Poland, probably on orders from Moscow. The exact circumstances of his death have never been fully revealed. Today stamps display Nowotko's picture. At the end of November 1989 the statue of Feliks Dzierżyński in the square next to the street bearing Nowotko's name was torn down. Now Nowotko Street is next to Bank Square. These changes of street names could be a good illustration of "objective" Hegelian history.

Henio was one of the most cheerful people I have ever known. He was always pleased with himself, perhaps too much so. But even if he had broken down under the interrogation and suddenly panicked for a moment, how had such a leap out the window been possible technically? There were three security policemen with him in that small room, and in keeping with the regulations and with unchanging practice, one of them was supposed to stand by the window and the window had to be closed. In any case, it was wintertime.

So he was thrown out the window. Alive? Defenestration has never been a Polish custom or a practice of the security forces. If it had been decided to murder him, there were methods less compromising and just as efficient. And so they threw a corpse out the window. But if he had died during the interrogation—and he would not have been the first—the security police knew what to do in cases like that: "There are witnesses in this world." There are doctors, for example. He could have died during the search, of course. And in a sudden panic they threw the body out the window. But the functionaries are trained to do nothing without an order. Unless someone hidden directed the murderers from a distance. One thing is certain: on that pavement in front of the building in which he lived lay the corpse of Henryk Holland.

I don't remember whether or not there was an obituary in *Warsaw Life*. But in any case over a hundred of us came to the funeral. The Powązki cemetery was swarming with undercover agents. "Just like the old Communist funerals before the war," said Edda Werfel, whom I met at the gate. She was an old party member. We looked around furtively. It seemed that we were sneaking into this funeral. As if it were an illegal demonstration. There was something shameful in our fear. We all felt the same way.

It was a bitter funeral. Without speeches, without funeral wreaths. It was only when the coffin was lowered into the grave on ropes that bouquets of dark chrysanthemums and a few orchids bought at the gate fell into the pit along with handfuls of earth. And then, I don't know who—perhaps it was Leszek Kołakowski—intoned the *Internationale*. That hymn, whose melody and words had long been dead and which, sung at countless official gatherings, now belonged to the ritual of conformity and submission, here, at Holland's funeral, unexpectedly resounded as a defiant challenge: "Arise, you wretched of the earth."

The Heart Attack

To Doctor Halina Kotlicka

I.

Two days before, I had been invited to lunch by friends on Aleja Róż. I was staying on Nabielak Street, right at the corner of Gagarin Street, where, a few houses farther down, almost opposite the gate to Łazienki Park, Zofia Nałkowska had sold cigarettes during the war. I had been to her house two or three times. I always came back through Łazienki Park. That particular morning I had nothing to do, I didn't have to hurry, so I decided to go through the park along by the Orangerie and then up toward the Belvedere. I walked for almost an hour; I could feel my heart in my throat and at least three different times I had to sit down on a bench.

As everyone knows, the world shrinks as we put childhood behind us. The Saxon Garden is full of mystery and still impossible for me to cross. I was left alone there as a child and got lost when I ran after a boy in a sailor suit on a tricycle who went down a side alley near Królewska Street, a hundred feet from the satyr with the chipped nose. The world that shrinks and grows tame as childhood recedes expands when old age sets in. Not horizontally but vertically. What was level becomes hilly; flat suddenly becomes steep. Houses without elevators suddenly acquire stories they didn't have before. Quaker Path, the street where I live in Stony Brook, seemed flat as a board to me for ten years. Two years ago, as I was walking back from the campus carrying a heavy briefcase (it had never seemed heavy before), I noticed that midway home my street went uphill, and halfway up I had to stop and put my briefcase down on the ground.

Of course I always knew that there was a Lower and a Higher Łazienki. But it was only then, at the time of my last walk before the heart attack, that I realized to my astonishment that the Lower Łazienki was lower and that the Higher Łazienki was higher. Almost as high as Giewont in the Tatras.

2.

The pain was dull. It was really very mild, but there was something strange about: it started at the breastbone but seemed not to end anywhere. The pain was slight yet somehow diffused throughout my entire body. I felt I had to lie down immediately. I was having lunch at the Journalists Club and I asked to be taken back to my apartment on Nabielak Street. I did not finish my coffee and I put out a half-smoked cigarette. It was only a week later, when I craved nicotine again, that I remembered the half-smoked cigarette, felt its taste in my throat, and regretted that I hadn't finished it.

Back in the house, I lay down, but the pain didn't go away. It continued to be mild and I was only surprised that, given its mildness, I did not feel like getting up or even talking. I was supposed to attend a party that afternoon, and I first sent word that I would be late, then that I would not come at all. The following morning at six I was supposed to leave for Cracow. If it hadn't been for that early-morning trip, I never would have called Dr. Kotlicka. "I have strange pains," I told her.

The ambulance arrived half an hour later. The attendants carried me on a stretcher. It seemed a superfluous ritual to me. At the emergency room on Stępińska Street, they asked me if I could walk to the electrocardiograph unit. It seemed ridiculous to me to think I couldn't cover that distance myself—it was only thirty or forty steps. I went back to the waiting room on my own. A few moments later the doctor on duty came in and said it was a heart attack. So I wouldn't be going to Cracow. I telephoned Irena Szymańska and asked her to notify everyone there that I would not be coming and that it was a heart attack. "Where are you, in the ICU?" At the time I didn't know what an ICU or an intensive care unit was, but the tone of her voice told me that something serious had happened. To me. I knew I should call Dr. Kotlicka immediately. "Let me talk to the doctor," she said. She must have yelled at the doctor on duty frightfully, because from inside, somewhere in the depths of my body, I heard her saying that I should be made to lie down and that she was sending an ambulance. It was not until I was put on the stretcher again that it finally dawned on me that I was having a heart attack. Up until then other people had heart attacks. All I knew about heart attacks was that one dies of them.

3.

The pain continued to be dull. But it seemed to be everywhere. Or rather it was as if I were detached from the pain. That is, it seemed to me as if I were leaving myself and the pain behind and going away somewhere. Just as one can leave oneself for a moment while on marijuana and, with a certain effort, come back again. And as happens after smoking marijuana, time slows down and feels different inside. And inside me the same dull pain was always there. I don't know how long I waited for the ambulance—a quarter of an hour or twenty-four hours.

I held someone's hand in the ambulance. Probably one of the nurses from Międzylesie. I was not scared. Later I remembered that I told her not to be scared and that I was only pretending to be in pain. And that none of it was real. What really hurt me was the intravenous injection. The needle was inserted into a vein of my right wrist, which had been immobilized. Perhaps the veins were too frail or too narrow, but it seemed as though the needle was constantly being withdrawn and then inserted again.

I knew I was being saved. Three or four heads were bent over me. But I felt myself being torn to pieces, the way one sometimes is in dreams full of hideous tortures—my right arm seemed detached from my body, as though it had been severed; the intravenous injection was connected to it, and that was the chief cause of pain; my left arm was bound and swathed so my blood pressure could be taken. My lips, to which a rubber oxygen tube was taped, seemed to be totally detached. I still was not scared. I must have lost and regained consciousness many times, but of those long hours of alien time (until three in the morning, as I was later told, I was not left alone even for an instant) I remember only the pricking of injections and a pair of eyes very near me. I knew that I was drifting away. "We're not going to drift off again today, you're not going to drift off again." I knew that someone said that to me sometime. But who and when? And I really wanted to drift off. So that the pain in my right arm would stop. Time and again I thought to myself that I was drifting off—without blood, without suffocation, with that pain which was so easy to leave behind. I had the sensation that I was drifting off into whiteness.

4.

"You almost got away from us several times yesterday," said the nurse who brought a basin of water the next morning. "Did you ever make a fuss last night!" the patient next to me chimed in. I couldn't respond, as the oxygen tube was still taped to my mouth. I couldn't sit up either; I felt my whole body wrapped in soft tubes that gripped me like the coils of a snake. Only later did I notice that those tubes were attached to five metal disks on my chest.

Now I knew what an ICU was. I was in the recovery room of the Railroad Union Hospital in Międzylesie. The two other patients who shared my room, one across from me and the other to my left, had also suffered heart attacks. This was the morning after the attack. After my attack. A heart attack always has its day and hour: when it begins and when it ends. The attack itself is brief. One lives in time either before the heart attack or after the heart attack.

In its brevity, dying of a heart attack is different from dying of cancer. This is true for the sick person and, to some extent, for his family and friends. By dying, I mean not the progress of the disease and the body's battle against it but the fear and dread of death experienced by the sick person and those closest to him. In my experience, dying was drifting away. For other heart-attack victims, dying is a piercing pain in the chest. For family and friends a heart attack is a series of late-night calls to the doctor on duty. Both for the family and for the victim, the dramaturgy of a heart attack is accelerated.

Dying of cancer takes weeks, months, sometimes years. It begins long before the diagnosis and often continues even after the verdict is reversed and the tumor is pronounced benign. I experienced the agony of prolonged waiting when, some twenty years ago, I had to undergo surgery for removal of what appeared in the X ray as a dark spot the size of a walnut on the upper lobe of my right lung. For weeks I saw the fear in Lidia's eyes. I described this agony in "A Short Treatise on Dying."

The experience of a heart attack is different. Once the attack is over, one is cured definitively or temporarily. Of course, another attack is possible; so is a second, a third, or a fourth. But the prognosis of death with coronary diseases has a different character than it does with cancer. And not only a different character but a different—I don't know what else to call it—metaphysic. Five years without metastasis counts as being cured of cancer. Once you are cured, "dying of cancer" takes the form of an incurable fear of metastasis. Dying of cancer is slow or rapid, continuous and gradual, but always without respite. Cancer is a death sentence with a reprieve. Dying is actually the reprieve. In English, an incurable illness is called a terminal illness. The dread and horror of cancer—so movingly described by Susan Sontag in her *Illness as Metaphor*—is that intransgressible terminus ad quem which confers on the illness the terrifying shape of a sentence, a destiny, a *fatum*. As if it were the work of dark forces from the other world. A heart attack has no terminus and there are no dark forces. There is only one's own heart, which has held up or failed.

The heart is a sack with two auricles and two chambers. This sack is a pump. The blood from the veins flows through the auricles to the chambers, from where it is expelled to the pulmonary arteries and the aorta. A heart attack is a wound. A part of the coronary muscle becomes atrophied and blocks the flow of blood. An attack is a necrosis of the heart—its partial death if one survives and its complete death if one does not. A wound to the heart heals, like all wounds, but like all wounds it leaves a scar. This scar remains to the end of one's life. The ECG is the most precise record of the heart's wounds. This record is a graph. The graphic memory of the heart attack is the underside of a wave, a valley instead of a peak in a maze of trajectories on cardiographic paper. The lines on our fingertips do not change from birth to death. They are the only infallible graph of our identity. The broken lines of the electro-cardiogram, their elevations and declivities, their summits and valleys chronicle the history of our heart.

5.

When I raised my head I saw a box the size of a small tele-vision set above the bed of the patient across from me. A sharp light like a dry-point needle relentlessly traced a pulsat-ing record from the electrocardiograph to the screen. Later, when I could prop myself up, I saw above my bed an identical luminous screen, which was connected to five electrodes on my chest. On the third or fourth day of my stay in the ICU, Halina Mikołajska came to visit me. When I sat up to hug her, she froze. She was not looking at me—she was staring at the screen. I remembered her in many roles and I remembered the many times on stage she had appeared petrified, her doe eyes wide-open and almost translucent, like Pallas Athena's, her small, silver-haired head incomparably mounted on a long and fragile neck. Never, in any of her roles, had I ever seen her so transfixed with terror. When I moved to greet her, two elec-trodes on my chest had slipped off and become detached. The luminous notation on the green screen stopped wiggling up and down and stretched out into a broad horizontal line. The nurse on duty instantly rushed up to my bed. A horizontal line on the screen indicates cardiac arrest. But in this case, it was only the electrodes that had fallen off. The nurse reattached them. Many weeks later, Halina told me that the dancing line on the screen above my tousled hair had come back to her in dreams.

But look, oh, look upon his heart
Like a scarlet ribbon hung
Or corals on a necklace strung.
A bleeding stripe there takes its start
   And stretches down from breast to feet.
   (Mickiewicz, *Forefathers' Eve,* trans. M. B. Peacock)

As I grew stronger, I would prop myself up on the pillows and stare intently at the screen above my bed. With each more energetic movement the luminous lines jumped on the screen as though suddenly startled. I gazed into my beating heart. "Look how my heart beats," I would say, placing Lidia's hand on my chest. *Look!* Only your fingers or mine could "see" the heart beating beneath warm and naked flesh. But now for the first time I *saw* the graph of a beating heart.

In the third week, when I was allowed to walk around, I often sneaked into the nurses' duty room at night. On eight small screens above a large table, the hearts beat in luminous zigzags. The heart of every patient in the recovery room was plugged into one of those little screens. If they didn't chase me out, I could gaze into those beating hearts for hours on end. Each heart beat differently; the zigzags of the luminous lines drew pointed or blunt teeth, moving like the fine stitching of a sewing machine or the sweeping strokes of a pen. But all the hearts were pulsating, and I was fascinated by that luminous pulse. In the dead of night I was spying on other people's hearts. There was something disturbingly erotic in this experience. The heart's pulse during those hospital nights seemed to me to be the pulse of sex.

6.

A hospital always exists as a separate place and a separate time, but in the recovery room, during the weeks of immobility, both time and place are even more distinctly set apart. Sartre wrote that characters and events in Faulkner's novels immediately retreat into the past like the landscape and highway seen through the rear window of a moving car. They are instantly in time past. Before they are, they already were.

In a *healthy* life, we stand firm in a kind of motionless movement, like the passengers on an escalator; we remain immobile but everything around us almost imperceptibly slides into what has been. Others grow older, but we age only in the mirror and in other people's eyes. In a *healthy* life, time is continuous, something outside of us, marked by a watch or a calendar, not something within us. The past is yesterday, the future tomorrow, but yesterday and tomorrow belong to the same continuum. Not only does a heart attack have its own hour of the day or night, but it is a cutting of time and a break in time. Everything is divided into preattack and postattack.

During the weeks of immobilization, only the preattack is present; at that point the break is perceived with exceptional sharpness. Immobilization is just that time and place apart, empty in itself, where the future—or the postattack—is a desperate and almost maniacal dream of repeating the preattack. The continuity of time and temporal sequentiality are violated or even completely destroyed. In more abstruse and technical terms, the diachrony of events is broken: the preattack is preserved within the synchronic memory and the entire future is only its projection, as in Beckett's *Happy Days* or perhaps more clearly in *Rockabyebaby*. The perception of time is a destruction within time, and hence the dramatic analogies to the experience of a heart attack. Time in hospitals is filled with boredom, like almost everything that takes place on stage in Chekhov. The real drama has been played out between the acts; on stage the characters talk only of what has been—like the patients in their hospital beds—even if, in talking of what has been, they use the future tense. All these analogies, though, are only partially helpful in describing the postattack experience of survival. But what is important in these analogies is the dramatization of time.

Someone's last book, last painting, or last musical composition can be interpreted simultaneously in two different ways: as simply the latest work in the ordinary course of events, in a bio-bibliographic chronology, or as something to be perceived in terms of the phenomenology of the end, as the last work preceding death. The last work is never conceived as being the *last,* but sometimes, as with Barthes's *Camera Lucida,* consciousness of approaching death seems to have accompanied the process of creation. In this phenomenology of the end, death transforms the final work into a last will and testament. It is through this approach that Shakespeare's *Tempest* has been quite flagrantly misread. Yet that is precisely how, in the postattack experience, the last events from before the break in time—the landscape and the people—the accidental affinities, are transformed into elective affinities. Accident becomes fate—fate as Hegel understood it. We confront our own fate as something *alien.* As an adversary. As a mortal foe. The metaphor is literal. The enemy is *death.*

A week before my heart attack I had gone to Cracow for a few days. My last night there I saw Wajda's *Hamlet* at Wawel, the castle of Polish kings. As we waited until almost eleven in front of the upper gate to the courtyard on that June night, people tossed garlands into the Vistula. It was part of the traditional ritual for Wanda, the legendary princess of Cracow. Gigantic spires appeared in the fireworks, as in a dream. It was as cold as in the real Elsinore. We sat on benches in the courtyard, bundled up in blankets and coats, warming each other's hands. Hamlet as envisioned by Wyspiański paced back and forth through the colonnades with a book in his hand. Gertrude foresaw everything. She knew every stone of Wawel. Ophelia, too, had figured it all out, but what could she do? She was an ugly old maid. Hamlet mistreated her, but he was the first man to desire her.

That night Ophelia, like Wanda, threw herself in the Vistula. These elements were only the bare bones of the tragedy. But the walls played their part too. They emerged in the light and fell back into the shadows. They were impenetrable. *Hamlet* is robbed of that impenetrability of stone walls when confined on stage within artificial canvas drops, as it usually is. I came back from the theater with T. through the deserted Planty. It was my first night walk through Cracow in seventeen or eighteen years. My last walk had been with Kazimierz Wyka, a year or two before my leaving Poland. I walked together with him once again, in Rome, a few months before his death. On via Giulia, we promised each other another long night walk through Cracow, from church to church, from bar to bar, from the market to the Piłsudski Mound. This time, I was to return to Cracow in a week. I did not return. I had a ticket for the 6:00 a.m. express. During the night I had the heart attack.

The third day after the attack, I asked for Proust's *Albertine disparue* and for *Tristan and Isolde*. At first I could read no more than a few pages a day. But for the first time I read Proust as if it were my own story. Albertine was gone. Everything that preceded the heart attack suddenly took on significance. It became unique and unrepeatable. Until then, tomorrow always seemed like yesterday. Albertine would come for the evening caress. As Mother would come to kiss Marcel good night. Albertine crashed into a tree. She was gone forever. I began to cry as I read of Albertine's death. For the first time since childhood I was crying over a book. I was crying over myself. My mother had died. I had lost Albertine.

I had read Proust three times before: twice from beginning to end and once picking and choosing. But now, in the intensive care unit, in my hospital bed next to the big syphon of oxygen, under the screen showing my own beating heart, I read Proust differently. I did not need any madeleine to recover things past. The preattack was still in me. I read Proust not to call back time past from oblivion but to repeat it when it could no longer be repeated. To find a way to live when, in the postattack, the preattack, the past imperfect, had become the past perfect. *Plusquamperfectum.*

Hamlet at Wawel Castle was one of dozens of *Hamlet*s that I have seen; the night walk through the empty Planty and the conversation with T. were one of many night walks and one of many night conversations that I have enjoyed. I knew that I could return in a week and once again walk through the dark Planty at night.

But when, in postattack, I lay in my hospital bed in Międzylesie, the *Hamlet* of a week ago became my last *Hamlet* and the walk through the Planty my last walk. And if I ever see *Hamlet* again or walk from Wawel through the Planty, it will be my first *Hamlet* and my first walk in postattack. Like death or even its shadow, a heart attack endows the people, events, and meetings from predeath (preattack) with symbolic meanings and marks of necessity. That night walk through the Planty was not only my last walk but my *only* walk.

After Albertine's death, I put Proust aside and read *Tristan and Isolde*. King Mark sends his faithful Tristan over the seas to bring back Isolde to be his bride. On the ship Tristan and Isolde share the same bed, separated by a sword. But one evening, as a storm approaches, Isolde's maid servant, Brangaine, brings them golden goblets containing a love potion intended for the future bride and groom. That night Tristan and Isolde remove the sword and sleep together as man and wife. Later Isolde marries King Mark, and Tristan is exiled. But perhaps the true story of Tristan and Isolde was different. They placed a sword between them in the bed on the ship, but on the very first night they slept together as unwed husband and wife. As the ship neared the shore where King Mark was waiting for his bride-to-be, Tristan and Isolde realized what they had done. Overcome with shame, they begged Brangaine to give them an eternal love potion. The adulterous couple became tragic lovers and passed into legend. They had no other choice. They had a heart attack together.

"My heart, my physical heart, / Is the object of medical research," Władysław Broniewski wrote in what is probably his most personal lyric poem. "My heart, my aching heart, / Is the object of sorrow. / There is one person too few in this empty room." On the rising and falling lines of the electrocardiogram one finds the mark of a wound to the heart that lasts until death. Even after the wound is healed. But the heart has still another memory and bears still other scars. A heart attack reactivates that memory. But not only a heart attack. Every brush with death.

My young friend David, the son of friends and my own son's high school classmate, wrote to me from a hospital in Jerusalem where he was waiting to be operated on for the removal of a cancerous tumor:

I found out about your illness last night. As you know, I am in pretty much the same predicament and so I can identify with you, though no one can know for sure what the threat of death means to another person. It still is very hard for me to express what I feel. I know most people think in such situations all you are concerned with is death and the fear of pain and dying, but that's not the case for me. I have been feeling everything much more intensely and life seems like an incredible thrill, both in the abstract and in the concrete. Perhaps you, too, feel the same way, especially at that point in your life when what you are working on has become more and more important. I do not know what more I can tell you.

David has always lived intensely. "And enamored with a mortal face . . ." almost as in Słowacki's "And enamored of your mortal face." The juxtaposition of these two lines, the inverted and the authentic text, reveals the universal experience. Death does not protect one from love; nor does love protect one from death. Albertine exists no more but always is. There is only dying in love and one's own dying. That is how I read Proust in the hospital in Międzylesie.

7.

"Watch out or it'll break," said Teresa, whom I called "The Clairvoyant" because she worked in the X-ray department. "You've got a porcelain tea cup inside there." There was no need to warn me. I felt as if my inside was made of glass. Particularly when, after two weeks, I was "mobilized." The process is almost a ritual. Other patients watch from their beds as the doctor leads you by the arm, then lets you go on your own. The distance from the bed to the window seems enormous. And the thing inside keeps on beating. Your arm is tightly wrapped. The doctor constantly takes your blood pressure.

On the first day I received a supply of "nitro." It is on the nightstand by the bed of each patient, a little vial of twenty tablets of nitroglycerin. When the pain grips you, you quickly place a tablet under your tongue; the blood vessels begin to dilate and the feeling of terror diminishes. Heart patients never go anywhere without their nitros. I keep this little vial in

my breast pocket like lifesavers. In the sanatorium in Nałęczów, after my hospital stay, I was given a small furry purse
for my nitros. Now it is a fetish I always carry it with me.

You carry "nitros" with you because you carry your heart
with you. In postattack experience, the heart is constantly
present: it is in you and yet it is a thing apart. You listen to
your own heart as if it were someone else's. But it is yours. It
twitches. You feel a cramp in your heart. "Doctor, my heart
hurt last night."

And it was only at the moment that I said it that I realized
that the heart really does hurt. And that I could feel inside
me everything that language says about the heart: I am light-
hearted, fainthearted, heavyhearted. And that my heart leaps
and that it can turn to stone. And what it means to break someone's heart. And what a blow to the heart is. I am pained at
my very heart; my heart maketh a noise in me; I cannot hold
my peace, because thou hast heard, O my soul, the sound of
the trumpt, the alarm of war. Destruction upon destruction
is cried; for the whole land is spoiled: suddenly are my tents
spoiled, and my curtains in a moment." (Jeremiah 4.19–20)
The "heart of darkness" really is a *heart* of darkness.

8.

Small posters with the caption "Save your heart!" hang in the
entrance hall and on the walls of all three floors at the sanatorium in Nałęczów. The red heart on them is perfectly symmetrical. But an aorta and a pulmonary artery, copied from
an anatomical atlas, unexpectedly protrude from the beautiful symbolic heart depicted on these posters at the sanatorium
for heart patients. Mild Nałęczów, situated in a basin between
two valleys, is famous for its microclimate. Mornings and
evenings are damp; nights are cool even during heat spells.
There are hardly ever wind storms. Five sanatoriums for heart
patients are located in Nałęczów. They are marked on a town
map posted at the main intersection, near the bus station and a
small marketplace where only apples were on sale at the time I
was a patient. The sign above the map reads: "Nałęczów heals

hearts." The hearts on the wooden map and on the post to which it is nailed have been carved with penknives and nail files. They are not as perfectly symmetrical as the poster hearts at the sanatorium. They are crooked. Like those on school desks or on the benches in Łazienki Park. These hearts, sometimes pierced by an arrow, have faded letters around them. Whose hearts are healed at Nałęczów? What sorts of hearts?

Buses leave the station every hour. Excursions of school children and tourists arrive by chartered bus. They go directly to the famous park, where there is an artificial lake with swans, a museum in the palace, and a café where ice cream is served. But even in the park it is easy to tell the tourists from the patients. The tourists speak in loud voices, wave their arms, and constantly hurry. For the heart patients, a stroll is like learning to walk. One of the alleys is marked by small posts at hundred-meter intervals. At the end of each interval there is a little bench. The patients from the sanatoriums walk slowly and solemnly; then, having performed that feat, they sit on the little benches and place their hands on their hearts.

On the last day before my departure from Nałęczów, a couple at the bus stop attracted my attention. I knew the man by sight. He was probably the oldest patient at the sanatorium; he was to undergo a serious heart operation. The girl was tanned; she must have spent her vacation in the mountains. Now she was standing on the step of a bus about to leave for Kazimierz. She was dressed all in white and there was something sad about her face.

He pointed to his heart
But says nothing to the shepherdess.
(Mickiewicz, *Forefathers' Eve,* trans. M. B. Peacock)

His eyes remained fixed on the girl until the bus left.

The Fifth Heart Attack

I.

Dying of a heart attack is easy. Death from a heart attack is apparently easy too. Death is always someone else's, even when it's our own. This is the only way we can imagine our own death. Death is always outside oneself, something done to one's body. Seven or eight years ago—a year before having bypass surgery in Stony Brook—I had my second heart attack, and a clinical death, while on a trip to Belgrade. I remember waking up several hours later (it was already daylight) and noticing two dark brown splotches on my chest—left by the electric plates that were applied to restart my heart when the jagged graph of my heartbeat disappeared from the monitor screen. Clinical death is simply a stopping of the heart. Within two minutes the flow of blood to the brain stops, and in another two minutes the brain dies. Death of the brain is irreversible. Sometimes prompt massage of the open heart (even in extremis) may reverse the irreversible. In my case a "shock box" was enough. The only thing I remember about my "death" is a slight piercing pain, as though a needle were being stuck through my ear. Maybe that's what dying is like.

My fifth heart attack began in the evening in bed. With a pain in my jaw under my dentures. I took the dentures out but the pain did not stop. Usually it would go away within a few minutes. I had had my first experience with that pain, then unfamiliar to me, a couple of months before my first heart attack. Lidia and I were on a short vacation with Julia Przyboś and Claude Weiss at the very tip of Long Island, which looks like the powerful jaws of a huge fish. But the surf is not threatening, the oncoming waves are gentle even when it's windy, and I have never seen such clean water, not even at the Masurian lakes. The sandy bottom was still visible to a depth of many feet; we could see shoals of small fish and gelatinous jellyfish with long hanging suckers. That summer the waters of Long Island were infested with jellyfish. The sting was painful, and even ammonia (the standard remedy) did not work. Early mornings were relatively free of jellyfish, and I used to swim before breakfast. One morning the water was exceptionally cold. That was when I first felt that sudden pain in my jaw. I was told after my first heart attack that that pain was a signal. Since then I'd had that pain often, sometimes two or three times a month, but it usually went away almost immediately after I put a nitroglycerin pill under my tongue and relaxed my body by spreading my legs apart. But sometimes the pain lasted longer. Lidia always reminded me not to leave the house without a vial of nitroglycerin pills. Sometimes the pain in my jaw would not go away after one pill, but two pills were always enough. That evening, though, the pain persisted even after three.

Within a few minutes it was followed by a burning pain just below the ribs. For a moment I took it for indigestion—the sensation is similar. But this time the pain started to travel up slowly but relentlessly. That was when the pain really began. And it was a pain that I well remembered. It is difficult to give a name to; it is hard to localize and not like other pains. At first it is dull rather than sharp and it seems as though it is centered in the chest and at the same time spread over the entire skin. When it began to hurt in my left forearm, I knew what it meant: the doctors always asked me about pain in my left arm. At that point Lidia called for the ambulance.

The ambulance people came and carried me out on a stretcher. By then I was starting to lose consciousness. But I remember our neighbor, the chef at a nearby French restaurant that Lidia and I never patronized—it was far too expensive—waving to me from his car. I didn't see much more: they put an oxygen mask over my face. I don't remember whether they gave me the IV in the ambulance or in the hospital.

The pain in my left chest wall was growing stronger and stronger. As if my chest were being slowly pulled apart. The doctor asked me to evaluate the pain on a scale of one to ten. I said "six," probably in Polish—I was beginning to mix up languages. And suddenly, with needles stuck in both my wrists (a painful experience since the nurse could not find the veins and succeeded only after repeated attempts), I started to laugh uncontrollably, causing the little oxygen tubes to fall out of my nostrils. The horrified doctor recoiled. The doctor's question took me back to the Warsaw of my youth, to the Legia sports club on Łazienkowska Street, where I used to go swimming every day after school. Every Sunday in autumn, when it was still warm, we boys used to evaluate the girls on a scale of one to ten. When my turn came on one girl I liked, I said "six." I no longer remember her name, but I do remember her black hair in braids. We saw each other regularly for a couple of weeks.

But the pain I felt was stronger than six. I said "six" out of politeness, trying to be brave. But in fact it was a crushing, continuous ache that seemed to spread inside my head.

When my ordeal was over and I was back home, Czesław Miłosz telephoned and asked me if I had suffered much pain. Of my whole heart attack that's what interested him most. He was afraid of the pain, not of the heart attack. In one of the most intimate and moving passages in his *Diary*, Gombrowicz wrote that he was outraged more by suffering than by death. He could not come to terms with the universal suffering of both human beings and animals in all their corporeality, with the torturing of their bodies, let alone of their souls. Pain for him was another cruelty of existence that could never be justified under any circumstances. Not even the suffering of a fly caught on flypaper or of a bug being squashed.

American medicine, I think, is more sensitive to pain than its European counterpart is. It wants to relieve the patient's suffering by any means, including drugs, of course. As soon as I arrived at the hospital, I was given an injection of morphine. The crushing chest pain slowly subsided. But in contrast to the prevailing European practice, that of American doctors and hospitals is not to spare either the patient or the patient's family even the most brutal truths. No concessions are made to one's sensitivities. Prior to an operation the patient signs an agreement and often is informed of his or her statistical chances of survival. Before my first open-heart surgery at Stony Brook the surgeon told Lidia and me that given my age and the pulmonary surgery that I had had years before to remove the upper lobe of my right lung, my chances stood at 80 percent. Then he told us that, just as in plumbing the old corroded pipes have to be replaced with new ones, coronary bypass surgery involves grafting veins taken from the patient's legs onto the obstructed arteries. Should I decide against surgery at this point, my chances of surviving the next year would be less than one in nine.

There is an admixture of the Puritan heritage in American medical ethics: neither the patient nor his or her family can be deprived of the right to make the fatal decision and to assume the ultimate responsibility for it; even the dying cannot be denied it as long as they cling to life. Death is not the only serious business; the last will and testament is a weighty matter too. Protestant severity in matters of duty to oneself and to one's family in dying and in marriage—quite alien to Polish custom—has survived to this day. "Is it a massive heart attack?" I asked before I got the shot of morphine. "A heart attack is a heart attack," I heard by way of answer. But the hospital had already told Lidia on the phone that I was having a heart attack.

At that point, still in the emergency room, I was given an injection of a new drug (or perhaps it was added to the IV infusion) that rapidly thins the blood so it can pass through the obstructed arteries and revive and resupply the starved heart muscle with nutrients. But this new drug, which had not been given to me for any of my previous heart attacks, also thins out everything else, including one's mind. I don't know how to describe it in any other way. Time and again, with ebbing consciousness, I kept entering the murky waters and rising back to the surface.

2.

There was a large electric clock with a white face and black hands on the wall directly opposite my bed. It was the first thing I saw after coming out of my hallucinations, and I think I saw it in my delirium too. The clock always indicated 3:05 or 3:07. That horrified me. In my delirium it seemed to me that hours passed between what were in fact two or three glances at the clock. The door of the ICU was perpetually open on the corridor. There was a large window in the corridor. Outside the window I could see the green sports field at Stony Brook, where I always took my morning walk, part of the exercise program I imposed on myself after my fourth heart attack. This empty space surrounded by giant maple trees whose leaves in autumn turned from russet to red and deep purple (much admired by my wife's mother and by my friend Roman Karst up to our last walk together before he died) now became transformed into the Szwajcarska Dolina, the Swiss Valley, seen from the windows of our Warsaw apartment on Aleja Róż. The window kept changing: at times it was only a stained glass of multicolored panes. The night was drawing to a close, but the clock showed its invariable five past three. And whatever was left of my consciousness let me suddenly realize that time must have stopped. And that was truly terrifying.

I had my fifth heart attack in late December 1990. Earlier that year, in June, I had been in another hospital for almost two weeks with pneumonia brought on by a new strain of streptococcus A. The bacteria is known as "hospital streptococcus"—its mutations were isolated in hospitals and have survived a battery of antibiotics, finally producing a new antibiotic-resistant strain. "Hospital streptococcus" pneumonia is often fatal. I was lucky. I had a very high fever for close to a week and was unconscious almost all that time, but I survived.

What I chiefly remember of my fifth heart attack are dreams. In one, a Spanish—or was it Puerto Rican?—theater ensemble consisting of men, women, and children came to the hospital room I was sharing with another patient. They were actors and musicians. I recognized right away what they were performing. It was a comic Italian opera. In my dream I even remembered the Italian title. And I recognized the melodies although I am totally tone-deaf. It was a singularly beautiful theater ensemble. One of the most beautiful I have ever seen. Young women in brightly colored, multilayered Gypsy skirts kicked their legs high. When, early the next morning, Lidia called me (I had the phone by the bed), I described to her the wonderful performance, only complaining that the musicians refused to leave and that all the children were sitting on my bed, screaming, and jumping around the room. And that the performance was over. "Help me," I shouted, "I can't get rid of them."

Of all the fantasies, hallucinations, and dreams, the Spanish theater stayed with me the longest. The first night was the worst, or there may have been only one night, for all I know. In that continuous dream I saw a succession of female nurses entering my room, always in threes and always different ones. They would pull the bedsheet off me and wrap it tightly around my head until I started to suffocate; then, when they had removed this hood from my head, they would unfasten the strings of my white hospital robe and expose my naked body. One after another the three would begin to stick pins into my penis. It wasn't painful, but I felt ashamed, and the nurses, looking like Ku Klux Klan members in their white hospital robes with white hoods, would keep nudging one another and giggling like schoolgirls. The pins were the straws I used to drink iced Coca-Cola. Then it was only one nurse who would come; she would stand in the doorway, lift her skirt up or unbutton her nurse's smock, and with an obscene gesture beckon me to follow her. I chased her down long corridors, but she kept disappearing behind doors that closed after her. Then I fell down and could not get up. At that point I woke up, fully conscious but still unable to move. I was tied to the bed. They told me that during the night they had tried to insert a catheter into my member and had had to tie my arms and legs because I kept pulling it out. I felt as if I were in a straitjacket.

When they untied me, I tried to call Lidia, only I could not remember the number. Each time Lidia called me she would repeat the number to me, but I could not memorize it. I tried to write it down but every time I would confuse the digits. In retrospect, the worst memory loss I had was after my fourth heart attack, when I went back to the hospital three weeks after the bypass at the Stony Brook hospital. That fourth attack was a "mild" one; the ECG did not register it but it showed up in the enzyme tests. I had other physical problems as well, including severe anemia that required blood transfusions. I remember calling Lidia at four in the morning asking to be taken home and telling her that I was in a foreign country and couldn't understand a word that was being said because they were speaking Spanish to me.

It was the last call I managed to dial myself. Shortly thereafter I was struck with speech and motor disorders. I could not recall the simplest words: *spoon, bell, urinal*. They seemed to be locked inside my head but could not find their way to my tongue. They couldn't be given a voice. They were simply notions without names. The signified lacking a signifier. I could only point with my index finger: "that." Like speaking a foreign language when a word escapes one's memory or one doesn't know it. "That" for a roll, "that" for a postage stamp, "that" for a cauliflower, "that" for a tie. Only "that" remained with me from language. I had a kind of aphasia that often follows a stroke. One has to relearn one's language.

Joe Chaikin tried to return to the theater two years after he had a stroke, but he was unable to memorize his role. I saw him in Los Angeles performing in a play specially conceived for him. Perhaps he even devised it himself. Chaikin sat in a chair behind a large table covered with an odd telegraph system of tangled strings. Colored cards with messages on them were attached to the strings and sent to Chaikin: "Go to the right," "Pour water into the glass," "Welcome, ladies and gentlemen," "I'm coming from nowhere." It was one of the most touching performances I have ever seen. And one of Chaikin's greatest roles. I remember seeing him as Woyzeck years ago. Büchner showed his genius in creating the scarcely literate Woyzeck, the first and—as far as I know—the only character in the entire history of drama who is unable to find words to express himself. Back then I found Chaikin's portrayal of Woyzeck not totally convincing. But now he was Woyzeck himself. A tragic, stuttering Woyzeck.

My "aphasia" was a motor malfunction as well. If a book fell from my bed, I could not pick it up. Either my fingers refused to cooperate at all or they tried too hard and got in one another's way. The signal failed to get through or, as in a bad telephone connection, it went to the wrong party. I repeatedly dialed numbers different from what I wanted.

Three times before I had had to face the diagnostic procedure called coronary angiography to determine which coronary arteries were blocked and how much: the first was in Belgrade after my second heart attack and my clinical death, the second before the bypasss surgery, and the third after my fifth heart attack at St. John's Hospital in Santa Monica. Angiograms are totally painless. The procedure is more frightening to hear about than to experience. The most unpleasant part was having my groin shaved at length and with great care by two female nurses. A cardiac catheter is inserted through an opening in the femoral artery in the groin and advanced against the arterial blood flow to the bulb of the aorta. The progress of the catheter—through main arteries to locate any narrowings or obstructions—is followed by an X-ray camera and projected on a screen. During the procedure the patient must remain still, but I almost spoiled it by constantly craning my neck trying to see my own living and throbbing heart and the tip of the catheter running across the screen.

I don't recall anything about my second angiogram; I must have been in a state of semiconsciousness. But I remember the third and last one. I kept lapsing into an oppressive half-sleep, followed by brief intervals of wakefulness during which I stared intently at the screen with my heart on it. In our garden in Stony Brook the canopy of maple trees is so dense that only rarely can the sun penetrate it. As I was lying immobile on the table it seemed to me for a moment that I was in our garden again lying on my back looking up at the canopy of the trees where the X-ray monitor floated with the catheter tip dancing across it. I must have dozed off again because when I opened my eyes I saw a screen that had been lowered in the middle of the stage for a performance of Euripides's *Orestes,* which I directed twenty years ago in Berkeley. On that screen I now saw Menelaus return from Troy to Mycenae, where Clytemnestra has been murdered by Orestes with the same double-edged ax that killed Agamemnon seven years before. In the next scene a drop of blood appeared on the blank screen, throwing out spiderlike tentacles that slowly filled the entire white expanse. The lighting designer for the Berkeley production was Toshiro Ogawa, a young Japanese. Toshiro came up with a device that he called the "fish tank." It was something totally new that he made especially for me. Toshiro was full of inventive ideas. The "fish tank" was an ordinary transparent glass filled with water into which a drop of a contrastive element—black or red ink— was added. The drop of ink would slowly turn into a jellyfish. A beam of reflector light was then directed at the glass, and the slowly dissolving drop of ink was projected onto the screen.

As I was wheeled back to my room after the angiogram, I saw Lidia standing in the corridor. Like a pillar of salt. Like Lot's wife when she turned her head to take one last look at her doomed town. But the angiogram results were unexpectedly encouraging. At least two major arteries that had been patched up with veins taken from my legs had not been damaged by the last attack. In a couple of days I was discharged from the hospital.

3.

"Don't count to five," my Stony Brook doctor had warned me after my fourth heart attack. But even back then, in the emergency room, I was not afraid. They say that the old fear death more than the young do. I doubt this is true; at any rate it is far from universal. Last year I was hit by a car while crossing the street on a green light and since then I am sometimes afraid to cross the street. But I am not afraid of dying. And I have become reconciled to the inevitability of death. My own and others'. Not reconciled to death itself—it is beyond our comprehension—but to its universal sway, from which there is no escape. The inevitability of my own death seemed less inevitable in my youth and for many years thereafter—in my twenties, thirties, forties, and even in my fifties. I do not mean death considered "theoretically" but death whose terror we know by the dryness of our throats, the pain in the pit of the stomach, the sudden contraction of the diaphragm. As a child I was terribly afraid of death. I would wake up screaming and my mother had trouble calming me down. I didn't want to die.

I have come to accept the death of friends, those of my generation and the next one. They have gone one after the other: Ludwik, Dawid, Franek, and Kazik from the Warsaw Circle of Polonists; all my friends from the first *Forge* and the founders of the Institute of Literary Research. After the recent deaths of Adolf Rudnicki and Stefan Żółkiewski I am the only one left from all the friends of my generation.

I hadn't seen Adolf for years. The last time was in Paris, I think. It was an unexpected meeting. I invited him to the Café de Flore on the boulevard St.-Germain. He was quite surprised when I ordered *deux fines*. Drinks were quite expensive at the Flore. "Are you very unhappy, Jan?" Adolf asked. I wasn't very unhappy, but I didn't say no. Adolf embraced me and said, "You see we are all unhappy."

Adolf come over to me in Warsaw—it was on my first trip back to Poland after seventeen years. At that point I spurned his friendly gesture; I was angry with him because of some remarks about me in his latest book. I remained bitter about this for quite a long time. Even on my last trip to Poland, in September and October 1990, I still couldn't force myself to go see him. I was told he was very ill, but Adolf was known for "wallowing" in real or imaginary "disasters" and I couldn't believe that he was really sick. I remember how, during that week in April 1943 when the Warsaw ghetto was burning, Adolf and I went there daily, following along the wall to Krasiński Square with its carousel, where, amidst laughter and squeals of pleasure, burning scraps from the ghetto floated in the air. Something else I remember too—memory makes its own choices: a long walk with Adolf in the rain on Piotrkowska Street in Łódź. Adolf gave me a book of his that had just come out; it was inscribed: "Having lived through the disaster together." This book, the only one with an inscription by Adolf that I ever had, was lost during one of our frequent moves, either from Łódź to Wrocław or from there to Warsaw, or possibly during our last move to America, when we took only a small portion of our library with us. We were to spend only one year abroad and then go back. And now I can't ask Adolf which of our many disasters he had in mind when he inscribed that book for me.

I didn't attend Adolf's funeral. Apparently only a few did, mostly women. Some old and some very young. Adolf would have been pleased. I didn't attend Stefan's funeral either. The last time I heard his voice was on the telephone. In October, shortly after my return from Poland, I called his wife to ask how Stefan was. It was the day he was sent home from the clinic. Stefan spoke in a stuttering whisper. But even in that whisper the voice of our former Hetman would break through for a brief moment—the famous booming voice commanding attention at the meetings of the Circle of Polonists, at the Institute of Literary Research, and at the Writers' Union on Krakowskie Przedmieście. In the last years of his life Stefan was very lonely. Many of his former followers had left him, along with Marxism.

I visited him twice at the clinic. He had an infarct of the cerebellum. I had never heard of such a thing, but I was told right away that it was fatal. Stefan's eyes were watery, and lying in that hospital bed he resembled a dying whale. For half a century this expiring whale had been the most loyal of my friends.

Tadeusz Kantor died a week or so before my fifth heart attack. He had been taken to the hospital from a rehearsal of his last production and died early the following morning. From the perspective offered by death, everything becomes a sign. As in Shakespeare's *Tempest*, both tragedy and comedy, where sometimes I feel I hear his voice. As in Kantor's *Today Is My Birthday* after *I Shall Never Return*. I last saw Kantor in Paris, at a festival devoted entirely to his work. The festival was Kantor's ultimate triumph. All of Paris came to see exhibitions of his pictures, and at all performances the house was full. There was a three-day symposium at the Pompidou Center; the sessions, which lasted from early morning to late afternoon, were widely attended, and the speeches and lectures by scholars and experts were punctuated by Kantor's incessant outbursts.

He screamed at every speaker during the symposium the

way he used to scream at his actors and technicians and everybody else during his rehearsals. He would roar and rage.
Everything was wrong. Either too early or too late, too close
or too far. And every day he was the star of the symposium,
too, as he always was on stage every evening. And as he always
was in Cracow, even when he was just walking down the
street. He was unique, a theater unto himself. I have compared
Kantor to Charon, who ferries the dead across the river Styx
and brings back the long-forgotten dead. Even if the dead return as marionettes. And Charon himself returns after each
trip. But Kantor, who brought about the return of the dead
to life, did not return. He slowly burned himself out in that
unyielding scream-quest for the Absolute Kantor. Until the
very end.

Every death creates a hole—in the ground and in ourselves.
All deaths are undeserved and always premature. But some
deaths seem to be particularly unjust, violating all the rules of
fairness, as if some sort of agreement between us and death
had not been kept, although we knew all along it was a trick.
Such were the deaths of the two Konstantys, Jeleński and
Puzyna. Not only did they die, they were abruptly snatched
away from us.

I last saw Kot (that's how Jeleński was known to his friends)
on a brief trip I made to Paris a year or so before his death.
He invited me to breakfast—a real Polish breakfast, not the
French *petit déjeneur*—at a bistro not far from where he lived. I
had already forgotten his address and had to refresh my memory by checking in an old address book. My memory is full
of holes too. But I still remember other Parisian breakfasts—
always around ten in the morning, a very early hour for Paris.

At those breakfasts Kot, like no one else in the world, was
at the same time both present and absent, yet always attentive
to what was being said. He had what is rare in a man: tenderness in the touch of his hand and in his look, in the tone of
his voice. But at intervals he seemed to go off somewhere else.
Then, as if realizing that he had drifted away, he would become
doubly attentive. At our last meeting his "absences" seemed
to be more frequent and to last longer. At one point I made a

personal remark about the infirmities of old age. That sparked his attention: "A long youth has been granted to us both and that's why we can't cope with old age," he said. I was astonished. The difference in age between us was only eight years, but Kot always seemed to me much younger than I was. In two portraits done by Leonor Fini, Kot is shown in all his radiant nakedness. He was still strikingly beautiful even now with his thinning hair, drooping mustache, and no longer fit and youthful figure. There was always something luminous about him. But during that breakfast, which proved to be our last, something like a shadow passed over his face. For a moment I had the impression it was the shadow of death, but I immediately dismissed the thought as absurd. Then suddenly Kot was youthful again as always. I don't know if he knew then that he was sick. And even if he had known, his inner discipline would not have allowed him to talk about it. Or perhaps he wanted to keep a distance from himself until the end. After Kot's death R. told me that when Kot was saying good-bye to her before her departure for America it was as if he were saying his last good-bye. He was taken to the hospital in a coma and never regained consciousness. M. told me that when he visited him in the hospital, Kot made a motion with his hand as if he wanted to greet M. He died a long and painful death. In the last weeks of his life he did not allow anyone to visit him in the hospital. Perhaps it was on doctor's orders or perhaps, again, Kot wanted to maintain that distance from himself until the end.

It was at the office of the theater journal *Dialog* in Warsaw that I saw Ket Puzyna for the last time. He had just returned from a trip to Paris. In his brand-new fashionable white suit he looked like a young boy; I had never seen him so well got up. "The girls have been taking care of me," he said. Ket always referred to the women who looked after him as "girls," and of course these included his *Frauzimmer* at *Dialog*.

In a year Ket was no more. In the summer, as he did every year, Ket had taken his vacation at the Masurian lakes. After a swim (the water was cold that summer), Ket experienced chest pains. He was taken to the hospital in nearby Augustów. The doctors said that he had survived a heart attack. Ket died two weeks later while being visited by friends. One of them, a young girl, brought him flowers. Ket smiled at her, turned his head, and wanted to say something. He didn't manage to.

The April 1990 issue of *Dialog* reached me late, as usual, but almost exactly on the first anniversary of Ket's death; it was the memorial number devoted to the former editor. Tadeusz Nyczek called his reminiscence "Only Waking Existence . . ." That title puzzled me. Only later did I realize that it was a quotation from one of Ket's poems. Ket used to send me his poems long before they came out in print; now I received a small gray book fifty pages long containing his entire poetic output, some twenty poems in all, under the title *Pebbles*. This little volume Ket prized more than anything else he wrote, more than his razor-sharp writings on theater. And more than his seminar papers and the Ph.D. dissertation he barely started to write, which he labeled "imponderabilia." Through those poems I came to a different Ket. I always suspected that he existed, especially when he visited us in Stony Brook, but the truth is that we never talked seriously except perhaps about the theater. And not lately: the theater had long since ceased to be of any serious interest to either of us. Except for Grotowski. But not as theater.

Only waking experience. Beautiful twenty-year-olds. Bitter sixty-year-olds. Puzyna turned sixty a few months before he died. I found in his poems the bitterness I knew only too well. In 1956 after the Polish October, I wrote, in the spirit of Camus, about a despair that is full of hope. But in Ket's poems, each heavy as a stone, there was more than bitterness. I especially remember a poem Ket wrote after seeing in some American museum a photograph showing a hanged man. The man had been hanged from a horse: he was ordered to stand on the saddle, the horse was spurred on, and the man was left suspended in midair. The saddle can still be seen at that museum. And the picture of the hanged man with his hat on his head.

Along with the bitterness there was also contempt in Ket's poems. Contempt he kept concealed in his smile, or was it only a slight curl of his lips?

Oh, no, my friends, no more
Mediterranean myths, Greek gods, no Palladas, . . .
No more oneiric visions, only waking experience,
Eyes wide open, bitter taste of curses.

I was to write a review of Ket's poetry. Ket was counting on it. I fell sick. Ket died. The only thing I wrote was a reminiscence, "Ket at High Noon." Always too little and always too late.

4.

True believers and true nonbelievers are at least alike in one thing: they are reconciled not to death but to its inevitability. There is no escape from one's death and there is no bargaining with it. This is the sole subject of *Everyman,* the late-fifteenth-century morality play that has never lost its power. Every man must die. Every man, and thus I, too, must die. Deeply religious and deeply areligious people have less anxiety and no doubts about the afterlife. Strong faith and unflagging skepticism are similar.

For a long time death seemed more comprehensible to me than did conception. In the natural order and even in the metaphysical order, to the extent that I could comprehend it. Every existence has its end, but its conception is more enigmatic. Even astrophysics offers more hypotheses about the end of our world than about its beginnings. Nothingness itself is more readily accessible to the mind, the senses, and the imagination than is the creation of something out of nothing—and all the more so in the human order than in nature. For a long time it seemed to me incomprehensible that as the result of a some convulsive motions of two bodies (Rochefoucauld called them comic) and the fusion of two fluids a new being is born, a being just like all of us and yet totally unique and unrepeatable. It has a soul, but when does that soul enter a new being? At the moment of conception or only when the heart starts beating, and where has the soul been stored before, in which of God's granaries? Christian theology has not been able to reach any clear, unequivocal conclusions. But one thing is clear in both anatomy and metaphysics: death comes when the heart stops beating.

In the carnivalesque imagination and wisdom—I learned this from Bakhtin—pregnant death, death the old woman who hatches, epitomizes the continuity of life. Man's loins and woman's womb lend indestructibility to what is consigned to death. And it is thanks to loins and womb that the human species survives.

"And the eyes of them both were opened, and they knew that they were naked." In the biblical myth of Adam and Eve the knowledge of sex is linked to death: "till thou return unto the ground; for out of it wast thou taken: for dust thou art and unto dust shalt thou return." And in the next chapter we read: "And Adam knew Eve his wife; and she conceived, and bare Cain, and said, 'I have gotten a man from the Lord.'" In the writings of the first-century church fathers, Christ is called a second Adam. In the Catholic version of Christ's story the sexual act is linked to death, but in a double negation: the immaculate conception and the resurrection of the Son of God.

In secular anthropology with ties to the ancient tradition, Eros and Thanatos are closely bound one to the other. On a Greek column representing a scene from *Alcestis* Thanatos is a beautiful naked youth whose hair is cut short, indicating mourning, and who holds a sword. This winged Grecian Death resembles Eros. The Eros on the Greek steles is a winged youth also, holding a torch as a sign of mourning. The messenger of frenetic love is also the messenger of Death. When you look into the eyes of your partner who is in the throes of orgasm, they are filmed over and unseeing. As if your partner were already on the other side: "I am dying." And from that oblivion we come back gasping for breath like a diver rising to the surface after having touched the bottom. And afterward we feel sad. We have just touched nothingness.

In my personal experience the assent to death has come about somewhat differently. Quite simply and in accord with the oldest tradition. Certainly not as in books. During my fifth heart attack, with needles constantly being stuck into my veins and my arm repeatedly being wrapped to check my fall-ing blood pressure, I kept looking at the photograph of my granddaughter that I had pinned on the wall of my hospital room. She was three months old then. She smiled at me. I have two children and a grandson twelve years old. But never be-fore had I thought that when I die they will remain. Until then I was too young to think about who would outlive me. But there is another reason, which I recognized only then, in the hospital bed. The baby girl had recently come from the other side. And that first smile of hers still had something of the other side about it.

To die of a heart attack is not so terrifying.

Santa Monica
January 1991

Selected List of Names and Organizations

This list has two purposes: to supply first names of persons where these are not given in the text and to provide additional information that may be helpful to the reader.

Alain (orig. Emile-Auguste Chartier) (1868–1951). French philosopher and essayist.

Anders, Władysław (1892–1970). Polish general and politician.

Andrzejewski, Jerzy (1909–1983). Polish writer. Leading figure of the opposition. 1976 co-founder of the opposition movement KOR.

Armia Krajowa (*see* Home Army).

Armia Ludowa (*see* People's Army).

Auderska, Halina (1904). Polish novelist.

Axer, Erwin (1917). Polish theater director.

Bartoszek, Hedda

Bataille, Henry Felix (1872–1922). French playwright and poet.

Bazhan, Mykola (Nikolai P.) (1904–1983). Ukrainian poet.

Beck, Józef (1894–1944). Polish colonel, minister of foreign affairs in prewar Poland. Died in Rumania.

Ben, Philippe

Bereza Kartuska. A concentration camp for political prisoners in interwar Poland.

Beria, Lavrenti Pavlovich (1899–1953). Russian Communist, closely associated with Stalin. 1938 became head of the Soviet secret police. 1953, after Stalin's death, arrested and shot.

Berling, Zygmunt (1896–1980). Polish general. During World War II, commander of the First Kościuszko Division (in the USSR).

Berman, Jakub (1901–1984). Polish politician. Second in importance to Bierut in postwar Polish politics. Member of the Politburo. 1954–56 deputy premier. 1957 expelled from the party.

Bertrand, Aloysius (1807–1841). French poet.

Białoszewski, Miron (1922–1983). Polish poet, playwright.

Bieńkowski, Władysław ("Władek") (1906). Polish politician. Prewar Communist, closely associated with Gomułka and the Polish Workers' party. Later joined the democratic opposition.

Bieńkowski, Zbigniew ("Zbyszek") (1913). Polish poet and literary critic.

Bierut, Bolesław (1892–1956). Polish president from 1944 to 1952. Later premier and first secretary of central committee. Responsible for implementing Stalinism in Poland.

Bobińska, Celina. Polish historian, daughter of Helena Bobińska.

Bobińska, Helena. Author of children's books.

Bocheński, Aleksander (1904). Polish writer and journalist.

Bogusławski, Wojciech (1757–1829). Polish playwright. Father of the Polish National Theatre.

Borejsza, Jerzy (1905–1952). Polish journalist, publisher, Communist.

Borwicz-Boruchowicz. Writer, journalist, activist in the militant Jewish underground.

Boy-Żeleński, Tadeusz (1874–1941). Polish literary and theater critic. Famous translator of French literature. Murdered by Germans in Lvov.

Braun, Jerzy (1901–1975). Polish poet and philosopher.

Bristigier, Julia (1902–1973). Director of the Ministry of Public Security. Active during the war in Lvov and Samarkand.

Broniewski, Władysław ("Władek," "Władzio") (1898–1962). Polish poet, socialist. Soldier in the Polish Legions organized by Piłsudski during World War I. Author of revolutionary and patriotic poems.

Brzękowski, Jan (1903–1983). Polish poet and critic.

Budzyńska, Celina (1908). Polish Communist activist. Her husband, Stanisław, was executed during the Great Purge of 1937. Left the party 1981 after the imposition of martial law.

Carnap, Rudolf (1891–1970). German philosopher and logician.

Ceauçescu, Nicolae (1918–1990). Rumanian politician. 1965

first secretary of the central committee of the Communist party. 1967 president of Rumania. Executed in 1990.

Chaikin, Joseph. American theater director.

Chwistek, Leon ("Leonek") (1884–1944). Polish philosopher, mathematician, logician, theorist of art, and painter.

Cyrankiewicz, Józef (1911–1989). Prime minister of the People's Republic of Poland from 1947 to 1952 and from 1954 to 1970. 1970–71 president of Poland.

Czechowicz, Jósef (1903–1939). Poet connected with the underground.

Dab-Kocioł, Marian

Dąbrowska, Maria (1889–1965). Polish novelist and essayist.

Denikin, Anton I. (1872–1947). Russian military leader. Commanded anti-Bolshevik forces in the South. 1920 emigrated.

Dubček, Aleksander (1921–1992). Political leader of Republic of Czechoslovakia. Member of Slovakian national minority. 1968 first secretary of Communist party. Initiator of "Prague Spring."

Dzerzhinsky, Felix Edmundovich (1877–1926). Son of Polish aristocrats. Leader of Bolshevik revolution and organizer of the Cheka (Russian secret police).

Ehrenburg, Ilya Grigoryevich (1891–1967). Russian journalist and novelist.

Erlich, Victor (1914). Russian-born American professor of Slavic languages and literatures.

Esslin, Martin (1918). Austrian-born theoretician of the Theatre of the Absurd. Currently living in London.

Fadeyev, Aleksander Aleksandrovich (1901–1956). Russian novelist whom Stalin appointed to head the Writers' Union. Participant in party's political persecution of writers. After a shift in Soviet internal politics, committed suicide.

Franko, Ivan Yakovlevich (1856–1916). Ukrainian writer and journalist.

Gałczyński, Konstanty Ildefons (1905–1953). Popular Polish poet who mixed wild fantasy with accessible language.

General Government. Portion of central Poland not annexed by the Soviet Union or by Germany in 1939, but placed under German rule. Divided into four areas: Cracow, Warsaw, Radom, and Lublin.

Gierek, Edward (1913). First secretary of the central committee of the Polish United Workers' party from December 1970 to 1980.

Ginczanka, Zuzanna ("Zuza") (orig. Sara Ginzburg) (1917–44). Polish poet.

Gombrowicz, Witold (1904–69).

Gomułka, Władysław (pseud. Wiesław) (1905–1982). 1956–70 first secretary of Polish United Workers' party. He represented a temporary democratization after 1956.

Grotowski, Jerzy (1933). Polish writer and director. Creator of the Poor Theatre.

Handelsman, Marceli (1882–1945). Polish historian.

Herling-Grudziński, Gustaw (1919). Polish writer, literary critic, journalist.

Hertz, Paweł (1918). Polish poet, prose writer, essayist, and translator.

Hoene-Wroński, Józef Maria (1776–1853). Polish philosopher and mathematician.

Hollender, Tadeusz (1910–1943). Polish poet, satiricist, and translator. Shot by Germans.

Home Army (Armia Krajowa). Conspiratorial Polish army that fought against the Germans on Polish soil during World War II. This 350,000-man army came under the direction of the Polish government in exile in London and was the principal force behind the Warsaw Uprising of 1944. The army was dissolved in 1945. Former soldiers were persecuted by the Communists after the war.

Home Delegation (Delegatura). The underground political body nominated by the Polish government in exile in London during World War II.

Ingarden, Roman (1893–1970). Polish philosopher and theorist of literature and art.

Irzykowski, Karol (1873–1944). Polish literary critic and writer.

Iwaszkiewicz, Jarosław (1894–1980). Polish writer, dramatist, essayist, and poet.

Jacob, Max (1876–1944). French poet and playwright.

Jakobson, Roman (1896–1982). Russian-born American linguist.

Jaruzelski, General Wojciech (1923). 1985–89 Polish head of state (chairman of Council of State). 1989–90 president of Polish People's Republic.

Jasienica, Paweł (orig. Leon L. Beynar) (1909–1970). Polish writer and historian.

Jastrun, Mieczysław (1903–1983). Polish poet, prose writer, essayist, translator.

Jędrychowski, Stefan (1910). Polish politician.

Jeziorański, Zdzisław. See Nowak, Jan.

Kaden-Bandrowski, Juliusz (1885–1944). Polish novelist and journalist.

Kasman, Leon (1905–1984). Polish Communist. Editor in chief of Communist daily *Trybuna Ludu* from 1948 to 1967 and member of central committee of Polish United Workers' party.

Kautsky, Karl (1854–1939). German Marxist.

Kliszko, Zenon (1908–1989). Prewar Communist. 1948 expelled from the central committee due to "right-nationalist" deviation. Closely associated with Gomułka. After 1956 occupied high positions in the party and government.

Kołakowski, Leszek (1927). Polish philosopher, essayist, writer. Marxist in his youth. Left Communist party in 1966. Later became critic of Marxism. Now an émigré in England.

Kołłątaj, Hugo (1750–1812). Polish philosopher, writer, poltician. Central figure in Polish enlightenment.

Komar, General Wacław (1909–1972). Director general of Ministry of Internal Affairs. Prewar Communist. Connected with the liberal wing of the Communist party.

KOR (Committee for Workers' Defense). Democratic opposition group established following violent suppression of workers' protest of price increases in the summer of 1976. The founding members of KOR included Jacek Kuroń, J. J. Lipski, Adam Michnik, Halina Mikołajska, Zbigniew Romaszewski.

Korczak, Janusz (pseud. of Henryk Goldszmit) (1878–1942).

Polish educator, physician, writer. Founder and leader of Jewish orphanage in Poland (1911–1942); voluntarily accompanied orphans to death camp.

Kościuszko, Tadeusz Andrzej Bonawentura (1746–1817). Polish patriot. Fought in American revolutionary army.

Kott, Aniela ("Lalutka") (1925–). JK's sister.

Kott, Kazimiera (née Wertenstein) (1888–1952). JK's mother.

Kott, Maurycy (1876–1942). JK's father.

Kowalewski, Janusz. Communist in prewar Poland. Later an emigré in England.

Krall, Hanna (1937). Polish journalist and writer.

Krasiński, Zygmunt (1812–1859). Polish poet and dramatist. One of Poland's three great romantic poets.

Kraus, Karl (1874–1936). Austrian critic and dramatist.

Krońska, née Krzemicka, Irena. Philosopher and translator.

Kroński, Tadeusz ("Tiger") (1907–1958). Polish philosopher.

Kruczkowski, Leon (1900–1962). Polish novelist and playwright aligned with the Communists. Deputy minister of culture and chairman of Writers' Union in Polish People's Republic.

Kultura. Most important newspaper of the postwar Polish emigration confronting political and cultural issues. [Founder and editor in chief was Jerzy Giedroyć.]

Kundera, Milan (1929). Czech writer and dramatist. Currently living in France.

Kuryluk, Karol. Polish journalist and writer. Postwar ambassador to Austria.

Kuźnica (The Forge). Weekly social and literary newspaper published from 1945 to 1950. Established at the initiative of Jerzy Borejsza by a group of intellectuals and writers affiliated with the Communist party.

Łaszowski, Alfred

Letter of the Thirty-four. Open letter dated March 14, 1964, from thirty-four writers and scientists to Prime Minister Cyrankiewicz to protest the state's cultural policies, including an increase in censorship.

Lipski, Jan Józef (or Józef Jan) ("Janek") (1926–1991). Polish literary historian and critic, journalist.

Łukasiewicz, Jan (1878–1956). Polish logician and mathematician.

Lukács, György (1885–1971). Hungarian writer, one of the foremost literary critics.

Malinowski, Bronisław (1884–1942). Famous Polish-born anthropologist.

Mandelstam, Osip Emiliyevich (1891–1938). Eminent Russian poet and essayist. Victim of Stalin's terror.

Maritain, Jacques (1882–1973). Eminent French philosopher. Raised Protestant; became Roman Catholic.

Matuszewski, Ryszard (1914). Polish literary critic.

Mayakovsky, Vladimir Vladimirovich (1893–1930). Russian poet and playwright. An important avant-garde poet who tried to serve the Revolution through his poetry.

Meyerson, Emilé (1858–1933). French philosopher and mathematician.

Michnik, Adam (1946). Polish historian, writer, essayist, dissident. A member of KOR, frequently imprisoned. 1980–82 adviser to Solidarity. 1989 elected representative in Sejm and editor in chief of the most popular Polish newspaper, *Gazeta Wyborcza*.

Miciński, Bolesław ("Bolek") (1911–1943). Polish philosopher, essayist, and poet.

Mickiewicz, Adam (1798–1855). Eminent Polish romantic poet.

Mikołajczyk, Stanisław (1901–1966). Member of Polish Peasants' party. On return from London, became vice-president of the soviet of writers. After 1947 an emigré in London.

Mikolajska, Halina (1925–1989).

Miłosz, Czesław (1911 in Lithuania). Polish poet, translator. 1951 emigrated to Paris; 1958 to the United States. 1980 winner of Nobel Prize for Literature.

Minc, Hilary (1905–1984). Until 1956, third most important politician in Communist Poland.

Moczar, Mieczysław (1913–1980). Active in Communist underground during the war. Chief of Internal Security.

Mukařovský, Jan. Czech linguist.

Nagy, Imre (1895?–1958). Hungarian Communist prime minister. Executed after the defeat of the 1956 Hungarian revolt.

Nałkowska, Zofia (1885–1954). Polish writer. Most important woman writer of the period between the wars.

Napierski, Stefan (orig. Stefan Marek Eiger) (1899–1940). Polish literary critic and poet.

Natolin and Puławy. Opposing factions of the Polish Workers' party during the 1950s and 1960s, named for their preferred meeting places—the Natolin palace and park and Puław-ska Street in Warsaw. The Natolin supporters were usually former partisans, conservative, pro-Russian and pro-Stalin, with nationalistic and anti-Semitic tendencies. The Puławy followers were more liberal and international and were usually intellectuals in contrast to the Natolin supporters, whose ranks included many of peasant stock.

Niesiołowski, Tymon (1882–1965). Polish painter.

Norwid, Cyprian Kamil (or Kamil Cyprian) (1821–1883). Polish poet, dramatist, prose writer, as well as sculptor and painter.

Nowak, Jan (orig. Jeziorański, Zdzisław). First director of the Polish section of Radio Free Europe. The "courier from Warsaw."

Ochab, Edward (1906–1989). Polish politician. Prewar Communist. 1956–57 became first secretary of the Polish United Workers' party when Bierut died. 1964–68 Polish head of state (chairman of Council of State). 1968 lost all his positions when he protested against the party's anti-Semitic campaign.

Orzeszkowa, Eliza (1841–1910). Polish novelist and social activist.

Panch, Petro (orig. Panchenko) (1891). Ukrainian writer.

Pasternak, Boris Leonidovich (1890–1960). Russian poet and prose writer. 1958 winner of Nobel Prize.

Pasternak, Leon (1910–1969). Polish Communist. Poet and prose writer.

PAX. Organization of "socially progressive" Catholics that began its official existence in 1952 but was really founded in 1945.

People's Army (Armia Ludowa). Underground Communist organization established January 1, 1944.

Pietrzak, Włodzimierz ("Włodek") (1913–1944). Polish literary critic, writer, and poet.

Piłsudski, Józef Klemens (1867–1935). Polish politician and general.

Plekhanov, Georgy Valentinovich (1856–1918). Russian revolutionary, Marxist theoretician and critic.

Polish Workers' party (PPR). Name of the Polish Communist party established by the underground in 1942. From its forced union with the Social-democratic party came the Polish United Workers' party, which existed until 1990.

Prosto z Mostu (Straight from the Shoulder). Monthly journal for literature, art, and politics, published from 1935 to 1939 in Warsaw under the editorial direction of Sergiusz Piasecki. Affiliated with right-wing nationalists.

Prus, Bolesław (orig. Aleksander Głowacki) (1847–1912). The most important Polish novelist of his time.

Pruszyński, Ksawery (1907–1950). Polish prose writer, journalist, and diplomat.

Przyboś, Julian (1901–1970). Polish poet and essayist.

Putrament, Jerzy (1910–1986). Polish Communist, writer, journalist.

Rakowski, Mieczysław (1926). Polish journalist and politician.

Różański, Jacek. Head of the Internal Security Department.

Rudnicki, Adolf (1912–1990). Polish prose writer and essayist. Since World War II has devoted his work to the tragedy of the Jews.

Schulz, Bruno (1892–1942). Polish writer and artist; one of the most original Polish writers of this century.

Shevchenko, Taras (1814–1861). Ukrainian romantic poet.

Sienkiewicz, Henryk (1846–1916). Polish writer, popular as author of historical novels. 1905 winner of Nobel Prize.

Słonimski, Antoni (1895–1976). Polish poet, journalist, novelist, playwright. Liberal humanist; important figure in Polish culture.

Słowacki, Juliusz (1809–1849). Major Polish romantic poet.

Sokorski, Włodzimierz ("Włodzio") (1908). Prewar Communist. Minister of Culture. Writer and journalist.

Sosiora, Vladimir (1897–1965). Ukranian poet.

Spychalski, Marshal Marian (1906–1980). Polish politician. 1968–70 Polish head of state (chairman of Council of State).

Staszewski, Stefan (1906–1989).

Stawar, Andrzej (orig. Dedwar Janusz) (1900–1961). Polish literary critic and translator. Communist theoretician and activist.

Steinhaus, Hugo (1887–1972). JK's father-in-law.

Stempowski, Jerzy (pseud. of Pawel Hostowiec) (1894–1969). Polish essayist and literary critic.

Straszewski, Stefan (1906–1989). Polish politician.

Supervielle, Jules (1884–1960). French writer. Divided his life between France and South America.

Światło, Józef. A defector in 1958.

Szemplińska, Elżbieta (1919). Polish poet and Communist.

Szmosz, Adolf (1900–1962). JK's maternal uncle.

Szymanowski, Karol (1882–1937). Polish composer of orchestral and chamber music, operas, and ballets.

Tarski, Alfred (1901–1983). Polish-born mathematician and logician. In U.S. after 1938.

Trybuna Ludu (Tribune of the People). Daily Communist newspaper, organ of the central committee of the Polish United Workers' party, published from 1948 until 1990. Transformed into *Trybuna*.

Turowicz, Jerzy (1912). Polish journalist and editor.

Tychyna, Pavlo

Tygodnik Powszechny (General Weekly). Weekly Catholic newspaper for culture and society. Published in Cracow since 1945.

Urban, Jerzy (1933). Journalist, satiricist. 1981 to 1989 official spokesman for General Jaruzelski's government.

Verbum. Catholic quarterly for culture. Published in Warsaw from 1934 to 1939.

Vlasov, Andrei (1900–1946).

Wajda, Andrzej. Polish director.

Wasilewska, Wanda (1905–1964). Polish novelist, Communist activist. Daughter of a famous Polish socialist. In Soviet Union after 1939.

Wat, Aleksander (1900–1967). Polish futurist poet, prose writer, translator.

Ważyk, Adam (1905–1982). Polish poet, translator of Russian and French poetry.

Wertenstein, Ludwik (1887-1947). JK's uncle.

Werten-Wertenstein, Maria (1888-1949). JK's aunt.

Wielopolski, Aleksander Marquis. (1803–1877). Polish politician.

Winawer, Bruno (1883–1944). Polish playwright, journalist, physicist.

Witkiewicz, Stanisław Ignacy (or Ignacy Stanisław) ("Witkacy") (1885–1939). Polish writer and painter, philosopher, art theoretician. Son of Stanisław Witkiewicz (1851–1915), a famous writer and architect.

Wittlin, Józef (1896–1976). Polish poet, novelist, translator.

Wolski-Piwowarczyk, Antoni-Władysław (?–1976).

Woroszylski, Wiktor (1927). Polish poet, prose writer, translator of Russian literature. Founding member of KOR.

Woszczerowicz, Jacek

Wyszyński, Stefan (1901–1981). Cardinal, primate of Poland from 1948 until his death. Political leader of Polish catholics during the time of political repression. Arrested in 1953, released from prison in October 1956.

Zagórski, Jerzy (1907–1984). Polish poet and translator.

Zawieyski, Jerzy (1902–1969). Polish writer, dramatist, Catholic politician.

Żeromski, Stefan (1864–1925). Polish novelist and playwright, concerned with political and social themes; still frequently read.

Zhdanov, Andrei Aleksandrovich (1896–1946). Russian Communist party functionary responsible for cultural Stalinism at its most repressive.

Żółkiewski, Stefan ("Hetman") (1911–1989). Theoretician of

Marxist literary criticism. Activist in the Communist underground during the Nazi occupation.

Żukrowski, Wojciech (1916). Polish writer.

Życie Warszawy (Warsaw Life). Warsaw daily newspaper.